EMANCIPATING PRAGMATISM

Modern and Contemporary Poetics

EMANCIPATING PRAGMATISM

Emerson, Jazz, and Experimental Writing

Michael Magee

THE UNIVERSITY OF ALABAMA PRESS

Tuscaloosa

Typeface: Perpetua

∞

The paper on which this book is printed meets the minimum requirements of American
National Standard for Information Science–Permanence of Paper for Printed Library
Materials, ANSI Z39.48–1984.

Library of Congress Cataloging-in-Publication Data

Magee, Michael, 1971–
    Emancipating pragmatism : Emerson, jazz, and experimental writing / Michael Magee.
        p. cm. — (Modern and contemporary poetics)
Includes bibliographical references (p.) and index.
    ISBN 0-8173-1390-7 (alk. paper) — ISBN 0-8173-5084-5 (pbk. : alk. paper)
    1. Emerson, Ralph Waldo, 1803–1882—Criticism and interpretation. 2. Literature,
Experimental—History and criticism. 3. Emerson, Ralph Waldo, 1803–1882—Influence.
4. Jazz—History and criticism. 5. Pragmatism in literature. 6. Music and literature. 7. Race
in literature. 8. Poetics. I. Title. II. Series.
    PS1638.M27 2004
    814'.3—dc22

                                                                              2003020879

Contents

Acknowledgments

"No teacher ever taught, that has so provided for his pupil's setting up independently." Whitman said this of Emerson; I say it of Lisa New. This project began one day in a graduate seminar when, after I had delivered a short presentation on Emerson, Lisa casually suggested that I "save those pages" for my dissertation. I had no intention of writing any more about Emerson, but the seed was planted. When Emerson finally took center stage, Lisa alternately indulged and guided me as I prodded the unlikeliest of characters into dialogue with the Concord sage and, for good measure, moved his scenes from the study to the streets.

Bob Perelman and Herman Beavers were just as influential to the casting. Bob is almost wholly responsible for introducing me to the world of experimental poetry. His stunning range as a scholar was a vital model as I crossed centuries and genres under the sign of pragmatism; his insistence that a certain amount of historicist rigor was necessary if such crossings were to be more than whimsical had a pervasive effect on the writing. In Herman Beavers I had a prominent Ellison scholar and poet to both encourage me and guide me around the pitfalls of my integrationist approach. Al Filreis and Farah Griffin have also been there from the beginning, reading work at various stages, making timely suggestions, and otherwise providing help and advice too numerous to mention. Last among my mentors I count Jean-Michel Rabate, without whose help I would not have had the privilege of studying at Penn, and Robert Cording, without whose inspiration I never would have applied.

The fingerprints of some dear friends are all over these chapters. John

Parker's thoughts on poetry and its relation to social conflict, his Marxist distrust of pragmatism, his cognizance of and commitment to the difficulty and possibilities of language—all made for many a talk-filled evening that time eventually distilled into writing. A group of young scholars who congregated around the Writers House at Penn in the mid-1990s were a constant resource: Kristen Gallagher, Louis Cabri, Mytili Jagannathan, Matt Hart, and John Heon. Then, too, Nate Chinen and George Blaustein, jazz musicians and writers both, served as resident musicologists with great patience. Lana Schwebel tutored me on the finer points of ballet and Balanchine. Several good friends farther off contributed as well: Phil Metres, Andrew Epstein, Jacques Debrot. The staff at the New York University Administrative Archive and the Thomas J. Dodd Research Center at the University of Connecticut were extremely helpful. Rutherford Witthus, a curator at the latter, was a vital resource. The editors and readers at a number of excellent journals—*Contemporary Literature; ESQ: A Journal of the American Renaissance; Kenning: A Newsletter of Contemporary Poetry, Poetics, Nonfiction Writing; Raritan; Review; Transactions of the Charles S. Peirce Society;* and *No: A Journal of the Arts*—provided suggestions that much improved this book. Likewise, I am in debt to Hank Lazer, Charles Bernstein, and an anonymous reader at the University of Alabama Press. Lastly, several of America's most talented writers and scholars have indulged my obsessions by talking with me at length and answering my letters: Harryette Mullen, Nathaniel Mackey, Bill Berkson, Lawrence Buell, Susan Howe, Robert G. O'Meally, Ann Lauterbach, Lorenzo Thomas, Richard Poirier, and Amiri Baraka stand out among them.

My family has been a constant source of emotional and intellectual support. My parents' affection has always been a buoy, but I am struck too by how their thoughts permeate the work: my dad's utopian vision of service to communities, my mom's speech that revealed to me that malapropism is a condescending word for the American vernacular in action. My younger siblings have always been my counselors. Mitch introduced me to jazz in the form of a Charlie Parker record when I was sixteen. Marc has spent many a late night rehashing the trials of our democracy with me. Meredith reminds me again and again by her actions that true intellectuals read, as Emerson once put it, "in the faces of the people."

My embarrassment of riches is increased tenfold by my wife, Susanna. I dedicate this work to her and to our two children. Anything I might say about myself would necessarily include her, and to describe the effect she has had on my identity would be to describe a life—impossible. I can only mention the small mercies. The opportunity to watch her care for America's sick and underserved has been my most valuable education. However, when I myself was diagnosed with a difficult illness during the writing of this book, she knew that what I needed most from her was not treatment but love, which she continues to give selflessly, daily. This is the blessing of my life.

Abbreviations

A   William Carlos Williams, *The Autobiography of William Carlos Williams* (New York: New Directions, 1967).

AG   William Carlos Williams, *In the American Grain* (New York: New Directions, 1956).

ASW   Len Gougeon and Joel Myerson, ed., *Emerson's Antislavery Writings* (New Haven: Yale University Press, 1995).

AW   Paul Goodman, "Advance-Guard Writing, 1900–1950," *The Kenyon Review,* 13:3 (Summer, 1951), 357–380.

BM   Susan Howe, *The Birth-mark: Unsettling the Wilderness in American Literary History* (Hanover, NH: Wesleyan University Press, 1993).

BP   LeRoi Jones (Amiri Baraka), *Blues People* (New York: William Morrow, 1963).

CE   Maryemma Graham and Amritjit Singh, eds., *Conversations with Ralph Ellison* (Jackson: University Press of Mississippi, 1995).

CEC   Joseph Slater, ed., *The Correspondence of Emerson and Carlyle* (New York: Columbia University Press, 1964).

CP   Frank O'Hara, *The Collected Poems of Frank O'Hara* (Berkeley: University of California Press, 1971).

CPT   Brad Gooch, *City Poet: The Life and Times of Frank O'Hara* (New York: Knopf, 1993).

CW   *The Complete Works of Ralph Waldo Emerson,* Centenary Edition, Vol. 2, ed., E. W. Emerson (Boston: Houghton Miflin, 1903–1904).

DE   Nathaniel Mackey, *Discrepant Engagement: Dissonance, Cross-Cultu-*

rality, and Experimental Writing (New York: Cambridge University Press, 1993).

EK   William Carlos Williams, *The Embodiment of Knowledge* (New York: New Directions, 1974).

GT   Ralph Ellison, *Going to the Territory* (New York: Vintage, 1979).

I   William Carlos Williams, *Imaginations* (New York: New Directions, 1970).

IM   Ralph Ellison, *Invisible Man* (New York: Vintage, 1952).

JMN   *The Journals and Miscellaneous Notebooks of Ralph Waldo Emerson,* ed. William H. Gilman and Ralph H. Orth et al., 16 vols. (Cambridge: Harvard University Press, Belknap Press, 1960–1982).

L   *The Letters of Ralph Waldo Emerson,* ed. Ralph L. Rusk and Eleanor Tilton, 10 vols. (New York: Columbia University Press, 1939–1996).

LW   John Dewey, *The Later Works, 1925–1953,* ed. Jo Ann Boydston, 17 vols. (Carbondale and Edwardsville: Southern Illinois University Press, 1984).

MW   John Dewey, *The Middle Works, 1899–1924,* ed. Jo Ann Boydston, 15 vols. (Carbondale and Edwardsville: Southern Illinois University Press, 1984).

P   William Carlos Williams, *Paterson* (New York: New Directions, 1992).

RR   Aldon Nielsen, *Reading Race: White American Poets and the Racial Discourse in the Twentieth Century* (Athens: The University of Georgia Press, 1988).

SA   Ralph Ellison, *Shadow and Act* (New York: Vintage, 1964).

SL   William Carlos Williams, *The Selected Letters of William Carlos Williams* (New York: McDowell, Obolensky, 1957).

SS   Frank O'Hara, *Standing Still and Walking in New York* (San Francisco: Grey Fox Press, 1983).

TE   Charles Woodbury, *Talks with Emerson* (New York: Baker and Taylor, 1890).

WJ   William James, *The Works of William James,* ed. Fredson Bowers, 16 vols. (Cambridge: Harvard University Press, 1981).

EMANCIPATING PRAGMATISM

I

Toward a Theory of Democratic Symbolic Action

> Doctor, do you believe in
> "the people," the Democracy? Do
> you still believe—in this
> swill-hole of corrupt cities?
> Do you, Doctor? Now?
> > William Carlos Williams, *Paterson*

There is Emerson and then there is Emerson. The pattern that repeats it-self—inevitably, endlessly—involves the critic arguing for a "true" Emer-son against one or the other past representation, sometimes to Emer-son's benefit, sometimes to his detriment. But the details tell the story. One might create a laudatory version of Emerson that would inspire as much disdain for him as a deeply critical one, and in fact the two might be related. "Emerson attended church on Sundays all his life with un-common regularity." This statement is a bald-faced lie, though no doubt a few critics over the years have taken it as gospel truth. Why did Charles W. Eliot write it, as he must have known it to be false?[1] "We are always coming up with the emphatic facts of history in our private experience," Emerson wrote. "All history becomes subjective."[2] History is a series of written texts whose words might be moved this way and that or, if all else fails, forged. The critic comes late to the game, and thus what John Dewey has said of philosophy is even more true of literary criticism: it is not "in any sense whatever a form of knowledge" but rather "a form of desire, of effort at action."[3] This is not to say that history isn't true—only that it becomes true, unfolding in time as a result of discovery, re-interpretation, and negotiation of meaning between readers. It is true whenever "we" agree on and believe the record.

The notebook in which Emerson recorded the vast majority of his thoughts on slavery and abolition, his "WO Liberty" notebook, was lost between 1903 and 1966. During this period no one apparently had any knowledge that it had *ever* existed. The antislavery writings of Emerson's that were extant were collected in a volume harmlessly entitled *Miscellanies*—and Emerson's interest in the cause of abolition, if it existed in the minds of scholars at all, was believed to be, at best, quite miscellaneous. Among those who believed otherwise were some prominent American pragmatists: William James, whose father was arranging lectures in New York for Emerson at a time when Emerson was delivering extremely controversial, vitriolic speeches on the Fugitive Slave Law; John Dewey, who was interested in fleshing out the implications of Emerson's role as the "philosopher of democracy"; and Ralph Ellison, who as an African American named after Emerson had obvious reasons for seeking out his namesake's opinions on slavery. The Emerson I plan to describe is largely *their* Emerson. If this Emerson seems unfamiliar, that is to some degree the point.

The fight over the meaning of Emerson's texts would certainly not have surprised him. Indeed, the Emerson I will describe was involved in such a fight. In chapter 2, I will suggest that Emerson's involvement in the struggle for abolition, or more generally emancipation, was a long time in the making, but for now I will simply leap into it. In the two decades following the publication of his first series of essays (1841), Emerson would spend a great deal of time arguing that cultural texts such as the Constitution and the Declaration of Independence must be read as contingent rather than codified texts and that this model of reading was the predicate by which the "rhetoric and rituals" of the republic could remain operative in practice as tools for the expansion of democracy. Otherwise, they were merely paper or, worse, impediments to the very ethic they supposedly promoted. "No forms," he would write, "neither constitutions, nor laws, nor covenants, nor churches nor bibles, are of any use in themselves. The devil nestles comfortably into them all" (CW 11:234). Far from being simply an abstract possibility, Emerson believed that the devil was already well into his work. The devil, so Emerson's story goes, is a free-wheeling interpreter of language living among passive literalists. Of course, as a freewheeling interpreter himself—and an advocate for that style of reading—Emerson's observations on the activity of the devil's minions are thick with irony; to read Emerson's characterization of Christianity as "a religion of dead dogs"[4] is to recognize just how severe he considered the crisis of slavery to be. "Of course they quote the bible, & Christ & Paul, to defend slavery," he mused in his "WO Liberty" journal, as if exasperated with all the passive literalists, "these are dead forms that will cover anything" (JMN 11:413). Texts such as the Bible and the Constitution, Emerson realized, were sites of social contestation, at once revered by the collective *for* their meaning and totally indeterminate *in* their meaning. Given this situation, he determined that "a literal, slavish following of precedents, as by a justice of the peace, is not for those who at this hour lead the destinies of this people" (CW 11:299–300).

If one were going to make an argument that the Bible or the Constitution stood for liberty and emancipation, one would have to eschew literalism as a potential strategy and, instead, embody those characteristics of liberty and emancipation and make a strong reading: "to interpret Christ, it needs a Christ," Emerson wrote, and "to make good the cause of freedom against slavery you must be . . . Declaration of Independence walking" (JMN 11:413).[5] This state of affairs presented an opportunity for anyone willing to present an interpretation, but it was an opportunity being grasped, by and large, by proslavery advocates and Northern apologists. "It is curious that now liberty is grown passive and defensive," Emerson lamented. "Slavery alone is inventive and aggressive, Slavery reads the constitution with a very shrewd & daring & innovating eye. Liberty is satisfied with the literal construction" (11:420). Of course the irony of this is that those representing slavery, while engaged in "wolfish interpretation," were loath to admit that their readings of cultural documents were anything but strictly literal. Emerson recognized this as a rhetorical game, a devious strategy.[6] Of Daniel Webster, two months after Webster had helped to make the Fugitive Slave Act into law, Emerson would write, "He praises Adams and Jefferson, but it is a past

Adams and Jefferson that his mind can entertain. A present Adams and Jefferson he would denounce. So with the eulogies of liberty in his writings—they are sentimentalism and youthful rhetoric" (CW 11:234, 204). Webster's paeans to liberty are precisely "eulogies" because they treat the concept of liberty as dead fact rather than as evolving, context-dependent principle. Likewise with Adams and Jefferson: Webster's praise is given under the conceit that the identities of those revolutionaries, what they represent, are codified and immutable. Emerson now had a rather horrifying practical example for his description, from "Self-Reliance," of the causal relationship between a reverence for "badges and names" on the one hand and the perpetuation of "large societies and dead institutions" on the other (2:51). Emerson himself was determined to disrupt the presumptions on which that causal relationship was based. Often such disruptions take the form of an edgy clearing of the air regarding signification. The country's most revered words, Emerson reminds in these moments, are not what they seem. Thus such gems as "democracy or other mumbo jumbo" appear in the journals (JMN 9:186), and, in the speeches, Emerson is constantly setting the record straight for anyone still invested in trusted American vocabularies. "Language has lost its meaning in the universal cant, Representative Government is really misrepresentative; Union is a conspiracy against the Northern States which the Northern States are to have the privilege of paying for; the adding of Cuba and Central America to the slave marts is enlarging the area of Freedom. Manifest Destiny, Democracy, Freedom, fine names for an ugly thing. They call it otto of rose and lavender,—I call it bilge-water" (11:259).

Emerson believed that convincing the nation that words such as *democracy* and *freedom* had come to signify their opposites was the prerequisite for the generation of new vocabularies—vocabularies that could better serve the principles on which such words as *freedom* and *democracy* were originally based. One can already see the change occurring here, as Emerson insists that representative means misrepresentative, free means slave, the word *democracy* is akin to bilgewater. He understood just how deeply reliant arguments for slavery and imperialistic government were on such words. They were the smoke screen behind which attacks on egalitarian activity were mounted—and they were incredibly persuasive. But Emerson's own attacks must have made arguments such as Webster's seem like those of the most inept confidence man. They are masterpieces of vitriol, and as such they betray the seriousness with which Emerson viewed his intervention. The following is an example from 1851:

> Mr. Everett, a man supposed aware of his own meaning, advises pathetically a reverence for the union. Yes but hides the other horn under his velvet? Does he mean that we shall lay hands on a man who has escaped from slavery to the soil of Massachusetts & so has done more for freedom than ten thousand orations, & tie him up & call in the Marshall, and say,—I am an orator for freedom; a great many fine sentences have I turned,—none has turned finer, except Mr. Webster,—in favor of plebeian strength against aristocracy; and, as my last and finest sentence of all, to show the young men of the land who have bought my book & clapped my sentences & copied them in their memory, how much I mean by them,—Mr. Marshall, here is a black man of my own age, & who does not know a great deal of Demosthenes, but who means what he says, whom we will now handcuff and commit to the custody of this very worthy gentleman who has come on from Georgia in search of him; I have no doubt he has much to say to him that is interesting & as the way is long I don't care if I give them a copy of my Concord & Lexington & Plymouth & Bunker Hill addresses to beguile their journey from Boston to the plantation whipping post? (JMN 11:359–60)

In this satire on the "orator for freedom" (a kind of miniature companion piece to "The American Scholar"), Emerson turns signification upside down. The final sentence—two hundred and twelve words long—is a rhetorical tour de force in which the "orator for freedom" betrays the bathetic and devious nature of his oration by the fact that his "finest sentence" is not a sentence at all—or, to be more precise, it is a sentence of a different sort. The final sentence of the orator for freedom is not a grammatical one but a penal one, a judicial decree, like those given out under the authority of the Fugitive Slave Law. This pun is not idle; it is

Emerson's reminder that the fine sentences of Everett and Webster, delivered at gatherings on the Fourth of July, are in the service of the sentences of Southern judges. Webster's sentences, the "finest" of all, are in fact the most menacing; they are of a piece with the "most worthy gentleman" from Georgia, the slave catcher. Emerson is not lamenting the fact that "most worthy gentleman" does not mean what it should; he is critiquing the whole discourse of "gentlemanliness" that is a subgenre of aristocratic discourse. We're meant to be reminded that this "orator for freedom" is supposed to be turning sentences "in favor of plebeian strength against aristocracy," not speaking up for "worthy gentleman," in fact, not participating in the discourse of "worthiness" at all.

The satire of the "orator for freedom" in Emerson's long sentence is only one half of a dialectic. In the second half, Emerson's de-authoritative tactics come to the fore. In the section involving "the young men of the land who have bought my book," one senses a self-critique, an anxiety that his theories have not been articulated well enough in terms of practice and, equally disturbing, that his sentences have failed to have their intended effect because they have failed *structurally,* as symbolic action. Rather than encouraging the contingent and collaborative development of meaning, they have been applauded and memorized. Emerson contrasts the young acolytes to the fugitive slave, "the man who has escaped from slavery to the soil of Massachusetts." Emerson insists on the fugitive slave's status as citizen as well as the fact that his actions, his will to freedom, supersedes, in effectiveness, any speeches *about* freedom. This latter recognition is akin to his observation that "the negro has saved himself and the white man very patronizingly says, I have saved you" (JMN 9:126). The black man who has "done more for freedom than ten thousand orations," is, Emerson says, "of my own age"—a characterization that suggests equality on two levels. First, he is equal to Emerson in years and thus not subject to such diminutions as "boy" or some equivalent. Second, he is of Emerson's "age," his era, in opposition to Webster and Everett who are from an older "age," one that Emerson would insist is quickly passing away in large part because of this fugitive man and the efforts of his fellow fugitives. Emerson seeks to find the symbolic equivalent for this man's will to freedom in his own prose, eschewing any attempt to describe the abstract principle of freedom. The styles, the rhetorical strategies, that marked so many annual addresses at Concord, Lexington, Plymouth, and Bunker Hill, were in essence eulogies and would only beguile someone currently striving toward freedom; they quoted old celebrations of liberty over the sounds of the whipping post. In contrast to such eulogies, Emerson intended to make sure there was no mistaking the fact that, like the black man of his own age, he meant what he said.

As I will detail in chapter 2, while Emerson's writing retains all of those elements of the "countering of diction" developed in the first and second series of essays, his vocabulary changes in accordance with changes in his own attitude toward the interconnectedness of public and private, theory and practice. This change is largely the result of a change in his definition of reading and of the reader. Ultimately, Emerson came to believe that "America" itself was a kind of text being read, its meaning a matter of collective decision. It followed that one's linguistic theory, one's view of how words generate meanings, had potentially large-scale social ramifications. In suggesting that words were "million-faced," Emerson came to realize, he was suggesting that social possibility was remakeable. He was suggesting that, as Richard Rorty has phrased it, "Large-scale change of belief is indistinguishable from large-scale change in the meanings of one's words."[7] One could go further in saying that Emerson was essentially banking on a theory of social change not unlike that which one finds in the pragmatist anthropology of Clifford Geertz, paying special attention to "the dynamic elements in social change that arise from the failure of cultural patterns to be perfectly congruent with the [current] forms of social organization." What Geertz points out so effectively is "that cultural structure and social structure are not mere reflexes of one another but independent, yet interdependent, variables." Incongruencies between cultural structure (dependent on expressive symbols that must be read) and social structure (the actual set of behaviors manifest in a given social system) will "give rise to social conflict, simply because the kind of social integration demonstrated by the [symbolically proposed] pattern is not congruent with the major patterns of integration in the society generally."[8] Emerson believed that his job as political symbolist (symbolic activist, we might call it) was to re-read and re-vision the *cultural* structure—the style, logical implication, and meaning of the cultures symbols—in such a way that it would be moved as far away as possible from the *social* structure. The more friction he could create between them (via an expansion of his proposed symbolic economy), the more likely was real social change in the direction of his egalitarian desires. As I will be arguing over the course of this book, Emerson was inventing a particular version of American pragmatism.

Words such as America, democracy, and freedom provided the most significant test for Emerson's symbolic activism because their influence was so extensive. As I've tried to show, Emerson often employed a tactic of disruption whereby he would deconstruct how a particular word was being employed by, say, Webster or Everett. The second half of that dialectic was to propose radically new definitions for those same words. These tactics harken back to his earlier impulses to "gazette" such hackneyed signifiers as "God" and "soul" in "reporting religious experience," though in these earlier instances it was the individual's possibilities of self-realization that he sought to free up.[9] One finds that in his later work, when Emerson proposes new definitions for culturally revered vocabulary, he insists that belief about language corresponds with belief about large-scale social action. "The use of symbols," he writes in "The Poet," "has a certain power of emancipation and exhilaration for all men" (CW 3:30). But by 1851 the idea of emancipation receives a much wider and much more public application:

> America is the idea of Emancipation
> abolish kingcraft, Slavery, feudalism, blackletter monopoly, pull down gallows, explode priestcraft, tariff, open the doors of the sea to all immigrants. Extemporize government, California, Texas, Lynch Law. All this covers selfgovernment. All proceeds on the belief that as the people have made a gov.t they can make another. . . . Mr. Webster thinks this union is a vast Prince Rupert's drop. . . . [Mr. Everett] has been reading in his Robertson instead of in the faces of the people. (JMN 11:406)

That "America is the idea of emancipation" is something Emerson might have said in "Self-Reliance" or "The Poet." But the capitalization of "emancipation" suggests something new, that the abstract concept is also the practical battle, that America, emancipation, and the emancipation of slavery are signifiers in a new vocabulary that would link language use to social action, rhetoric to rituals. Emerson drives home this point by following up with a feverish litany of practical applications. This litany is part call to action, part imagining of future possibility, part system of analogy. Emerson's use of commands—abolish, pull down, explode, open, extemporize—marks an insistence on his part that these social actions are covered under the rubric "America." Those commands also suggest a causal relationship whereby abolishing, pulling down, and exploding leads to opening and extemporizing. The dialectic of tearing down old vocabularies and proposing new ones, which I noted earlier in the passage on the "orator of freedom," is at work here as well. The sweeping analogies between America, emancipation, self-government, and the host of real contemporary issues Emerson names are a kind of purposeful shorthand intended to syntactically resemble swift social change, rooted, according to Emerson, in the fundamental belief of the people in America as a revisable entity. The ability to "make another" America is causally linked to making another *definition* of America. Webster takes the opposite view of America—that it is too fragile to withstand remaking. America is like Prince Rupert's drop, the glasswork seemingly strong and luminescent but in truth easily shattered. Emerson's criticism of Everett is to the point as well. Everett reads Robertson's *History of America* instead of reading America itself, in its currently evolving form, embodied "in the faces of the people." For Everett, America *is* history, its status as signifier long ago determined. Reading "in the faces of the people" is an antidote to that view of American culture that would privilege a reified past over evolving possibilities.

In "The Fortune of the Republic," Emerson announces, "We shall be a multitude of people" and extends on the journal description of "doors wide open" above. Those doors, he says, are wide open "to every race and skin, white men, red men, yellow men, black men" (CW 11:541). For a philosopher who had come to adopt what we would now call a pragmatist view of language—a view of language as the malleable reflection of logical space and cultural belief—social and racial pluralism had major ramifications. It is one thing for Emerson to write "language is made," but it is quite another for him to follow with the rhetorical question, "Who has not helped to make it?" (JMN 9:353). This question suggests a broadly collaborative model for the creation of the American vernacular. And then, it is another thing still for him to link the development of that vernacular to the maintenance of "the real union, that is, the will to keep and renew union." "This alone," he wrote to his skeptical future biographer Oliver Wendell Holmes, "gives any tension to the dead letter."[10] What James Livingston has written about Lincoln is equally true of Emerson, that Lincoln recognized "that the United States could remain true to its original principles and purposes only by changing radically, so that the condition of republican continuity had become revolutionary discontinuity."[11] Emerson's description of the relationship between a developing American vernacular and a perpetually renewable union has received little critical consideration, but it is absolutely crucial to how we construct not only his own philosophy but its impact on the American literature and philosophy that followed.

What does it mean for Ralph Ellison to say that he "inherited the language of Emerson"?[12] If we attempt to answer this question by isolating the implied exchange—by reducing it to a simple matter of "influence" or lack thereof—we run the risk of missing its broader significance. Ellison's claim to inheritance comprises an implicit argument about the meaning and direction of pragmatism, American literature, and the role of symbolic action in American culture. There are, however, reasons to keep a particularly close eye on Emerson when examining this nexus. The first and most obvious is that Emerson's influence on that nexus (pragmatism, American literature, symbolic action in American culture) is pervasive. The second is that, largely as a result of having been named after Emerson (for us, the happiest of accidents), Ellison uses Emerson's work as a touchstone for his more extensive concerns. What I propose to do here is explore the avenues by which Ellison comes to consider jazz as the predominant form of pragmatist artistic practice and democratic symbolic action in the twentieth century. I suggest that we begin with Burke and work our way back through the pragmatist canon toward Ellison's namesake, Emerson. Doing so provides a foundation on which to construct an argument regarding Ellison's re-visioning of pragmatism. In chapter 3, I will engage in a more specific consideration of the role Emerson plays in Ellison's vision, for one reason: because Ellison's signifying on Emerson in *Invisible Man* represents his most nuanced description of the process by which jazz music and African American culture lay claim to the tradition of American pragmatism. In Ellison's hands, pragmatism is, like America itself, "jazz-shaped," and his insistence on this point has major consequences for anyone attempting to describe "pragmatism proper."

The revival of pragmatism in philosophy and literary studies over the last decade has revealed a tradition more nuanced, more subtly shaded than even a radical pluralist like William James could have hoped. An important feature of the new scholarship is its insistence that several twentieth-century black intellectuals be considered major pragmatists in conscious dialogue with classical pragmatism. In *The American Evasion of Philosophy,* Cornel West places W. E. B. DuBois squarely (if somewhat antagonistically) in the pragmatist canon.[13] More recently, philosophers such as Leonard Harris, Nancy Fraser, Judith Green, and Richard Shusterman have argued that Alain Locke should be understood as a key voice in the pragmatist tradition.[14] Not surprisingly, these thinkers are, to use John Dewey's words, "animated . . . by the strivings of men to achieve democracy." In this regard I include myself among them. I will make the case that Ralph Ellison is an even more vital figure in the current revival—not least because he understands the role that African American culture played in the *development* of pragmatism, as one of its pretexts, and thus is better equipped to disclose that "anticipatory arena where actuality and possibility, past and present, are allowed to collaborate on a history of the future."[15] As Ross Posnock has argued, the incongruency between Horace Kallen's race-focused cultural pluralism and Dewey's pragmatist pluralism (both inspired by James) has obscured the role played by African American thinkers in the development of pragmatism, most notably DuBois and Locke.[16] Posnock notes that Ellison draws on "this rich counter-tradition" within pragmatism: "Starting with DuBois's 'kingdom of culture' (1903), including Dewey's dissent from Kallen (1915–1916) and Locke's rejection of 'cultural purism' and theorizing of cosmopolitanism in the twenties and thirties, this lineage creatively appropriates an antiseparatist Jamesian pluralism whose byword is 'reciprocity rather than identity.'"[17] But there are good reasons to consider Ellison the preeminent African American pragmatist and indeed a pivotal revisionist of the pragmatist tradition exemplified by James, Dewey, and Burke. In chapter 2, I describe the role African Americans play in Emerson's thinking, and in doing so I complicate and extend Posnock's argument: whereas DuBois and Locke are for Posnock "Jamesian pragmatists" appropriating and revising James's thought, James himself is the unwitting inheritor of a tradition of African American symbolic action. Pragmatists who ignore "race matters," then, are inherently self-ironizing and indeed self-defeating. In arguing this case I am very much following in the footsteps of Ellison.

In his essays and novels, Ellison carries on a dialogue with Emerson and Burke through which he rearticulates pragmatism's connection to African American culture. In returning to Emerson, Ellison recalls the uncanny truth about pragmatism, that it is "the partial creation of black people." Most importantly, Ellison naturalizes the implicit pragmatism of jazz, a move that complements and amplifies the return to Emerson by once again disrupting the notion of lineage and appropriation. The turn to jazz has major aesthetic implications as well, enacting a bridge between Emerson's "experimenter" and the jazz improviser, while suggesting that this trajectory exemplifies pragmatism's view of, in Dewey's words, "art as experience."

Ellison acts on a basic premise about language and culture perhaps best put in the following quote from William James, with which he would have been in deep agreement: "Distinctions between the lawful and the unlawful in conduct, or between the correct and incorrect in speech, have grown up incidentally among the interrelations of men's experiences in detail; and in no other way do distinctions between the true and the false in belief ever grow up. . . . Previous idiom; new slang or metaphor or oddity that hits the public taste—and presto, a new idiom is made. Previous truth; fresh facts: and our mind finds a new truth."[18] What James was pointing toward at the turn of the century was the process by which the nation's various vernacular communities (makers of new slang, metaphors, idioms, "oddities") effect changes in the beliefs of the larger community (their sense of lawfulness, correctness, truth) by way of linguistic or symbolic intervention. In analogizing "new idiom" to "new truth," James, like Emerson, was anticipating Rorty's observation that "large-scale change of belief is indistinguishable from large-scale change in the meanings of one's words." But in emphasizing that word changes are *idiomatic,* a matter principally of "slangs" and "oddities," he was pointing down a road that led not toward Rorty but toward Ellison.[19] James, I mean to suggest, was beginning to map out the consequences of Emerson's insistence that "we shall be a multitude of people . . . every race and skin, white men, red men, yellow men, black men," a community of living proof that "there never was such a combination as this of ours, and the rules to meet it are not set down in any history" (CW 11:538, 541). Ellison, more than any other pragmatist, gave critical attention to the role ethnic diversity plays in pragmatism's necessary and perpetual reinvention of itself.

Returning to James's discussion of the idiom: A multitude of people from a multitude of linguistic traditions will, when faced with the prospect of expressing themselves in the logical space of a second language, create a multitude of new idioms. And here we should be specific about what an idiom is and what it *does.* Most generally, it is a "dialect or style of speaking peculiar to a people," but more specifically, it is "a construction or expression of one language whose parts correspond to elements in another language but whose total structure or meaning is not matched in the same way in the second language." The structural or epistemological incongruity signaled by an idiom has important consequences: As an expression, an idiom's "meaning is not predictable from the usual meanings of its constituent elements or from the general grammatical rules of a language."[20] James understood an idiom to be more than a consequence of deterministic social forces. An idiom, he would say, is an act that "create[s] the world's salvation so far as it makes room for itself"—it is an

expansion of logical possibility arising out of social incongruity and pre-
scribing social change. As such, the idiom has a central role in the pragmatic method, particularly when that method is, as James understood it
to be, the manifestation of republican desires, "the idea of a world growing not integrally put piecemeal by the contributions of its several parts
. . . a social scheme of cooperative work genuinely to be done." When
James says "languages, as is well known, tolerate much choice of expression and many dialects," he is not only being descriptive but *prescriptive,*
not just telling us what it is but *what it should be* (WJ 1:138, 140, 33). He
is laying the groundwork for what Ellison would later call "the American
vernacular as symbolic action."

To invoke this phrase is to, conveniently, begin at the end, a kind of
signifying Ellison might have found humorous. As Albert Schweitzer
Chair in the Humanities at New York University in the 1970s, Ellison
repeatedly taught a course entitled "The American Vernacular as Symbolic Action." The course took as its base "the Declaration of Independence, the Constitution, and the Bill of Rights," as well as the work of
"such literary men as Emerson, Thoreau, Whitman and Lincoln" and made
extensive use of Burke's concept of "language as symbolic action."[21] This
is where I'd like to begin, with a brief but important discussion of Burke's
significance to Ellison and Burke's debt to pragmatism. In 1937, Ellison
attended a lecture of Burke's called "The Rhetoric of Hitler's 'Battle.'"
That lecture left a deep and lasting impression on him. Eight years later
he would write to Burke: "You gave me the first instrument with which
I could orient myself. . . . I am writing a novel now and perhaps if it is
worthwhile it will be my most effective way of saying thanks." While I
take Ellison at his word here, I would also want to extend the implications of Ellison's note of thanks by arguing that the "instrument" that
Burke gave Ellison was, in a word, pragmatism[22] and that Ellison's even
more significant "orientation" involves making sense of Burke in relation
to Emerson. Out of that connection comes the Ellisonian concept of "the
novel as a function of American democracy."[23]

While I don't disregard Ellison's claim that "Burke's terms, purpose
to passion to perception" provided the framework for *Invisible Man*'s
"three-part division" (CE 14), I don't believe that this framework repre-

sents Burke's real "gift" to Ellison. Again, I go back to the seminal essay on Hitler's *Mein Kampf:* "What I learned from Burke," Ellison says, "was not so much the technique of fiction but the nature of literature and the way ideas and language operate in literary form. . . . I began to learn something of the nature of literature, society, social class, and psychology as they related to literary form. I began to grasp how language operates, both in literature and as an agency of oral communication" (CE 363–64). What Ellison took from Burke's essay was a point that Frank Lentricchia, thinking of Burke, has stated succinctly in this way: "Not all social power is literary power, but all literary power is social power. . . . The literary act is a social act."[24] Something like this represents Ellison's basic premise about Burke's concept of language as symbolic action: that as a kind of social power, writing can serve as a function of either social oppressiveness and stagnation or social flexibility and change and that one can manipulate language in the service of either goal by paying attention to how it *operates,* to what it *does.* Taking this as Ellison's understanding, two things jump out at me (and I suspect jumped out at Ellison) in Burke's description of Hitler's rhetoric. The first describes its design: "The efficiency of Hitlerism is the efficiency of the one voice, implemented throughout a total organization. The trinity of government which he finally offers is: *popularity* of the leader, *force* to back the popularity and popularity and force maintained together long enough to become backed by *tradition*" (213). Burke's critique of Hitler (which, as I will detail in chapter 2, resembles Emerson's critique of Carlyle) involves throwing light on a strategy whereby force of statement and endless repetition (by both speaker and auditors), taking place in a symbolic vacuum (a space kept clean of all linguistic interference), leads to the entrenchment of both symbolic and political hierarchies. Burke takes what was at the time the rather unpopular step of considering Hitler's writing seriously in order to illustrate how complicit our language is in the maintenance of our politics.

Of course the complicity between language and politics is as much opportunity as it is disaster. The second point I'd like to highlight is Burke's suggestion of an antidote. He quotes Hitler as saying that "a Babel of opinions cannot serve as the basis of a political fighting movement"

(206) and makes this keen observation: what Hitler can't tolerate, Burke says, is the "vocal diaspora" (200). The phrase is meant of course to recall the Jewish diaspora, and in that sense the political dangers of Hitlerism are all too clear. But it is also meant to signify a dispersion of voices generally, voices, that is, of minorities living among prevailing majorities— and therein lies its *rhetorical* significance. Fascism's aversion to the vocal diaspora lies in the fact that the diaspora calls into question the hierarchical grades of value on which the rhetoric of fascism depends. The "efficiency of the one voice" is, potentially, trumped by the flexibility, creativity, and productivity of the *polyvocal*. This is, I believe, how Ellison would have read the comparison. Indeed, he must have greatly appreciated the joke that Burke tells in the course of his critique, that in America it is not our *virtues* that are staving off fascism but rather "*conflict among our vices. Our vices cannot get together in a grand united front of prejudices; and the result of this frustration,*" Burke says, "*speaks . . . in the name of democracy*" (192). Emerson once noted similarly, though less sardonically, "a court or an aristocracy, which must always be a small minority, can more easily run into follies than a republic, which has too many observers" (CW 11:517). Ellison would have recognized in both statements an implicit validation of American subcommunities, particularly those communities most likely to frustrate the efficiency of the one hegemonic voice, encouraging in its place a social model based on what Ellison called "antagonistic cooperation."[25] In Burke's description of Hitler's rhetoric and its social import, Ellison recognized a counter-description, one that emphasized the central role played by vernacular communities in expanding egalitarian ideals. And he would not have missed, either, Burke's suggestion that American thinkers were particularly equipped for both the application of a rhetorical theory of form to fascist discourse as well as for the suggestion of an alternative to that discourse. American thinkers, Burke said in that same lecture, were "a people trained in pragmatism" (192).

I emphasize Burke's interest in pragmatism not only because Burke's work owes so much to the work of Emerson, James, and Dewey but because it is in the context of pragmatism that Ellison's interest in Burke makes the most sense. All of these writers are involved in an investigation of how a rhetorical theory of form might be wedded to a desire for democracy. Their work gives evidence, in varying degrees, to Cornel West's claim that American pragmatism's "basic impulse is a plebeian radicalism that fuels an antipatrician rebelliousness for the moral aim of enriching individuals and expanding democracy." Thus it is not simply an aside when James ends "What Pragmatism Means" by saying of the pragmatic method, "you can see already how democratic she is."[26] One needs this full palate, I'm suggesting, in order to make sense of precisely what Ellison means by "the American vernacular as symbolic action" and why that phrase acts as a touchstone for Ellison's changes to pragmatist discourse. With that phrase in mind, I'd like to direct Burke's concept of "language as symbolic action" toward John Dewey. Dewey, I hope, will serve as a middle term on our way to a more specific discussion of Ellison.

The following is one of Burke's more lucid descriptions of language as symbolic action, in regard to poetry: "The general approach to the poem might be called 'pragmatic' in this sense: It assumes that a poem's structure is to be described most accurately by thinking always of the poem's function. It assumes that the poem is designed to 'do something' for the poet and his readers, and that we can make the most relevant observations about its design by considering the poem as the embodiment of this act . . . this pragmatic view of the poem . . . through the emphasis upon the act promptly integrates considerations of 'form' and 'content.'" Burke's "pragmatic view of the poem" has as its antecedent Dewey's stipulation that "in the act [of writing] there is no distinction between, but perfect integration of manner and content, form and substance."[27] I note this not to privilege Dewey over Burke via his "originality" but simply as a way of pointing out that the concept of language as symbolic action that Ellison found so useful might be located in Dewey's work as well. Why is this important? The answer has to do with the way the concept of symbolic action "integrates considerations of 'form' and 'content.'" As Burke explains in the quotation above, when one speaks of symbolic action, there is a presumption that motives (political, social, psychological, economic) are manifested in design. What might be considered merely "content" (say, a political point of view) according to another paradigm has, according to pragmatism, formal consequences. Conversely (and this is equally important), *form* (syntax, grammar, poetics) is considered as *a kind of content,* as socially substantive, as having, potentially, a social function.[28] Burke, Dewey, and Ellison are all in agreement on this point. Again, why then discuss Dewey? Because Dewey is most useful in illuminating what Ellison means by "the novel as a function of American democracy" and explaining why his idea of "the American vernacular as symbolic action" constitutes a redirection of pragmatist discourse.

Dewey describes pragmatist philosophy as a kind of democratic symbolic action and calls Emerson and James "the philosophers of democracy." Most importantly, he describes what a philosophy that acted as a function of democracy might look like. "A philosophy animated, be it consciously or unconsciously, by the strivings of men to achieve democracy will construe liberty as meaning a universe in which there is real uncertainty and contingency, a world which is not all in, and never will be, a world which in some respect is incomplete and in the making, and in these respects may be made this way or that according as men judge, prize, love and labor . . . a genuine field of novelty, of real and unpredictable increments to existence, a field for experimentation and invention" (MW 11:50). Dewey considers philosophy in the same way that Burke considers the poem: as a particular kind of *motivated* discourse. He assumes, that is, that a philosophical discourse, one of Emerson's, for instance, is designed to do something, and he considers that discourse "as the embodiment of that act." Dewey insists that philosophy is not a form of objective or abstract knowledge but rather "a form of desire, of effort at action." Thus if Emerson writes, as he does in "Montaigne," "the philosophy we want is one of fluxions and mobility" (CW 4:160), Dewey wouldn't hesitate to relate this to Emerson's political desires, his interest in "the strivings of men to achieve democracy" and his contemporaneous agitation in favor of emancipation. He would, in all likelihood, point out that Emerson here construes philosophy as a *desire*—not a written transcription of an abstract truth but something we "want." Moreover, he would find in Emerson's style—his "paragraphs incomprehensible"—similar motivations: a will toward unpredictability in the name of experimentation and invention. What this has to do specifically with sustaining egalitarian politics and democratic institutions, I will make more explicit in chapter 2. Emerson theorized that the strivings of people to achieve democracy in "America" was predicated on the ability to revise the definition of America and the definitions at work in its founding documents. There needed to be, in Emerson's words, a "belief [among Americans] that as the people have made a government, they can make another" (JMN 11:406). And this belief could best be fostered by a corresponding belief that the generation and maintenance of meaning was an unpredictable and ongoing affair.

Though I jump ahead somewhat in doing so, I'll say now that Ellison's theory is similar: "Out of the democratic principles set down on paper in the Constitution and the Bill of Rights," Ellison says, Americans "were improvising themselves into a nation, scraping together a conscious culture out of various dialects, idioms, lingos, and methodologies of America's diverse peoples and regions" (CE 336). Emerson, Dewey, and Ellison would all agree that a rhetoric that emphasizes its improvisational, experimental qualities is acting symbolically in favor of an improvised republic, a nation whose "grammar" is flexible enough to allow it to revise itself according to, as James would say, "the collectivity of experience's demands." Still, it's worth paying attention to the distinctions in emphasis among these writers, distinctions that imply that they are part of a continuum rather than a camp. In the above quotation, Ellison describes the key operators in political and cultural improvisation as the "various dialects, idioms, lingos, and methodologies of America's diverse people." As we have seen, Emerson and, to a lesser degree, James point toward the role cultural diversity necessarily plays in the development of American pragmatism. But neither is nearly as insistent on this point as Ellison. In another philosophical paradigm this distinction might seem negligible, but in the context of pragmatism, as James would have insisted, changes in vocabulary constitute equivalent changes in belief, in philosophy. The vernacular improvisation, the idiomatic *reinterpretation,* which Ellison argues was the method by which the Constitution became a functional and *functioning* document in American experience, is the same method that Ellison himself applies to the founding documents of pragmatism. In some cases he is directly signifying on work by pragmatists such as Burke and Emerson. But in *all* cases we can take his work as a general signifying improvisation on pragmatism. To do so is to read creatively in the direction of a new definition of "what pragmatism means."

I'd like to focus on one final passage from Dewey as a way to deepen our understanding of what I'm calling Ellison's "method" in anticipation of his greatest illustration of that method, *Invisible Man.* The passage reveals Dewey to be as much artist as philosopher:

> Man excels in complexity and minuteness of differentiations. This very fact constitutes the necessity for many more comprehensive and exact relationships among the constituents of his being. Important as are the distinctions and relations thus made possible, the story does not end here. There are more opportunities for resistance and tension, more drafts upon experience and invention, and therefore more novelty in action, greater range and depth of insight and increase of poignancy of feeling. As an organism increases in complexity, the rhythms of struggle and consummation in its relation to its environment are varied and prolonged, and they come to include within themselves an endless variety of subrhythms. The designs of living are widened and enriched. Fulfillment is more massive and more subtly shaded. . . . The process of organic life *is* variation. . . . Demand for variety is the manifestation of the fact that being alive we seek to live, until we are cowed by fear or dulled by routine. The need of life itself pushes out into the unknown. (LW 10:29, 172–73)

In this passage, Dewey is performing one of the older philosophical tasks—he is describing the nature of man. Dewey's performance, however, strays—purposefully—well outside the boundaries of traditional, abstract philosophizing. I would go so far as to say that Dewey doesn't particularly care whether his description of man is "true" or "real" or not. The "being" Dewey describes—with its "constituents," its "rhythms of struggle and consummation"—is, rather, a philosophical, sociological, psychological, and aesthetic description of action as pragmatism would have it, as Dewey would *want* it. Rhetorically, the passage functions by suggesting a series of "necessities" that are the predicates of "opportunities" for "insight," "enrichment," and "fulfillment." In his emphasis of "invention" and "novelty," "complexity" and "variety" over that process by which one is "dulled by routine," Dewey seems to promote an experimental aesthetic and ethic that is fueled by "more comprehensive and exact relationships among the constituents."[29] In using a word like "constituents," Dewey tips his hand, signifying that his description is not only aesthetic, philosophical, and biological, but sociopolitical. A word like "constituents" in this context asks us to introduce its various meanings, to make "the parts" cousin to "the voters." Dewey describes a deficiency (the necessity for "more . . . relationships," the death state of dull routine) and suggests a solution (the processes of invention and variation) and the benefits of that solution (widened designs, an enrichment of life). When bodies "come to include within themselves an endless variety of subrhythms" and, empowered by this inclusion, "push out into the unknown," living itself is enriched—good things happen. In Dewey's "body" (corporeal body, body politic, body of art), boundaries and categories are fluid, and invention is the result of tension resolved in the expansion of design and the reconfiguration of structures.

If Dewey is so adept at putting philosophical speculation in the service of "the strivings of men to achieve democracy," what accounts for the necessity of Ellison? The answer lies, I believe, in Dewey's vocabulary, particularly if we contextualize that vocabulary according to the period in which it was employed, 1934. Dewey's terms, despite the scope of their application, remain in some sense resistant to all but the most aggressive interpretation. I don't intend this as an attack on Dewey; he presumed that only aggressive interpretation in accordance with cultural change keeps any writing vital. But he also presumed that the pragmatic method would be sustained not only by the aggressive redirection of old vocabularies but by the invention of new ones. And so with these presumptions in mind, I'd offer the following insight: Dewey's writing, circa 1934, never exactly admits race or ethnicity as a category relevant to the expansion of democratic designs that he calls for. "Variety" never quite reveals itself to be "diversity" in the way we've come to understand this latter term. And even if we take "the constituents" to be "the voters," the complicated relation of this second term to American racism never really materializes. The shoe doesn't drop. I would speculate that one explanation for the "resistance" of Dewey's vocabulary is that Dewey himself—as a philosopher who equates the operations of language and the operations of culture—offers no specific description of the role ethnicity plays in the formation of the American vernacular. Again, this is less a critique than a description of a *gap* that requires a *transition*. For me it constitutes the necessity of Ellison.

One interesting aspect of Ellison's thinking around pragmatism is that he is the first person since Emerson to offer an insistent and sustained description of the pragmatist method that relates it causally to the struggle by Americans (both empowered and disenfranchised) to make sense of their cultural identity vis-à-vis the symbolic agency of their founding documents. To put it simply, Emerson and Ellison take the Declaration of Independence, the Constitution, and the Bill of Rights as exhibits A, B, and C in their historicized description of how language operates and what it can do. The ramifications of their insistence need to be made clear. These "exhibits" were *active documents* against which the *acted* document of culture could be compared. As Ellison put it in a 1956 letter to his friend Albert Murray, African Americans had "turned the Supreme Court into the forum of liberty it was intended to be, and the Constitution of the United States into a briar patch in which the nimble people, the willing people, have a chance. And that's what *it* was intend[ed] to be."[30] Emerson and Ellison took their radically democratic interpretations of the nation's founding documents, coupled them with a belief that, as Geertz has said, "cultural forms can be treated as texts, as imaginative works built out of social materials,"[31] and then proceeded to do an ongoing, decades-long comparative study. What such a methodology gave them was a means to continue returning to the social text where symbolic systems involving race had obvious theoretical importance. As I will discuss in the next chapter, Emerson was led by that methodology to consider the actions of African Americans as of basic and revelatory importance to his conception of liminal selfhood as it relates to self-reliance. Ellison was led by the same methodology to a careful and lifelong examination of the American vernacular.

In a course description for "The American Vernacular as Symbolic Action," Ellison wrote: "After having started with proper English usage as an inherited (and aristocratic) norm, the former English colonials gradually developed their own democratic vernacular speech. An improvised language . . . the basic symbolic agency through which the British colonials gradually transformed themselves into 'Americans.' Through the vernacular they inspirited their fledgling social forms and political processes with the egalitarian principles of democracy laid down by the Founders of the Republic."[32] Ellison makes an argument about language as symbolic agency analogous to the one Dewey makes about philosophy. Dewey describes how a philosophy "committed to a metaphysical feudalism" whose goal was "to show the rationality of this or that existent hierarchical grading of values and schemes of life" is transformed by figures such as Emerson and James into a democratic philosophy (MW 11:52). Ellison offers a similar description of how the king's English became, through improvisation, the American vernacular. It became, that is, a form of democratic symbolic action. When he describes how the vernacular was transformed into "splendidly pragmatic literary agency," he is thinking of Emerson, Whitman, and Melville, as well as himself.

Again, though, we should resist reading Ellison's list of "pragmatic literary agents" as the description of a camp, except in the loosest sense. Consider his use of the term "inherited" in the preceding passage. Inheriting "proper English usage" is nearly synonymous with *changing* proper English usage. As improvising, displaced heirs, Americans had to adapt their inheritance to "experience's demands." Now consider the fact that Ellison says that he "inherited the language of Emerson." Ellison understood that, whatever his affinities with Emerson (and the affinities are sometimes uncanny), as a displaced heir he would have to change "the language of Emerson" in order to use it. Ellison's changes to pragmatism's vocabulary are uniquely important symbolic acts.

I will offer one resonant example that I think bears comparison to Dewey's meditation on man discussed earlier. In this passage from "The Novel as a Function of American Democracy," Ellison describes the development of the American vernacular in more detail. Notice how his emphases and metaphors differ from Dewey's:

In this country there is no absolute separation of groups. The American language, this rich, marvelous, relatively unexplored organ, is the creation of many, many people, and it began with the Indians. . . . We forget, conveniently sometimes, that the language we speak is not English, although it is based on English. We forget that *our language is such a flexible instrument* because it has had *so many dissonances thrown into it*—from Africa, from Mexico, from Spain, from, God knows, everywhere. And yet it has been reduced to a working and flexible, highly poetic language. . . . In this sense our national style is a product of these elusive variations of styles, manners and customs which emerged from *our many subcommunities*. (GT, 316–17, emphasis added)

I find the tonal similarity between this passage and the earlier passage from Dewey remarkable. Dewey makes the *body* implicitly both a *country* (full of constituents) and a *language* (created in "drafts" and composed of rhythms). Ellison makes the *language* implicitly both a *country* (he simply dispenses with the logic that would separate "this country" and "the American language") and a *body* (or, at least, an organ). Both writers characterize this multisymbolic "body" as "rich, marvelous," and "unexplored" (Dewey uses "enriched," "opportunities," "fulfillment," "the unknown"). Both make an argument for a democratic state energized by a conception of both individual and group identity as perpetually *becoming* rather than *being*. And both link an "experimental attitude" to "the mood of personal moral responsibility for democracy."[33] Still, these similarities should not impede us from considering what I believe are key differences. In Ellison's terminology, Dewey's description of "subrhythms" becomes explicitly "sub*communities*." And these communities are specifically multicultural: the real movers in the transition from proper English usage to American vernacular speech are "the Indians" as well as arrivants "from Africa, from Mexico, from Spain, from, God knows, everywhere."

Ellison describes the dynamic between American subcommunities and the American community as a whole similarly to how Nathaniel Mackey describes the dynamic between individual artists and the larger groups to which they belong. Mackey describes "the role of eccentric individuals

[individuals *out of the center*] whose contributions come to be identified with the very culture that may have initially rejected them" and goes on to explain this phenomenon by noting that "in matters of artistic othering individual expression both reflects and redefines the collective, realigns, refracts it." In like manner, Ellison describes how American subcommunities simultaneously reflect and redefine, realign, refract American culture generally. I make this connection between Mackey and Ellison because both writers have as their model for this dynamic jazz music and jazz musicians. The jazz musician—who, Ellison says, always plays both "within and against the group" (SA 234)—constantly reflects and redefines the ensemble in which he plays. Likewise, the ensemble reflects and redefines the larger community to which it belongs.[34] This jazz ensemble model deeply informs Ellison's sense of the American vernacular and, thus, his role as a pragmatist. Again, consider his variation on Dewey's model: Dewey's description of how "the rhythms of struggle and consummation" widen the culture's "designs" becomes, in Ellison's hands, a description of how "dissonance" acts to produce that "flexible instrument" he calls our "national style."

Ellison uses the term dissonance—a word he purposely culls from the jazz idiom—to describe a vital tool at work in the central dialectic of the American vernacular: if on the one hand its flexibility lends it a "capacity for creating order out of chaos," its insistent use of dissonance allows it to also "creat[e] confusion out of no longer tenable forms of order."[35] Dissonance, then, is never absolute dissonance; it acts and resonates where "no longer tenable forms of order" lack the logical space to accommodate it. Dissonance is a tactical "interruption of our composure," as Robert Duncan would say.[36] Avant-garde jazz trumpeter Booker Little has described the rhetorical motives behind his use of dissonance in this way: "The more dissonance, the bigger the sound. It sounds like more horns; in fact you can't always tell how many there are. And your shadings can be more varied. Dissonance is a tool to achieve these things. . . . I can't think in terms of wrong notes—in fact I don't hear any notes as being wrong. It's a matter of knowing how to integrate the notes."[37] Notice how Little refuses to make a priori judgments about right and wrong in regard to the notes being played; right and wrong are decided in the course of integration. In the process of integrating the dissonant notes, one achieves the "bigger sound," the polyvocal effect of "more horns" (representative, I would say, of "more constituents"). Integration involves the accommodation of new varieties in shading. (It's uncanny to me how Little's characterization of the way in which one's "shadings can be more varied" echoes Dewey's description of the way in which the body's rhythms "are varied . . . and more subtly shaded.") Ellison and Little have a similar understanding of dissonance as symbolic action in a jazz ensemble, a fact unsurprising given how steeped in the jazz tradition both artists are. And I would suggest that in the passage on "the American language," Ellison's employment of jazz metaphors in what is essentially a pragmatist description of language is a purposeful use of dissonance vis-à-vis the pragmatist tradition, an attempt on his part to make it a more "flexible instrument." As a pragmatist, Ellison "consider[ed] himself," in Burke's words, "as involved in the process . . . recognize[ed] that one discovers 'reality' in accordance with one's terminology."[38] He knew that the introduction of the idioms of jazz into pragmatist aesthetic discourse would force that discourse into a specific and extensive consideration of what "the Negro cultural idiom and style have contributed to the form and content of American culture."[39] Ellison was employing what Burke called "planned incongruity" on the pragmatist canon itself. As Burke explains: "Planned incongruity should be deliberately cultivated for the purpose of experimentally wrenching apart all those molecular combinations of adjective and noun, substantive and verb, which still remain with us. . . . Imagine beginning your course of study precisely by depriving yourself of this familiarity, attempting to understand motives and purposes by avoiding as much as possible the clues handed you ready made in the texture of language itself."[40] Obviously, Ellison understood that the implications of his rewriting went well beyond any isolated claim for the centrality of jazz as a form of pragmatist artistic practice. Ellison is always broadening the scope of his remarks, making sure that they are not taken to be relevant only to art, philosophy, psychology, or politics but, rather, as part of a web of signification that touches all these areas of cultural expression.[41] American culture, and indeed pragmatism, Ellison insists, is "jazz-shaped." And, like the jazzman, Ellison the writer puts "democracy into aesthetic action."[42]

I'm here. I come after you yesterday
I couldn't find you. Doctor, I'm in a bad
fix; I want you to do something for me.

"old man Hemby," African American patient of Williams Carlos Williams, as described in *In the American Grain*

In the context of this book, William Carlos Williams might be thought of as Ellison's ghostly double. I cannot move forward without some explanation of the role he has played in my thinking about pragmatism, the motivation he has provided for my construction of detours on the pragmatist corridor. To a remarkable degree, the older Williams was shadowing Ellison (quite unconsciously) in the years directly preceding and following the publication of *Invisible Man*. In the same year, 1945, that Ellison began corresponding with Burke (and "writing a novel" as the "most effective way to say thanks" to him), Williams (who had been friends with Burke for twenty-five years) was complaining to Burke that the first book of *Paterson* was a failure. (For this complaint Burke let Williams have it, telling him in a letter that at least he "might have believed in his own poem."[43]) I find it particularly useful to think of Williams and Ellison as competing for Burke's attention from this point forward—or competing, rather, over the subsequent direction of American pragmatism. This may seem to some an odd competition since Williams's and Ellison's understanding of writing as a function of American democracy are so closely aligned—but there is a value, I'd suggest, in considering Williams and Ellison as involved in a "cutting session," what Ellison describes as a "contest of improvisational skill and physical endurance between two or more musicians" (SA 208). In jazz, such a contest generally involves a base text, a blueprint, the chord changes, say, to a "standard" tune. Likewise in my fictionalized scenario: Williams and Ellison are playing over the accompaniment harmonies to pragmatism.

Ellison wins the day—not least because he understands the role that African American culture played in the development of pragmatism and thus is better equipped to disclose that "anticipatory arena where actuality and possibility, past and present, are allowed to collaborate on a history of the future." Ellison naturalizes the implicit pragmatism of jazz: where contact with African American culture is an impediment to Williams's pragmatic method, it is the prime mover in Ellison's. The year 1945 also marks Williams's one sustained effort to engage jazz music on the aesthetic level. It is a failed effort, and one that needs to be understood in terms of his pragmatism. Race is a roadblock for Williams, though he knows enough to keep bumping up against it. His accidents are informative, and I will discuss some of them in anticipation of my discussions of both Emerson's abolitionism and Ellison's jazz-shaped writing, key detours in the alternative route (root) of pragmatism I hope to describe.

The development of a theory of democratic symbolic action negotiated through and/or between Emerson, James, Dewey, and Burke was as important to Williams's artistic growth as it would be to Ellison's. Like Ellison, Williams was encouraged by these pragmatists to pay special attention to the American vernacular, which he, too, believed was "the basic symbolic agency through which the British colonials gradually transformed themselves into Americans." In my discussion of Ellison, I have analogized this quotation to Dewey's attack on "metaphysical feudalism." Interestingly, Williams sounds most like Ellison when he is specifically drawing on Dewey's work, as in the following, from a 1944 letter to Horace Gregory: "There has to be a recognition by the intellectual heads (Eliot among them) of the work-a-day local culture of the United States. In fact, there can be no general culture unless it is bedded, as he says, in a locality—something I have been saying for a generation: that there is no universal except in the local. I myself took it from Dewey. So it is not new."[44] Williams was expressing here what he had expressed a thousand times before: that the artist, the intellectual, needed to hash out what it meant to be what he called a "United Stateser." "Yes it's ugly," he would say defiantly of that moniker, "there is no word to say it better." The adoption of an "ugly" name (first publicized in the Declaration of Independence) was one way to insist that "the American background is America."[45] And whether D. H. Lawrence was right in all cases when he said "the local in America is America itself," he certainly was right in the case of William Carlos Williams.

What Williams wrote to Gregory also came up in "The Poem *Paterson*," where he noted, "John Dewey had said (I discovered it quite by chance), 'The local is the only universal, upon that all art builds.' "[46] Williams intended this statement as a gloss on his motivations *for* writing *Paterson* as well as for his choice of design *in* writing it. The suggestion that he discovered the quote "quite by accident" is a canard; it appeared in an essay entitled "Americanism and Localism" in the June 1920 issue of *The Dial* (two months before Williams's great poem "Portrait of a Lady" appeared there), where Williams had been following Dewey's work closely. This was a fertile period to be keeping an eye on Dewey: his essay "Philosophy and Democracy" had been published two years before. There, he insisted that "philosophy is a form of desire, of effort at action" and described (as quoted earlier) what a democratic philosophy might look like. There, he called "free verse" a "deliberate action . . . an experiment with the world to see what it will stand for, what it will promote, and what frustrate" (MW 11:43, 48–50).[47] Dewey was suggesting that "experimental" poetry (free verse being one such "experiment") was a type of democratic symbolic action, designed to see whether the world would stand for and promote, or conversely frustrate, democracy, whether the linguistic structures of the poem would be consonant with or dissonant to the social structures against which the poem acted.

Williams was primed to accept these connections among philosophy, democracy, and poetic form. In 1917 he'd published *Al Que Quiere! or The Pleasures of Democracy,* its egalitarian Spanish title ("To Him Who Wants It") signifying the desire for a new (though Whitmanian) relationship between reader and writer and coming on the heels of his decision to abandon poetic standardization, for instance, the capitalized letters at the beginning of each line. In the same month that Williams read Dewey's "Americanism and Localism," he had also published an irreverently American poem called "Spirit of '76" in *Poetry,* poking fun at editor Harriet Monroe's habit of capitalizing his left margin against his wishes. Dewey's essay, then, was ammunition for a poet who often felt as if he was under

siege. "We have been too anxious to get away from home," Dewey wrote.
"Naturally that took us to Europe though we fancied we were going
around America."[48] The distinction he was making was between "local
color" and an American writing that, grounded in the experiences of
American *localities,* would act as a function of democracy. For Williams
it must have been fire of a real order, with the accompanying anxiety of
influence. When Burke greeted Williams's manuscript of philosophical
essays (which would become *The Embodiment of Knowledge*) by worrying
that it owed too much to Dewey, Williams wrote back, "If I could convince myself or have anyone else convince me that I were merely following in the steps of Dewey, I'd vomit and quit—at any time. But for the
moment I don't believe it—the poetry is offered not too confidently as
proof" (SL 138). In this sheepish disavowal, Williams registers his nervousness about a lack of originality rather than any specific disagreement
with Dewey. Burke could hardly have responded otherwise. *The Embodiment of Knowledge* is a pretty good rendering of the philosophic advances
Dewey had made through the 1920s, which is to say, it is an attack on
metaphysical feudalism in favor of a pragmatic approach to knowledge:
"Philosophy has been the chief offender in this respect with its pursuit of
'the Absolute' which is nothing whatever—outside of philosophy," Williams wrote. "Yet, men believe in each category as it is brought out, exactly as they believed in dynasties and kings formerly."[49] During this
same period (1929, in this case), Williams would even gloss Burke's writing with Dewey's concept of Americanism and localism, writing, "One
has to learn what the meaning of the local is, for universal purposes. The
local is the only thing that is universal. . . . Burke seems to me to be
stalled in the right place" (I 358). But Burke's and Williams's anxieties
are of little interest to me—the point is that Williams was developing his
aesthetic under the influence of pragmatism. Moreover, he was reading
pragmatism as Ellison was, as a kind of democratic symbolic action.
Hence, the Deweyan "local" and the democratic are finally synonymous
for Williams, as in the following: "to be democratic, local (in the sense
of being attached with integrity to experience)" (I 351).

As a reader of his own poetry, it is of paramount importance to Williams that he "show how the language he practices varies from English"

because he believes, as any pragmatist does, that in that language resides the imminent ideology of the culture.[50] A language designed to support aristocratic practice would have to be changed if it were to foster and support democratic practices. As Williams himself put it, "It is impossible for any group of people to change their habits until the language has first given them the means to state their objective, this is the only permissible use of 'ideals'" (EK 118). By 1920 he was already dismantling Anglocentric language and motifs in his poems. One such poem was "Portrait of a Lady," which, as I have already mentioned, appeared two months after Dewey's "Americanism and Localism" in *The Dial* and serves as an apt companion to that essay. Here is the poem in full:

PORTRAIT OF A LADY
Your thighs are appletrees
whose blossoms touch the sky.
Which sky? The sky
where Watteau hung a lady's
slipper. Your knees
are a southern breeze—or
a gust of snow. Agh! what
sort of man was Fragonard?
—as if that answered
anything. Ah, yes—below
the knees, since the tune
drops that way, it is
one of those white summer days,
the tall grass of your ankles
flickers upon the shore—
Which shore?—
the sand clings to my lips—
Which shore?
Agh, petals maybe. How
should I know?
Which shore? Which shore?
I said petals from an appletree.

The poem is an assault on English metaphor through dialogic interruption, though even before the irritating questioner (who I would like to read as the "Lady" herself) begins her obstruction, one is struck by the visual inadequacies of the metaphor and, soon, by its arbitrariness: "The sky / where Watteau hung a lady's / slipper"—Williams has gotten his paintings mixed up (the speaker is thinking of Fragonard's *The Swing*), but the nonchalance, the seeming randomness, of his answer suggests that it doesn't matter much. Likewise with his next attempt, "Your knees / are a southern breeze—or / a gust of snow." The first choice of metaphor seems dictated entirely by sound; it is a joke on the symbolic constraints brought about by the need to rhyme, the metaphor quickly undone by the suggestion of an alternate metaphor that is in fact the *opposite* of the first. (It is also a pretty clear relative of Dickinson's use of dashes and "multiple choice"—the kind one finds in a poem like "The brain—is wider than the sky," for instance.) The speaker's guttural "Agh!" is a gesture toward dispensing with metaphor entirely, even as he seems to have realized his mistake regarding the painting. Who cares? the poem implies. From this point forward anything that might be construed as "high" or "English" speech is suffused with irony. "Ah, yes . . . it is / one of those white summer days"—here we have something quite intentionally similar to the "peculiarly English" portrait with which Henry James begins his *Portrait of a Lady:* "Under certain circumstances there are few hours in life more agreeable than the hour dedicated to the ceremony known as afternoon tea."[51] But Williams has spliced into the middle of his proper speech a sort of gag, indicating that the poem is in the process of being written: "below / the knees, since the tune / drops that way"—Williams is working his way down the page. This insistence on the act of writing over and against the "portrait" was another version of his insistence on the local. As he put it in reference to Burke, "writing is made up of words, of nothing else. These have a contour and complexion imposed upon them by the weather, by the shapes of men's lives in places" (I 357). "Which shore? Which shore?" That's the question, the one the lady keeps insisting on, the one that frustrates attempts at portraiture. It too is a joke—the pun on "sure" signifying on the speaker's lack of surety. The insistence on location is meant to remind the male speaker and the reader what shore they were dealing with: this Lady, in contrast to James's and Eliot's, was on the *American* shore, and she was making the point that Williams himself was always making: "that observation about us engenders the very opposite of what we seek: triviality, crassness and intellectual bankruptcy" (I 351). For my money, "Portrait of a Lady" is Williams's most explicitly feminist poem (it may have helped that he had appetizing targets in James and, particularly, Eliot to play off of). The American woman speaks, but more importantly, she is entangled with the other speaker in the poem—it is impossible to unravel who states the final two questions. As Brian Bremen has said in reference to *In the American Grain,* in Williams's best work "notions of 'identification' and 'empathy' maintain this paradox of identity and difference by moving beyond power relations to achieve greater intersubjective understanding."[52] At the conclusion of "Portrait of a Lady," we cannot call the two characters identical, but they are, as I say, *entangled*—and the poem is prolegomenon to some future expression of their intersubjective identity.

The intersubjectivity that Bremen highlights is best captured, perhaps, by Williams's claim that his poetry came from "the mouths of Polish mothers" (A 311).[53] This claim has as its correlative an incident described in *In the American Grain*. In the chapter on Aaron Burr (Williams's archetypal democratic activist), "The Virtue of History," Williams writes:

> A while ago, just here, I heard a Polish woman saying to her daughter: "You bust your coat with your fifty sweaters."
>
> What's that: you bust your coat with your fifty sweaters? It's immediacy, its sensual quality, a pure observation, its lack of irritation, its lack of pretense, its playful exaggeration, its repose, its sense of design, its openness, its gayety, its unconstraint. It frees, it creates itself . . . not a scheme, nor a system of procedure—but careless truth. . . . Burr's life was of that stuff. It is *this* that is trying to escape in a democracy. (AG 206)

Williams is describing something very near to what Ellison called "the American vernacular as symbolic action." Bremen is right to conclude that, in this instance especially, Williams's politics "includes the voices that other writers either omit, repress, or seek to silence" (182). Equally important, though, is the attention Williams gives to the very *structure* of those voices he includes. Williams had that same sense of the importance of the idiom that I have already located in James and Ellison. What he appreciates, what he attempts to incorporate into his own practice, as in "You bust your coat with your fifty sweaters," is the challenge it poses to proper usage via what Emerson called "a spontaneity which forgets usages" (CW 3:68). It represents the storehouse of possible language in the process of radical structural change. What's that? Williams asks sincerely of this new unit of organization making room for itself.[54] I am reminded of another observation of Dewey's from the essay "Americanism and Localism" that surely must have caught Williams's eye. Dewey writes of American immigrants—particularly those "recalcitrants who are denounced" for not succumbing to "Americanization"—"One gathers of course that Americanization consists in learning a language strangely known as English. But perhaps they are too busy making the American language to devote much time to studying the English" (685). I have said that Dewey's writing never exactly admits race or ethnicity as a category relevant to the expansion of democratic designs that he calls for; he offers no specific description of the role ethnicity plays in the formation of the American vernacular. "Americanism and Localism" reveals my statements to be at best half-truths. But the possibilities latent in the connection between vernacular expression and pragmatist theory remain undeveloped in Dewey. In the context of his massive corpus we can take the four pages of "Americanism and Localism" as a furtive suggestion not capitalized on, something he left others to pursue. Williams, finding this germ in *The Dial* and already thinking along similar lines, and Ellison, well versed in Emersonian pragmatism and profoundly attentive to the American vernacular, do pursue it.

With his eye on incidents such as this one with the Polish mother, Bremen links Williams to Burke along those same lines on which I have linked Burke and Ellison. Williams recognized, says Bremen, that "the American 'identity' is made up of that 'Babel of voices,' that 'corporate we' that Burke 'identifies' in *Attitudes to History*" (179). There is surely a great deal of truth to that statement but I would want to adopt the same pragmatic insistence that Williams did, that propositions such as Bremen's must be "proven in each case" (EK 79). "It should be clear," continues Bremen, "that a tradition that rigorously excludes the voices of women and minorities effectively relegates these groups to a subordinate silence." With this proviso in mind, I would like to address Williams's approach to African Americans and African American culture. My basic point is this: that, as I have said before, Williams knows enough to continually dip his toe into African American cultural space—he understands intuitively the relevance of that space and its activities to his own work, but in those moments when black voices and symbolic activities begin to mediate his expression, a response akin to silencing does occur. I do not want to elevate this phenomenon too dramatically, to make it stand in for the oppression of a culture. To put it plainly, Williams needs black people a lot more than they need him. I want to read the cultural exchange for its missed opportunities, as a way to emphasize Ellison's significance to an alternative model of pragmatism.

One cathectic moment in the history of Williams's involvement with African Americans occurs in the chapter of *In the American Grain* entitled "The Advent of the Slaves" (208–11). Indeed that chapter might serve as a guide to Williams's later attempts to engage African American culture. In it, Williams describes a father and son, both of whom were his patients. Of the son, "M.," he writes, "Language grows in the original from his laughing lips," quotes several lines of his speech ("Cocaine for horses, cocaine for mules, IN THE TRENCHES!"), and continues, "The relief is never ending, never failing." Williams is echoing here (unconsciously I expect) his response to Duchamp's *Nude Descending a Staircase,* which he saw at the Armory Show in 1913: "I laughed out loud when I first saw it, happily, with relief" (A 134). Coming toward the end of *In the American Grain,* on the heels of his discussion of the Polish mother's vernacular speech as symbolic action ("it is this that is trying to escape in a democracy"), we ought to take this implicit conflation of avant-garde art and black vernacular speech seriously. The American vernacular is front and center at the conclusion of this book, so much so that we are encouraged to consider the speech of these two black men (despite the chronological impossibility) as the prototype even for Edgar Allan Poe's inventions. What Poe (who "faced inland") shares in common with these men, Williams implies, "is that of proving even the most preposterous of his inventions plausible . . . and by the very extreme of their play, by so much more do they hold up the actuality of that which he conceives" (230). At bottom, Poe's language operates the way slang operates, growing up pragmatically, without "rigid canons of what shall count as proof" (WJ 1:44).

To me, the most intriguing moment in *In the American Grain* occurs when Williams says of the son in "Advent of the Slaves," "I wish I might write a book of his improvisations in slang. I wish I might write a play in collaboration with him" (211). The possibilities and the limitations, the abilities and incapacities of Williams are all here. A collaborative play based on improvisations in slang. Collaborative improvisation. Does Williams even know that he is signifying on jazz here? And suggesting a writing practice that would be, in Ellison's sense, "jazz-shaped"? Vaguely, I suspect. Regardless, the mood here is subjunctive: Williams wishes that he might, but the implication is that he certainly won't. And even his actual forays into this area of African American vernacular are imbued with a sense of the inevitably missed opportunity. Of the father, Williams writes, "I once made several pages of notes upon his conversation—but I lost them." The implication here is that chance has dashed any future attempt to use the father's speech in some way, any possibility that it might have mediated Williams's poetic expression. The full picture though is much more complex. The unrealized opportunities that Williams alludes to in this passage on the father and son can be explained in part by his misunderstanding of black speech and culture.

As Aldon Nielsen has written, Williams "was not terribly concerned with thinking straight and studying hard about Afro-Americans."[55] Thus, Ellison's sense of black vernacular English as a collaborative improvisation that, in turn, is a crucial, often dissonant, voicing in the improvisation of the American vernacular as a whole is absent in Williams. Though he hints at collaborative possibilities (and even, occasionally, at an analogy to jazz), they are continually undercut by his most basic premise about the black speaker: "Language grows in the original from his laughing lips." It is a backhanded compliment, this gesture toward the "existential blank out of which Williams believes the black improvises his own authenticity, his own unencumbered being." Nielsen comments wryly about such gestures that "there appears to be an enormous price to pay if the black other is to accept this opportunity to achieve his primordial creativity" (81–82). Williams cannot really envision a collaboration with these black men because he does not see black speech as collaborative, which is to say, black speech, for Williams, does not arise out of specific social contexts, does not mediate, and is not mediated by other forms of speech. Each speech act by a man like Hemby grows "original" from a romanticized, plush void. Thus, contact with black speech is, for Williams, more comfortably explained by the metaphor of *discovery* (he finds it already intact, he copies it down) than by the concept of interaction. Williams's tendency to view black speech and black speakers as emerging from a naught is a disastrous misstep that haunts his discussions of the American idiom till the end.

Again, though, I would prefer not to attribute mythic proportions to Williams's difficulties. Williams is not Icarus drowning but rather a poet whose available language is insufficient for the task of explaining or engaging central aspects of American culture. When he's *explaining,* say, some aspect of black culture, he's terrible. When he's *engaging* it, we are at least privy to an informative and sometimes complex encounter worthy of more than our condescension. Such encounters are often loaded with irony (as when old man Hemby tells him, "I'm here. I come after you yesterday but I couldn't find you. Doctor, I'm in a bad fix; I want you to do something for me.") And, however mistakenly, they do mediate Williams's expression. As Nielsen points out, "even as Williams is stuffing black music into a white envelope . . . he is mailing a cultural letter bomb," and "as mistaken as Williams may be, the example of jazz aids him in the transformation of American verse."[56] The epicenter of Williams's engagement with black culture is that year I mentioned before, 1945. It is the year when, after seeing New Orleans jazz musician Bunk Johnson play in New York, he wrote his "jazz poem," "Ol' Bunk's Band," and began his collaborative "black novel," *Man Orchid,* with his friend Fred Miller and, later, Lydia Carlin.[57] Much of the material that would become book 3 of *Paterson*—the book in which African American women take center stage—was already conceived as well.

The ironies of Williams's attempts to engage and represent black culture are thick indeed. There is the fact that he went eagerly, with Miller, to see Johnson play under the impression that he was getting the genuine article, *jazz,* without even the faintest knowledge of what had been going on for five years at Minton's Playhouse on 118th Street, where Thelonious Monk, Charlie Parker, and others (including, for that matter, audience member Ralph Ellison) collaborated on a history of the future of jazz. There is the fact that the model for the black protagonist in *Man Orchid* (Bucklin Moon, whom Williams and Miller had talked to at the Bunk Johnson show and had mistaken for a light-skinned black man) was in fact white. (As Mackey has said, "Two white writers sit down to create a black protagonist whose model is another white writer. The ironies and contradictions needn't be belabored.") The comic missteps involved in producing these works have already been dealt with at length in the excellent critical work of Nielsen, Mackey, and Sergio Rizzo, as well as in the biographical work of Paul Mariani.[58] Mackey's reading of "Ol' Bunk's Band" is deft in its rendering of both the problems and the promise of Williams's one significant engagement with jazz. The poem reads in part,

> These are men! the gaunt, unfore-
>   sold, the vocal,
> blatant, Stand up, stand up! the
>   slap of a bass-string.
> Pick, ping! The horn, the
>   hollow horn
> long drawn out, a hound deep
>   tone—
> Choking, choking!
> . . . .

            These are men
     beneath
whose force the melody limps—
     to
proclaim, proclaims—Run and
     lie down,
in slow measures, to rest and
     not never
need no more! These are men!
     Men!

Mackey reads the poem's symbolic play between men, dogs, and limping
in this way:

> The "hound deep / tone," reminding us that Johnson played in
> a band known as the Yelping Hound Band in 1930, also conjures a
> sense of underdog status which brings the orphaned or outcast poet
> into solidarity with an outcast people. The repeated assertion,
> "These are men!" plays against an implied but unstated "treated like
> dogs."
>   Threaded into this implicit counterpoint are the lines "These are
> men / beneath / whose force the melody limps," where "limps"
> reflects critically on a crippling social order. . . . Looking at *Pater-*
> *son,* which hadn't been underway long when "Ol' Bunk's Band" was
> written, one finds the same complex of figures: dogs, lameness,
> limping. (DE 242)

The lines from *Paterson* that Mackey has in mind are from the preface,
where Williams poses his protagonist as "just another dog / among a lot
of dogs" and writes, "Only the lame stands—on / three legs" (3). Mackey
reads these lines and "Ol' Bunk's Band" creatively, in the direction of "the
Fon-Yoruba orisha of the crossroads, the lame dancer Legba," as well as
toward one of Ellison's underdog characters in *Invisible Man,* Brother
Tarp. Williams's limping dog, Mackey argues, is like Legba, "the mas-

ter of polyrhythmicity and heterogeneity," in that "he suffers not from deformity but multiformity"; he is "an emblem of heterogeneous wholeness" (243–45). Taking the liberties that Williams's language allows, Mackey extends Williams's poems in directions Williams himself could never have predicted. His activity suggests that the real poem is the poem renewed in the act of reading, and I would want to extend the possibilities of Mackey's reading by noting another contribution to the construction of Williams's dog, from Dewey's *Art as Experience:* "The live animal is fully present, all there, in all its actions." Dewey continues, "In its wary glances, its sharp sniffings, its abrupt cocking of ears. The dog is never pedantic nor academic." Here we are again—on the symbolic ground where pragmatism and jazz interact, where the African American reflects, redefines, realigns, refracts the "American" in that territory that Ellison would map in such detail.

Yet, with Williams, nagging questions remain. What if "These are men!" is not a gesture of solidarity with men who have been "treated like dogs" and figured as "boys" but merely—or even partly—a Maileresque romanticization of black masculinity? Fred Miller, in the course of his collaboration on *Man Orchid,* had interjected nervously in one of its chapters, "Why the orchid?—to begin with. There's the old, tiresome and at bottom snobbish literary assumption that the Negro in America is an exotic bloom. Negro equals jungle." Mackey notes that the orchid's "phallic appearance plays upon a stereotypic black male sexuality. The distance from this to Norman Mailer's 'Jazz is orgasm' isn't very great" (DE 250).[59] Again, what if the members of Bunk's band are *objectified,* rendered significant, through this *Man Orchid* metaphor? Coming to terms with this possibility necessarily limits one's ability to read "Ol' Bunk's Band" as democratic symbolic action. To quote Dewey, treated as "artistic objects," these men "are separated from both conditions of origin and operation in experience, a wall is built around them that renders almost opaque their general significance" (LW 10:9). The thought that Williams has separated the band from its "conditions of origin" should remind us of Williams's tendency to view black expression as primordial. In the mantra "these are men," we should also hear the echo of the opening lines of "Advent of the Slaves": "these were just men of a certain mettle who came to America in ships, like the rest. The minor differences of condition were of no importance—the mere condition of their coming is of no importance" (AG 208). That Williams ignores the middle passage as an experience relevant to the development of African American culture informs his view of that culture circa 1945. (Or, perhaps it is the other way around: his view of twentieth-century black people informs his belief that the middle passage was of no consequence.) His ignorance helps account for the fact that it is *we* as readers who must reinstate the irony that Williams apparently misses in his description of old man Hemby: "In the hold of the vessel when they were packing porgies, ice and fish filling the hold of a schooner in heavy layers, it was he who could stay down there at work the longest" (211). As he is not always aware that he is signifying on jazz, Williams apparently didn't realize he was signifying on the middle passage in relating this story of "heavy layers" in the hold of a ship. Likewise, the significance of "Ol' Bunk's Band" might be revivified by the kind of search and rescue in which Mackey engages, but one's sense of Williams's own limitations remains.

As both Mackey and Nielsen point out, "One measure of *Man Orchid*'s flawed embrace of otherness is the prominence in it of Williams's all too familiar feud with Eliot, a feud into which he pulls Bunk Johnson." In this feud, "Johnson has no voice but the one that Williams gives him" (DE 249).[60] In "The Great American Novel," Williams provides a more generic version of this feud in which the black man comes to his aid against European culture: "I hate every symphony, every opera as much as a Negro should hate *Il Trovatore,*" he writes. Note the syntax: "I hate . . . as a Negro *should* hate." Williams's belief that black people should hate European music says much about his confusion regarding jazz. Cecil Taylor reflects a widespread approach among jazz musicians when he says, "I am not afraid of European influences. The point is to use them—as Ellington did—as part of my life as an American Negro."[61] Indeed, one can imagine any number of jazz musicians—from Louis Armstrong to Ornette Coleman—quoting from or otherwise manipulating, say, Verdi's "Anvil Chorus" in the course of improvisation.[62] Ellison analogized the jazz musician's approach to his own use of other writers: "Anywhere I find a critic who has an idea or concept that seems useful, I grab it. Eclecticism is the word. Like a jazz musician who creates his own style out of the styles around him" (CE 364). This is, incidentally, the way Ellison approaches Eliot. Ellison, who chose epigraphs from Eliot's work for both his novels, was always fond of pointing out just how "full of American folklore" was Eliot's work (a much more subversive method of critiquing Eliot's privileging of classical tradition, it seems to me) and felt free to take this or that from Eliot without anxieties about agreement or disagreement, love or hatred. He could do this because he had faith in the *method* by which he engaged Eliot. If Williams's address to Eliot is Manichaean, Ellison's is idiomatic. Ellison treats Eliot the way American speakers treat English, not by rejecting it but by altering it. (Mackey notes a similar approach to Eliot in the work of Barbadian poet Edward Kamau Brathwaite.[63]) The joke turns out to be that there's nothing very American (which is to say, nothing very democratic) about Williams's approach to Eliot.

Ellison was fond of pointing out that "that which cannot gain authority from tradition may borrow it with a mask," and his view of racial identity was such that he could see how "the 'darky' act makes brothers of us all. America is a land of masking jokers." Blackness, in this sense, was a construct behind which all sorts of activities—by African Americans and European Americans alike—might occur.[64] But if Ellison believed that masking put the lie to rigid assertions of identity, he was also keen to the various motives behind the employment of such masks, which could be worn "for good and evil . . . for purposes of aggression as well as for defense; when we are projecting the future and preserving the past" (SA 54–55). Louis Armstrong might employ an "African" mask in order to "manipulate you deaf, dumb and blind," taking "liberties with kings, queens and presidents" and projecting the future after having diverted the attention of those who would stop him (52, 150). Abraham Lincoln might play dumb—the mask of "the simple country lawyer"—for the advantage it gave him when "the chips were down" (55). But Ellison could also point out that "out of the counterfeiting of the black American's identity there arises a profound doubt in the white man's mind as to the authenticity of his own image of himself" (53). I think Ellison would have seen Williams as jumping rather frenetically between these two poles: assuming various black masks as a gesture of solidarity (how-

ever mistaken) with Bunk Johnson and disdain for Eliot and what he represented, and then the abrupt and anxious throwing off of these masks,
an assertion of his role in the intellectual world in which, ultimately, he
didn't believe black people played a very large part. In the chapter of *In
the American Grain* that followed "The Advent of the Slaves"—"Descent"
—Williams revealed just how persuaded he was by the very logic to
which he was ostensibly opposed. "It is imperative that we *sink*. But from
a low position it is impossible to answer those who know all the Latin
and some of the Sanskrit names, much French and perhaps one or two
other literatures. Their riposte is: Knownothingism. But we cannot climb
every tree in that world of birds. But where foreign values are held to be
a desideratum, he who is buried and speaks thickly—is lost" (214). The
passage has the quality of an internal monologue. And the jolting reversals—"But . . . "But . . . But"—recalls the familiar cartoon of a man
with an angel on one shoulder and the devil on the other. Williams has
accepted the terms and grades of value of the hierarchy he intends to
critique. That he sees the "low position" as the positive one hardly solves
his problem since his symbolic activities remain circumscribed by the debate over high and low. Just as the "noble savage" was never anything
more than a negotiation of terms already available within European co-
lonialism, the fact that Williams found it "imperative that we sink" would
not have disturbed a symbolic system like Eliot's very much at all. Miller
recognized this same dilemma in Williams's *Man Orchid* chapters, and it
led him to consider writing "an attack on the estheticization of the Negro
in gen[era]l and our hero in particular!" reminding Williams that "to regard the black as an object of aesthetic interest was still to regard him as
an object . . . and to do that was to deny him his humanity."[65] One wonders what might have happened had Williams understood this proviso as
absolutely central to his project—had he recognized that all his talk of
"the American Idiom" was undercut by his failure to heed it—just as one
wonders what might have happened if he had followed through on his
idea, contemporaneous with the beginning of *Man Orchid,* to start an inter-
racial magazine. As Nielsen has speculated, "the enterprise might well
have altered the course of Williams's subsequent work and of American
letters generally" (RR 81).

Rizzo offers us a version of "what might have been" in the course of his argument that *Paterson* "is determined by the crisis of representing racial difference." His argument focuses on the "Beautiful Thing" episode in book 3, part of which had been written and published in 1937 as "Paterson: Episode 17." In these poems, Paterson addresses and interacts with a black woman who has apparently been gang-raped by rival New Jersey gangs. If " 'Episode 17' can be seen as a masculine effort to contain the anxieties of difference (black) femininity provokes," Rizzo reasons, then "*Paterson*'s return to '*Paterson:* Episode 17' could be read as Williams's attempt to grapple with the criticism leveled by Fred Miller in the process of their collaboration on *Man Orchid*."[66] In Rizzo's scenario, Williams addresses Miller's critique in two significant ways. First, he inserts a black woman speaker into book 3 in the form of an actual letter procured from his friend Kathleen Hoagland written to her maid Gladys Enalls from Enalls's girlfriend Dolly ("DJB"). In that letter we have something like Williams's earlier use of words from the Polish mother that prompted Bremen to suggest that Williams's politics "includes the voices that other writers either omit, repress, or seek to silence." The letter ends,

> Tell Raymond I said   I bubetut hatche isus cashutute
> Just a new way of talking kid. It is called (Tut) maybe you heard
> of it. Well here hoping you can read it[67]

Rizzo is certainly right that in this instance "what Williams appreciates in Black English and the game of Tut is the aesthetic validity of emerging voices and their subjective creativity as they struggle to represent themselves within their American idiom[s]" (202). "Tut," whatever its basic rules may be, is "a new way of talking" and in that sense is a logical space that has not yet been rigidly codified. To read it only as coded denotation ("I bet he is cute"?) is to miss the *connotative* aspects of the form itself. By not giving away the code, by not translating, Dolly implies that she and Gladys can collaborate on meaning; they are both active and shaping in relation to the code: "here hoping you can read it." Likewise, Tut is treated as potentially active and shaping vis-à-vis the inherited code that is English. Tut is a form of American speech.

Dolly's "new way of talking" is contrasted in book 3 with Beautiful Thing's speechlessness, which, in his rewriting of episiode 17, Williams suggests is partly the result of his own compulsion to silence her. Among the lines added to the original episode are the following:

Your clothes (I said) quickly, while
your beauty is attainable.

　　　Put them on the chair
(I said. Then in a fury, for which I am
ashamed)
　　　You smell as though you need
a bath. Take off your clothes and purify
yourself . .
And let me purify myself
　　　　　　　　　　—to look at you,
　　　　　　　　to look at you (I said)

(Then, my anger rising)　　　TAKE OFF YOUR
CLOTHES! I didn't ask you

to take off your skin . I said your
clothes, your clothes. You smell
like a whore. I ask you to bathe in my
opinions, the astonishing virtue of your
lost body (I said) .

　　　　　　　　　—that you might
send me hurtling to the moon
　　.　　.　　let me look at you (I
said, weeping)
　　　　　　　(P 106)

Here we have something comparable to Williams's deconstruction of portraiture in "Portrait of a Lady." The iterative disruption "(I said)" implies that Williams is revisiting a scene that has already taken place; a scene in which he is revealed as complicit with those who have done violence to Beautiful Thing; in which his obsession with *purification* belies his denial of racist motives ("I didn't ask you / to take off your skin"); and in which *speaking,* since it is not dialogic, turns out to be only a form of *looking* (to look at you, / to look at you . . . let me look at you"). That Williams discovers, in the course of his looking, "astonishing virtue" only contributes to our sense of his refusal to interact. He has accepted what in almost every other case (every case that does not involve people of color), he would reject, namely, a "spectator theory of knowledge," whereby Beautiful Thing's naked body would be, in Dewey's words "a reality fixed and complete in itself . . . so fixed in its regal aloofness that it is a king to any beholding mind that may gaze upon it." Williams, I am suggesting, has in this case embraced a form of aristocratic symbolic action. That Beautiful Thing's image is figured as king (or queen, as it were) only serves to ironize his denial of her subjectivity. And though the scene, which ends with Williams's character weeping, clearly contains an element of self-critique, he fails to build on the promise of that critique— his figuration of Beautiful Thing ends where it began: she is "black plush, a dark flame" (P 128).

One grows tired of waiting for Williams to deliver the goods. In the fall of 1957, Williams did an interview with Mike Wallace in which he said the following: "We poets have to talk in a language which is not English. It is the American idiom. . . . It has as much originality as jazz" (P 222). These lines ended up in book 5 of Paterson in 1958. During this same period, younger poets deeply influenced by Williams, poets such as Frank O'Hara and Amiri Baraka, began showing up at the Five Spot, a jazz club in the Bowery where, in August 1957, Thelonious Monk and John Coltrane began a six-month gig. The cultural exchange that the Five Spot inspirited—an exchange that I will discuss at length in chapter 4— is anticipated half-consciously by Williams in book 5, where, under the sign of connection between the American idiom and jazz, we find a list of names that includes Bessie Smith and Gertrude Stein, Allen Ginsberg,

Gilbert Sorrentino, Mezz Mezzrow, and Jackson Pollock. These were names that, along with those of O'Hara, Baraka, Robert Creeley, Monk, Robert Duncan, Ornette Coleman, and many others, one was likely to find in Baraka's journal of the period, *Yugen*. Indeed, Williams's poem "A Formal Design" appeared in *Yugen* 5 (1959) alongside O'Hara's poem "Ode on Causality," part of which had been written at the Five Spot. But whatever promise these webs imply in relation to Williams's thought and poetry, it never pans out. One finds that as late as March 1961, Williams wrote to Baraka to praise *Yugen*. But, contemporaneously, one finds this, from a November 1960 interview with Walter Sutton:

> WCW: But in jazz music even the saxophone sounds are not advanced enough from the primitive to interest me at all. I don't like jazz. The artists in Paris rave about jazz, but it's too tiresome, it's too much the same thing.
> WS: There's not enough variability?
> WCW: Not variability at all. Not subtle. And if you've got to be sexually excited by it, it shows you to be a boob. It merely excites; there's no subtlety at all.[68]

There is no usefulness in taking this apart as an example of Williams's racist misconceptions any more than has already been done. The point is this: that for all the casual analogizing between the American idiom and jazz we are inspired to do when reading Williams, he himself did not understand the analogy adequately. We ought to turn to Ralph Ellison if we want that analogy fleshed out. And to understand what poets like Baraka and O'Hara were up to at the close of Williams's life (such will be the subject of chapter 4), we're better off looking to Ellison—and, even, to Emerson for answers.

There is one final irony on which I would like to close. In "The Great American Novel," Williams writes, "We care nothing at all for the complacent Concordites? We can look at that imitative phase with its erudite Holmeses, Thoreaus, and Emersons. With one word we can damn it: England" (I 211). In his zeal to draw a bold line between the American and the English, Williams missed out on an opportunity that might have changed the course of his thinking considerably. For to equate Emerson with Holmes was to indulge in an old historical error perpetuated by Holmes himself. As I will detail in chapter 2, Holmes and Emerson differed violently on an important contemporary issue: the issue of slavery and emancipation. Holmes's disdain for Emerson's abolitionism (which was sometimes manifested as attacks on Holmes) motivated him to essentially erase it from the record in his seminal biography of Emerson. In lumping them together casually, Williams showed himself to be one of the many suckers of history, that "tall tale told by inattentive idealists," as Ellison once put it. Williams's apparent failure to discover Emerson's abolitionist essays was his loss. But for the radical democrat, lament must take a backseat to the revelation of a workable set of terms.

2

The Motives of Emancipated Prose

Emerson and the Collaborating Reader

Whilst I insist on the doctrine of the independence and the inspiration of the individual, I do not cripple but exalt the social action . . . to each man the largest liberty compatible with the liberty of every other man. No citizen will go wrong who upon any question leans to the side of general liberty.

Ralph Waldo Emerson, "Lecture on Slavery"

One may without presumption believe that even if Emerson has no system, nonetheless he is the prophet and herald of any system which democracy may henceforth construct and hold by, and that when democracy has articulated itself, it will have no difficulty in finding itself already proposed in Emerson.

John Dewey, "Ralph Waldo Emerson"

In the 1840s and 1850s, as his involvement in the abolitionist movement grew more intense, Emerson recognized a distinction between what he most often thought of as democratic and aristocratic linguistic structure and, more specifically, how the "democratic" structures—or what he often simply called "the forms"—were highly dependent on a collaborating reader. A reader who took advantage of the contingency of language could, in a sense, turn reading into a form of writing. Likewise, a writer could encourage this possibility latent in the act of reading by emphasizing the contingent nature of his or her writing. The result would be a text that functioned like a symbolic republic: "It is our republican doctrine," Emerson wrote, "that the wide variety of opinions is an advantage . . . a living soul contending with living souls. It is, in every expression, an-

tagonized." Emerson increasingly aspired toward such "antagonized expression" in his own writing in the hope that it might become a site for
the generation of new possible vocabularies. The impression of "contrast,
change, interruption" that he cultivated in his prose was, he believed,
"necessary to new activity and new combinations" (CW 11:398, 533).
This causal relationship was the means by which a democratic vernacular
might be continuously generated, functioning symbolically just as democracy proper needed to function. As he wrote in a letter criticizing
Oliver Wendell Holmes for not supporting abolition, "the real union" was
"the will to keep and renew union. . . . This alone gives any tension to
the dead letter" (L 3:18).[1] Likewise, a democratic vernacular would have
to be supremely flexible, placing no a priori limits on what it might substantially become. Emerson's own writing can be *transitional,* in Jonathan
Levin's sense of that term, and, at the same time, "deploy thought as a
weapon to enable more effective action," as Cornel West says of Emersonian pragmatism. In fact in Emerson's case the two are causally linked.[2]

Central to Emerson's argument was an ever-increasing insistence that
theory must be articulated in terms of practice and that language and
linguistic structures must be understood as socially symbolic acts. That
the South had developed "not a democratic but an aristocratic complexion," for instance, could be explained in part by its reliance on and reverence for rhetoric and rituals that emphasized "immemorial usage" (CW
11:319). This was language-as-hierocracy, sanctioned and assembled according to its level of ossification, and the social apparatus it perpetuated
was equally hierarchical and equally entrenched. In contrast, a democratic rhetoric would be characterized by "a spontaneity which forgets
usages" (3:68), that is, a spontaneity that made language and social practice subject to the constant changes within individuals and communities
and that served as catalyst for a shift from usage to *usefulness.*

Emerson recognized that "immemorial usage" could have the ironic
effect of turning the meaning of a word like "liberty" into its opposite.
"What avails the correctness of the theory, when the practice is despot-
ism?" Emerson despaired in 1854. "Nothing remains but to begin at the
beginning to call every man in America to counsel, Representatives do
not represent, we must take new order & see how to make represen-

tatives represent us" (JMN 14:421, 423). This change in the scope of his address—outward toward "every man in America"—is a crucial moment in the development of American pragmatism. In "What Pragmatism Means," William James suggests that pragmatism is a *method* that "lies in the midst of our theories like a corridor in a hotel." In each room might be a man with his own private theory "but they all own the corridor, and all must pass through it if they want a practicable way of getting into or out of their respective rooms." Abolition, then, was Emerson's entrance into the corridor of social practice, his way of testing the "probable truth" of theory by measuring it, as James would say, against "the collectivity of experience's demands" (WJ 1:32, 44). Asking the question, "What's the Use of Calling Emerson a Pragmatist?" Stanley Cavell has noted that "Emerson retains stretches of the vocabulary of philosophy but divests it of its old claims to mastery. This is why his writing is difficult in a way no other American philosopher's (save Thoreau's) has been, certainly not that of James or of Dewey." But, in answer to Cavell's question, Emerson is not simply difficult—he *practices* difficulty in the face of myriad "old claims to mastery."[3] One use of such a distinction—the use of identifying Emerson as, in essence, a pragmatist—is that it allows us to see that Emerson's linguistic experimentation does not exist either in isolation from or opposition to his involvement in the social problems of his day. Rather, Emerson enlists "emancipated" language in the struggle for emancipation.

This chapter, then, begins with an oft-noted observation regarding the post-structural texture of Emerson's writing and ends with an explanation of how the deconstructive thrust of that writing becomes integrated with Emerson's abolitionist, radically democratic politics. To borrow a paradoxical phrase from Ralph Ellison, "the end is in the beginning and lies far ahead."[4] I am in basic agreement with those contemporary critics (Bloom, Packer, Cavell, Poirier, Carton, Levin come immediately to mind) who have argued variously that Emerson's style affects or necessitates a particular kind of reading strategy, one in which the onus of connection, logical systemization, analogy, is felt to be squarely the responsibility of the reader.[5] In "Experience," Emerson writes, "I am a fragment and this is a fragment of me" (CW 3:83). One draws an "accurate" portrait of Emerson from this moment at his or her peril; accuracy becomes an entirely relative term. Instead, such self-representations by Emerson force us to consider his language as contextual; that is, his language ceases to mean anything until we have constructed it as vehicle, until we have recognized his "fragments" as a series of tools lent *by* Emerson rather than as a representation *of* Emerson. In "Self-Reliance," he gives us a description of identity in the form of a riddle: "We pass for what we are" (2:58). This seems on the surface to be a tautological joke, one that Emerson was fond of telling; in the subsequent paragraph he provides another, "Always scorn appearances and you always may" (2:59). Tautology makes us suspicious of linearity, collapses our faith in cause and effect. Thus it is one of Emerson's many methods for discouraging the attempt to discover his meaning by parsing his sentences.

But "we pass for what we are" works on several levels. In addition to being a grammatical game, it is a riddle on identity. It forces us to consider the position on identity opposite from the one provided by common sense. Common sense tells us that when we pass for something it is precisely because we are *not that thing*. Emerson suggests that identity —what we *are*—is what we are, at any given moment, passing for. Moreover, he suggests that what we are "passing" for is always about to "pass."[6] This elaborate bit of punning on identity is central to Emerson's method. If such a description of the liminal and constructed self sounds like a particularly "postmodern" theory of selfhood, it would not be the first time that Emerson was accused of being one of postmodernism's chief forerunners. Harold Bloom, who perhaps inaugurates the connection between Emerson and post-structuralism in the critical discourse, calls this tactic, by which Emerson links the contingency of his selfhood to the contingency of his prose, the tactic of "evasion." Bloom says, counterintuitively, that evasion is "the center" of Emerson's philosophy and that this evasion accounts for the fact that "no two disciples can agree upon Emerson's doctrine."[7]

Emerson's motive for such evasion is not so much a will to agonistic misreading so deeply felt that it extends to what he believes to be his prior selves; rather, his evasion is a will to collaboration based on the democratic structure of language, a will to foster proactively creative reading where any resolution of meaning is based on contextualized "respect to the present hour" (CW 3:60). I draw this distinction regarding Emerson's motive because it will become later directly related to his social activism in a way that challenges almost all of our received ideas about Emerson as canonical literary figure, from his role as activist to his influence on contemporary writing. (Juliana Spahr's book *Everybody's Autonomy: Connective Reading and Collective Identity,* for instance, reads contemporary experimental writing practice as marked by "a collective attention to the multiple, an attention to the diversity of response in the name of individual rights" that foregrounds "the politics and dynamics of reading itself."[8] Emerson fairly invents this kind of attention, and the genealogy of American experimental writing is shot through with his readers and their admirers.) "Liberty," Emerson will say, "is aggressive," and the preservation of liberty, he came to realize, was chiefly in the hands of the aggressive reader. The crisis in which the Constitution had been allowed to stand for slavery was a crisis of language and a crisis of reading: "slavery reads the constitution with a shrewd & daring & innovating eye. Liberty is satisfied with a literal construction" (CW 11:244, 420). That this was the context in which Emerson continued to develop his linguistic philosophy through the *Second Series* essays and into essays such as "Emancipation in the British West Indies," as well as seemingly less political ones such as "Montaigne," is crucial to our understanding of the motives of his rhetoric, the motives of the various experimental devices described by post-structurally inclined critics of Emerson.

In the years following the publication of his second series of essays, the boundaries of nature, language, and politics in Emerson's thinking become more fluid than they had ever been. "As the globe keeps its identity by perpetual change," he would say in "The Fortune of the Republic," "so our civil system, by perpetual appeal to the people and acceptance of its reforms" (CW 11:529). In like manner he would go on to argue that the American vernacular itself must have perpetual change at its core. That personal self-reliance was dependent on a particularly fluid sense of the boundaries between writer and reader and thus on the contingency of signification was a lesson Emerson had learned early. That the contingency of signification was the predicate by which texts—such as

the Constitution, the Declaration of Independence, and indeed his own
—became sites of social contestation; that the desire for an expansion of
democracy was futile without an attempt to "realize our rhetoric and our
rituals" (11:530)[9] in a language that was democratic in its very structure
and that was conceived of as socially symbolic act—these were lessons
Emerson learned during his long involvement with abolitionism. Emerson came to realize that, as Clifford Geertz has put it, "cultural forms
can be treated as texts, as imaginative works built out of social materials"
and that "cultural acts, the construction, apprehension, and utilization of
symbolic forms, are social events like any other; they are as public as
marriage and as observable as agriculture."[10] In light of this recognition,
Emerson brought the full weight of his intellect to bear on the cultural
texts he saw before him, advocating for a model of reading that he believed would provide the cultural pressure necessary for the abolition of
slavery and the expansion of democracy.

Though recent scholarship on Emerson's relation to both abolitionism
and the pragmatism of James and Dewey bolsters the conclusions I am
drawing here, those conclusions still fly in the face of a great deal of conventional critical wisdom, which has had it for a long time that Emerson
was pushed reluctantly into abolitionism and that his activity and involvement constituted a departure from his more philosophical calling. But as
Len Gougeon has said (and shown in his important book, *Virtue's Hero*),
"Some of the most deep-seated scholarly commonplaces regarding Emerson's relationship to the important reforms of his day are based upon
assumptions that have obtained credibility almost solely on the basis of
historical reiteration rather than historical fact."[11] The ramifications of
these "deep-seated scholarly commonplaces" extend well beyond the issue of creating an accurate historical record—they have influenced how
critics reconstruct Emerson's view of American culture, his position vis-
à-vis continental philosophy, his sense of the role of women and ethnic
minorities in American life and literature, and many other areas of Emerson scholarship.[12]

Anita Patterson's *From Emerson to King* is a recent and characteristic
example of this "reconstruction" of Emerson. In a book that focuses al-

most exclusively on Emerson's theories of race and "ownership," it is striking, if symptomatic, that Patterson would choose to neglect this remarkable quatrain from Emerson's "Boston Hymn," read in the Boston Music Hall to a cheering crowd, which included many former slaves,[13] on January 1, 1863: "Pay Ransom to the owner / And fill the bag to the brim. / Who is the owner? The slave is the owner, / And ever was. Pay him" (CW 9:204). The unequivocal nature of "Boston Hymn" belies Patterson's portrait of him as an equivocator. Indeed, her central premise— that there is a contradiction between Emerson's "democratic ethos" and "the racialism that circumscribes his notion of the representative self"[14] —never addresses the fact that this contradiction is not simple, stable, or it turns out, long lasting. As I will argue a bit later in this chapter, while Patterson's "contradiction" *may* be operative in "Self-Reliance" (1841), it disappears under the heat of Emerson's study of slavery, the slave trade, and, in particular, his vitriolic response to the Fugitive Slave Law. What remains is contradiction of another sort: the countering of diction, a rhetorical strategy by which Emerson could now throw himself headlong into abolitionism without occupying a hierarchical position vis-à-vis the "many well-advised persons" involved in the struggle, "this work of humanity," as he called it (CW 11:100).

My argument, then, differs starkly from John Carlos Rowe's position that "Emerson's political writings from 1844 to 1863 remain so profoundly divided internally between transcendentalist values and practical politics as to be practically useless, except as far as the value of their political rhetoric might be measured."[15] As von Frank has shown, "Rowe's discussion of Emerson's stance sets off as a category unto itself the texts that are important to Gougeon's case for Emerson's social commitment."[16] Moreover, in taking the transcendentalism of *Nature* as the very definition of Emerson the philosopher, Rowe sets up a formula whereby any divergence from that transcendentalism is not a sign of Emerson's thought in *transition* (to use one of Emerson's favorite words) but is rather a betrayal of Emerson's true philosophical beliefs, albeit a noble one done in the name of an admirable cause. While von Frank has done much to explain how Emerson's early transcendentalism is more politically efficacious than his critics would allow, I concede to Rowe his point that "In *Nature*

(1836), the transcendental spirit is approached by the 'man thinking' who uses language in a decidedly patriarchal fashion."[17] What I do not concede is any implication that Emerson's complicity with something like Kant's "transcendental ego" at an early stage in his career as a thinker remains a central, or even tangential, aspect of his philosophy. Sometime around 1840 Emerson begins to write himself out of a transcendental view that "in the function of knowing . . . The Reality becomes a mere empty *locus*" (WJ 8:343) and into a view of thought as *interaction* that I can only identify as pragmatist.[18] Rowe wants to separate Emerson the writer and Emerson the speechmaker. To do so is to ignore the fact that despite an occasional false start, Emerson develops a theory of democratic symbolic action that makes "aesthetic dissent" a form of political dissent; preceding both pragmatist philosophers like James and Dewey and cultural critics like Rowe, Emerson banks on a belief that language is material.[19]

"The sugar they raised was excellent. Nobody tasted blood in it" (CW 11:124). So goes Emerson's stunningly succinct comment in 1844 on the mystified commodity and the politics of production. In the same speech he suggests that "Language must be raked . . . to tell what Negro slavery has been" (11:102). This latter statement is not a situational departure from transcendentalism but an insistence on the materiality of language. As there is blood, unrecognized, in the cane, so it is with words. Likewise, Emerson's famous description of Montaigne's writing—"Cut these words and they would bleed" (4:168)[20]—is an invitation that marks his insistence that language is embodied; this sentence deserves to be placed alongside Douglass's equally famous and remarkable statement from his 1845 *Narrative,* "My feet have been so cracked with the frost that the pen with which I am writing might be laid in the gashes."[21] Both Douglass and Emerson create a space for the cultural critique of linguistic usage while simultaneously promoting a view of language as "vehicular and transitive" (CW 3:34) as characterized by "fluxions and mobility" (4:160); language is not the special province of a group, tradition, court, or other organizing body.[22]

While earlier historicist work such as Bercovitch's and Jehlen's had no recourse to Gougeon's historical research, the decision by historicist critics such as Patterson not to draw on that research is perplexing.[23] The result is an often absurd reduction: for Christopher Newfield, Emerson is "a white supremacist," while Patterson falls back on innuendo: "the point is that [Emerson] never did—publically, visibly, literally—go to prison, and so the question of whether he shares a spiritual affinity with black American slaves is left wide open."[24] As I will discuss in detail a bit later, Emerson did indeed share an affinity with black American slaves, one that changed the course of his thinking and of American philosophy. To read Patterson's statement that Emerson "accepted the violent, racist policy of westward expansion" is to know that she either never read or simply ignored pronouncements by Emerson such as the following: "Language has lost its meaning in the universal cant, Representative Government is really misrepresentative; Union is a conspiracy against the Northern States which the Northern States are to have the privilege of paying for; the adding of Cuba and Central America to the slave marts is enlarging the area of Freedom. Manifest Destiny, Democracy, Freedom, fine names for an ugly thing. They call it otto of rose and lavender,—I call it bilge-water" (CW 11:259).

Patterson's misconceptions regarding Emerson's abolitionism are unfortunate, as they affect the two most interesting aspects of her work: 1) her attention to the way in which a consideration of race moves Emerson toward a notion of the self as socially constructed; and 2) the way in which Emerson's work assists later African American thinkers such as DuBois, King, and West in developing an oppositional political philosophy. I would like to look briefly at a passage from "Fate" (1860) quoted by Patterson before moving on to my central argument regarding the way in which Emerson's radically democratic abolitionism is integrated with his linguistic philosophy. Here is the quote: "One key, one solution to the mysteries of human conditions, one solution to the old knots of fate, freedom, and foreknowledge, exists, the propounding, namely, of the double consciousness. A man must ride alternately on the horses of his private and public nature. . . . To offset the drag of temperament and race, which pulls down, learn this lesson, namely, that by the cunning co-presence of two elements, which is throughout nature, whatever lames or paralyzes you, draws in with it the divinity, in some form, to

repay" (CW 6:47–48). While Patterson admits that Emerson "does confront the important question of positionality and the particular, racial
conditions of his own speech with considerable directness," and while
she clearly recognizes the debt that DuBois owes to "Fate's" description
of "double consciousness" as "the creative tension between voluntary and
involuntary aspects of political obligation," she overlooks the transvaluation of the word "race" undertaken by Emerson in this passage. Beginning with the presumption of Emerson's racism and complicity with the
"violent policy of westerward expansion," Patterson can only read "Fate"
as a fascinating possibility for DuBois's redirection.[25] It is more than this.
In fact, taken in the context of Emerson's contemporaneous antislavery
writings, it is clear that "Fate" precedes DuBois's work in its radical use
of the term "race" and its positioning of African Americans as the "gifted,"
forerunners of American possibility.[26] To absorb the full impact of Emerson's signifying, one needs to read the portion of the above quote from
"Fate" that Patterson has excised:

> A man must ride alternately on the horses of his public and private
> nature, as the equestrians in the circus throw themselves nimbly
> from horse to horse, or plant one foot on the back of one and the
> other foot on the back of the other. So when a man is the victim of
> his fate, has sciatica in his loins and cramp in his mind; a club-foot
> and a club in his wit; a sour face and a selfish temper; a strut in his
> gate and a conceit in his affection; or is ground to powder by the
> vice of his race;—he is to rally on his relation to the Universe,
> which his ruin benefits. Leaving the daemon who suffers, he is to
> take sides with the Deity who secures universal benefit by his pain.

The distinction between public and private, which, as it does for DuBois,
informs racial distinction, is not simply "alternate" here—it is "nimble,"
flexible. ("See how fate *slides* into freedom and freedom into fate," Emerson writes earlier in the essay. "Observe how far the roots of every crea-
ture run, or find if you can a point where there is no connection" [CW
6:36]—bringing his observation from "Circles" that "the surface on which
we now stand, is not fixed, but *sliding*" [CW 2:314, emphasis added] to

bear on the issue of race.) Likewise, "race" is a radically flexible term in this passage.

The logic of these sentences would seem to make race as significant or insignificant as a sour face, a strut in one's gate, conceit in one's affection. (Earlier in the essay Emerson simply defines "man" as "the latest race" [CW 6:36], and in his 1855 "Lecture on Slavery," he specifically employs the term "race" to signify not a specific group but rather the liminal American republic poised for emancipation: the "real function . . . of our race is to liberty" [ASW 105].) The troping play ("a club-foot and a club in his wit" leaping from physical to mental and punning on human "clubs") destabilizes the "fated-ness" of these categories. Emerson's examples do move from the most material to the most abstract, and perhaps race is meant as the highest abstraction, though one that still has the material force to ground us to powder, unless this too is meant as an abstraction. Most significant for our purposes is whether "race" works here to differentiate between groups—who is "ground to powder by the vice of his race"? Those critics who portray Emerson as complicit with the ideology of Manifest Destiny would have us believe that race here signifies people of color and would point to Emerson's infamous suggestion that Negroes have "guano in their destiny" (CW 6:16) as proof. "Guano," though, most obviously signifies not any innate vice but rather the middle passage and slavery itself: "They are ferried over the Atlantic and carted over America, to ditch and to drudge, to make corn cheap and then to lie down prematurely to make a spot of green grass on the prairie" (6:16–17). Notice that the word "prematurely" serves to mark the death of slaves as a social, rather than natural, process.[27] "Guano" stands in for Emerson's recognition that, as he said in 1844, "the white has, for ages, done what he could to keep the negro in that hoggish state. His laws have been furies" (11:140). Indeed, the only race described as having vices in "Fate" is Emerson's own: "Who likes to believe that he has, hidden in his skull, spine, and pelvis, all the vices of a Saxon or Celtic race, which will be sure to pull him down,—with what grandeur of hope and resolve is he fired,—into a selfish, huckstering, servile, dodging animal?" (6:34–35). Whither white supremacy in the face of such questions? Following this passage, Emerson makes a very important transition: "A man," he writes, "must thank his defects and stand in some terror of his talents" (6:35). As I will presently explain, this strategic universalism provides a logical space where Emerson's reader can opt out of racial categories by embodying the democratic ethos of African Americans; it is akin to his 1844 observation that Frederick Douglass, as the "anti-slave," renders "black or white . . . an insignifcance. Why at night all men are black" (JMN 9:124).

Had Patterson not begun with the presumption that Emerson was an unmitigated racist, had she looked more carefully at the correspondences between "Fate" and the antislavery writings of the same period, she might have recognized Emerson's proposal that "limitation is power that shall be" (6:35) as directly related to his view of African Americans: of "the injured Negro," he writes, "in his very wrongs is his strength. . . . It is certain that . . . all just men, all intelligent agents, must take the part of the black man against the white man" (ASW 37). Patterson's argument that African Americans employ "the Emersonian tradition" in their "development of an innovative poetics of protest"[28] omits two key facts: that Emersonianism owes a debt to antebellum African Americans and that Emerson largely predicted their development of an innovative poetics of protest. As I will explain toward the end of this chapter, over the course of his antislavery writings, Emerson developed an argument regarding the African American's ironic position in a nation undergoing radical transformation. Ralph Ellison has expressed the irony in this way: "Given the reality of slavery and the denial of social mobility to blacks, it is ironic that they were placed by that very circumstance in the position of having the greatest freedom to create specifically *American* cultural idioms" (CE 336). Emerson and his namesake Ellison are alike in equating democracy with idiomatic invention. The remainder of this chapter will be concerned with the consequences of Emerson's integration of democratic politics, the symbolic action of African Americans, and his oft-noted interest in de-authorizing his own texts. Emerson's destabilization of racial hierarchy is in keeping with, and in fact necessary to, his own de-authorization. As I will explain toward the end of the chapter, in the context of his abolitionist commitments, Emerson called this de-authorization, "the might of liberty in my weakness."

The misconceptions regarding Emerson's views on race and abolitionism noted above have influenced how we view what Kenneth Burke
might call "the motives of Emerson's rhetoric." Even before he became
deeply involved with the issue of emancipation, Emerson was intensely
engaged in a consideration of individual liberty as represented by the individual reader. The distinction to make between Emerson's work before
and after 1844 pivots on the scope of his address. The strong sense of
collective enterprise that Emerson developed over two decades beginning in 1844 would have been foreign to him at the time he was prepar-
ing his first series of essays in the late 1830s. Emerson's deep suspicion of
the impediments imposed on individual authority by collective, historically sanctioned wisdom led him to adopt a rhetoric that emphasized the
local and immediate "I" and "you" over the dubiously large and corporate
"we." The way in which Emerson approached the philosophical com-
plexities of "History" and "Self-Reliance" depended heavily on a style developed in conversation and letter writing, one that never failed to remind the auditor that "the ear and the tongue are two organs of one
nature" (CW 2:84) and never failed to remind the reader that, as he once
told a young Williams College student named Charles Woodbury, "you
only read to start your own team."[29]

What Emerson set out to do in the early essays was to alter the structure by which "this idea of authorship controls our appreciation of the
works themselves" (JMN 13:79). That "author" was root of "authority"
was an idea the ramifications of which Emerson keenly understood; to
alter the balance of authority in the text, he would have to alter the
reader's conception of the author and, ultimately, of the self. As Richard
Poirier has said, "The strongest evidence for me of Emerson's own genius
is that his way of writing simultaneously affirms and calls into doubt his,
or anyone else's, individual authority over language, the language he himself chooses to use."[30] In order to de-authorize his texts, Emerson needed
to adopt an extremely fluid sense of both language and selfhood. At least
since "The American Scholar" (1837), Emerson had insisted that "there is
then creative reading as well as creative writing" (CW 1:93) and had
given consideration to how the latter might foster the former.[31] His conclusions, more often than not, had to do with the way in which the radi-

cal contingency of language (what we now describe with Derrida as the process by which "the absence of the transcendental signified extends the domain and interplay of signification *ad infinitum*"[32]) was the necessary ground for any description of a radically democratic relationship between writer and reader. "Every word we speak is million-faced or convertible into an indefinite number of applications," Emerson wrote in 1841. "If it were not so we could read no book. Your remark would only fit your case and not mine" (JMN 8:157).

Barbara Packer notes an early "incident in which Emerson interrupted his delivery of a sermon to say quietly to his congregation: 'The sentence which I have just read I do not now believe,' and then went on to the next page."[33] This quizzical event is, even at this early date in Emerson's development, less "honesty" than strategy. Rhetorically, it undermines that aspect of sermonizing that distances minister from parishioners, that reifies his place in the pulpit. In "History," Emerson acts toward the reader much as he did toward his congregation, stopping dead during one of his characteristically hyperbolic assertions to exclaim, "Is there something overweening in this claim? Then I reject all I have written, for what is the use of pretending to know what we know not?" (CW 2:39).

It is hard to describe one's reaction upon first reading lines such as these. You think to yourself, What does he mean he rejects all he has written? before consenting to his insistence that "we cannot spend the day in explanation" (2:52). As you run into more of his stops and starts, his diversions and detours, you begin to believe him when he says, for instance, in "Circles": "Do not set the least value on what I do, as if I pretend to settle anything as true or false. I unsettle all things. No facts are to me sacred; none are profane; I simply experiment, an endless seeker, with no past at my back" (2:318). Moments such as these are, it should be said, crucial to the development of what will become the pragmatism of James and Dewey. They precede and predict James's stipulation that "pragmatism has, in fact, no prejudices whatever, no obstructive dogmas, no rigid canons of what shall count as proof" (WJ 1:43–44). In addition, they anticipate Dewey's description of the artist as a "born experimenter": "only because the artist operates experimentally," Dewey says, "does he open new fields of experience" (LW 10:148–49). Dewey's sense of Emerson as "the philosopher of democracy" is absolutely dependent on the way that Emerson's experimental stance toward language and the generation of meaning encourages the reader to recognize that his or her act "involves activities that are comparable to those of the creator" (10:58). Whatever meaning he or she then decides is being created, he or she will be averse to any concern with whether Emerson would *approve*. Approval, as it were, is not part of the formula. Indeed, how could it be, given the structural ambiguities of the work and the way in which those ambiguities, the freeing up of signification's potential, seem to act as guiding principle? Stanley Cavell frames the issue well in saying, "Emerson is I believe commonly felt to play fast and loose with something like contradiction in his writing; but I am speaking of a sense in which contradiction, the countering of diction, is the genesis of his writing of philosophy."[34] Contradiction, as Cavell suggests, is somehow both mood and strategy, born of Emerson's recognition of both the inevitability of linguistic fragmentation and its usefulness.

Emerson's very grammar, what he called "paragraphs incomprehensible, each sentence an infinitely repellent particle,"[35] was constructed to persuade the reader into genuine dialogue. Everyone who has read Emerson (and many who haven't) remembers his adage that "consistency is the hobgoblin of little minds," but too little attention has been paid to Emerson's definition of "consistency." "Our consistency," Emerson says, is "a reverence for our past act or word" (2:56). In essays such as "History," "Self-Reliance," and "Circles," Emerson cultivated what he would call "a spontaneity which forgets usages" (3:68). Usage for Emerson primarily meant linguistic usage, not only the catalog of what one might say (the policing of ideas) but of how one might say it (the policing of grammar). On a large scale, usage was historically and culturally determined; on a local scale, authorially determined. As such, Emerson set out in that first series of essays to radically call into question both history and author. In the following passage, from the beginning of his essay "History," Emerson takes aim at teleological conceptions of history (indeed at historical narrative generally) not in the form of a polemic but a riddle: "Of the works of this mind history is the record. Its genius is illustrated by the whole series of days. Man is explicable by nothing less than all his history.

Without hurry, without rest, the human spirit goes forth from the beginning to embody every faculty, every thought, every emotion, which belongs to it in appropriate events. But the thought is always prior to the fact; all the facts of history preexist in the mind as laws" (CW 2:3).

If history is the record of the mind, and all the facts of history preexist in the mind, then Emerson has provided us with an odd tautology: history is the record of all the facts of history. (As Gertrude Stein would later put it, "Let me recite what history teaches. History teaches.") In between this tautology, Emerson can allow himself to stray outside the parameters of logical necessity because his goal is not to construct an argument, a fact that becomes painfully clear for any reader who attempts to follow the lines of argumentation: Is the "it" that begins the second sentence "history" or the "universal mind"? Is "*his* history" in the third sentence to be differentiated from the history of the first sentence? When he says that "the human spirit goes forth from the beginning *to embody* every faculty," does he mean "in order to embody," "to inevitably embody," or "in an attempt to embody"? And what to make of "appropriate events," which is to say, by what or whose standards are we to judge them appropriate or inappropriate? The ambiguity forces one to react to the passage rather than attempt to "understand" it; it forces one to develop one's own strategy for reading it.

Emerson's contradiction has, as its motivation, an extremely serious understanding of how words, and indeed grammar, functioned as what he called "organization tyrannizing over character."[36] When in "Self-Reliance" he wrote "I am ashamed to think how easily we capitulate to badges and names, to large societies and dead institutions" (CW 2:51), he meant to suggest not only a list of ills but an equation whereby "badges and names" were the apparatus through which "large societies and dead institutions" sustained their authority and influence. Emerson's answer to this process was a revolution of the reader: "the student is to read history actively and not passively," he writes, "to esteem his own life the text" (2:7–8). When Emerson says "history is to be read and written" (2:38), when he suggests that the reader reply to the authorial "patriarch . . . in the same pitch of voice" (2:84) in which that patriarch has written, he is suggesting that reading is a kind of writing. This principle, this conflation

of reading and writing as practices so collaborative as to be almost synonymous, is the platform from which he prophecies that "we shall not
always set so high a price on a few texts, a few lives" (2:67). It is, I mean
to suggest, the beginning point for his vision of what we might call the
democratization of language, a process by which the hierarchical structure of language itself is thrown into stark relief and, then, into doubt.[37]

I have mentioned Charles Woodbury, and his relationship with Emerson provides an interesting and useful model of the relationship between
reader and writer as Emerson understood it during the period in which
he wrote "Self-Reliance." The fact that Woodbury's "talks with Emerson"
actually occurred in 1865 should tell us something: Emerson doesn't
abandon this model in later years so much as expand the arena in which
it might be practiced. His relationships with individual young scholars—
which at one time were the central manifestation of his egalitarian desires—were, by 1865, just one element in a broad nexus of democratic
activities. For now though, it is worth examining Emerson's relationship
with Woodbury in isolation, as an example of his earliest considerations
of rhetorically how to foster individual liberty. Emerson met Woodbury
during a visit to Williams College, where he had been invited to lecture.
The visit had all the symbolic trappings of a disrespect for authority that
Woodbury clearly found energizing; announcements of Emerson's visit
"blistered every available space, even trespassing upon such respected
preserves as the chapel, library doors and the fence about the residence
of Dr. Hopkins, president" (TE 3–4). Emerson's most enduring lessons
about authority, however, came in the form of informal "talks" he had
with Woodbury over the next five years. These talks focused most often
on the subjects of reading and writing, and Emerson's critique of authority was characteristically self-directed.

The style Emerson employed in these talks with Woodbury was a style
that he had developed over the course of three decades. In these talks
Emerson foregrounds both the rhetorical and contingent nature of language as a way to suggest the collaborative possibilities involved in any
language exchange. The following example serves to illustrate how Emerson sets those possibilities in motion. In a discussion of writing methods,
he says, "the most interesting writing is that which does not quite satisfy

the reader. . . . A little guessing does him no harm, so I would assist him with no connections" (22). This piece of advice is characteristic of how Emerson's sentences (particularly those sentences that position themselves as "advice") tend to operate. First, they tend to bridge theory and practice: "A little guessing does him no harm" is an abstract statement about "the reader"; "I would assist him with no connections" is specifically directed at young Charles Woodbury about to sit down and begin writing. Second, Emerson tends to direct his sentences, seemingly as they are being written, toward, and sometimes past, the extremities of logical coherence. The word "so" in the second sentence above implies that the second clause is intended to confirm the one that precedes it, as "therefore" or "hence" would. But Emerson must be employing that syntactical structure toward different ends: "a little guessing" implies *some* connections; "*no* connections" implies *a lot* of guessing. How to read around this contradiction?

One can argue that "a little guessing" is purposeful understatement, that Emerson meant "a lot of guessing" all along. This possibility seems insufficient since to simply replace "a little" with "a lot" in our minds changes the tone of "does him no harm" by throwing that proposition into doubt. We hear the phrase differently, as we would hear a significant difference between "a little running never hurt anyone" and "a lot of running never hurt anyone." A more likely argument would be that Emerson is pursuing not a coherence in logic but something more evasive, something like a coherence in mood, the narrative for which we as readers must construct; in doing so, we might say that Emerson begins in a mood to provide the opportunity for "a little guessing" and decides not to *change* that mood but to *elevate* it. In "so I would" we hear both an increase in pressure, taking it up a notch, and a decrease in authorial responsibility, a distancing not unlike "if it were me." As readers we feel both the burden of our role as narrators (this isn't Emerson we have discovered but something we've made and are calling "Emerson") and the pleasure created by that narrative, a pleasure based largely on the belief that, since Emerson provided us with "no connections," he must have wanted it this way.[38] Our sense of what Emerson must have wanted (a sense infused with the knowledge that this is the biggest guess of all) comes principally from our reading of the syntax of his sentence. As such, that sentence begins to seem more and more like a comment on itself. "So" being a false connection, this sentence literally assists us with "no connections." In "not quite satisfy[ing] the reader," the sentence becomes "the most interesting writing"—-at least, that is the gamble Emerson seems to have taken.

What occurs on the level of the sentence in the above example occurs in the following example on the level of the paragraph. Here we have an instance of Emerson ostensibly giving the most practical advice, what to read and what not to read, based on his sense of the proximity of the act of reading to the act of writing:

> Reading is closely related to writing. While the mind is plastic there should be care as to its impressions. The new facts should come from nature, fresh, buoyant, inspiring, exact. Later in life, when there is less danger of imitating those traits of expression through which information has been received, facts may be gleaned from a wider field. But now you shall not read these books"—pointing— "Preston or Bancroft or Motley. Prescott is a thorough man. Bancroft reads enormously, always understands his subject. Motley is painstaking, but too mechanical. So are they all. (24)

Emerson's chief fear regarding Prescott, Bancroft, and Motley is an aesthetic one; it has less to do with the information they have to offer than with "those traits of expression through which information [is] received." These three writers, Emerson suggests, employ a rhetoric of thoroughness and lucidity that is implicitly hierarchical; the enormity of one's reading, the clarity of one's expositions, are the markers by which writer distances him- or herself from reader. To imitate such rhetoric (as Emerson fears the young Charles Woodbury might) would be to adopt its logic, the logic inherent in an apprentice model of knowledge acquisition and creative possibility. Contrast this to Emerson's own model, even in this seemingly paternalistic paragraph. Notice how the authoritative command "you shall not read these books" is unraveled by the oracular excess of the final sentence, "So are they all." This sentence is a good example of why Emerson's essays demand (or at least reward) a poetic model of reading. Here the inversion of subject and verb result in four equal stresses, "so are they all," with a corresponding (and causal) loss of specificity. Were he to have begun the sentence "they are all," it would have demanded an adjective—"mechanical"—and the connection to the previous sentence would have established a referent. If he had chosen to simply say "they all are," the word "all" would be the single stressed word: "they *all* are." The specificity of the stress effects a casualness in tone, leaving open the possibility that "all" means "all three of them."

But "so are they all" is grand and vague. It suggests vast biblical inclusions such as "Blessed are they all" (Tobit 13:12) and "So all Israel shall be saved" (Rom. 11:26) and equally large exclusions such as "neither because they are the seed of Abraham are they all children" (Rom. 9:6–7).[39] At the very least the sentence seems to encourage Woodbury to include everyone on Emerson's bookshelf at the time, and it seems to drift toward the inclusion of writers generally. Taken in this latter way, "you shall not read these books" comes to mean something closer to the absurd proposition "you shall not read." How to take such an admonition from a voracious reader standing in front of his bookshelf? We are left again not to understand what he means but to guess at what he implies—in this case, an extremely subversive model of reading "closely related," as he says at the beginning of the paragraph, "to writing." Unable to make sense of "you shall not read" on the level of strict denotation, one fishes about for other, connotative possibilities.

The model described here is the vehicle by which, as Emerson's most famous "student" Whitman once put it, "Emersonianism breeds the giant which destroys itself."[40] One becomes an Emersonian, Whitman suggested, by abandoning "Emerson" as a denotative or *denotating* entity. A few pages later Emerson offers Woodbury another related piece of advice: "Do not attempt to be a great reader," he says. "The glance reveals what the gaze obscures" (27). The "great reader" is presumably the one reading Prescott, Bancroft, and Motley (or gazing at them, in Emerson's characterization). "The glance" implies a method of reading vertiginously, free from that model by which the reader seeks to "always understand his subject." Rather, reading becomes just another activity that falls prey to Emerson's observation that "direct strokes never gave us power to make; all our blows *glance,* all our hits are accidents," as he states it in "Experience" (CW 3:49–50, emphasis added). But if the gaze affords the comfort of directness, then the glance affords the possibility of something much more radical: the freeing up of the reader's creative potential via the freeing of signification itself. "Books belong to the eyes that see them" (3:50), Emerson writes, but, we should presume, only if those eyes are glancing.

What Emerson is really after here is a disruption, via the glance, of what John Dewey calls "the spectator theory of knowledge." Dewey, in describing that theory, offers what we might take as an important insight into the political possibilities inherent in Emerson's disruption: "The real object is the object so fixed in its regal aloofness that it is a king to any beholding mind that may gaze upon it." The model of reading based on the gaze, which Emerson criticizes in his advice to Charles Woodbury, is an aristocratic model of reading. The model based on the glance, which he promotes, is a democratic model. In Emerson's discussions with Woodbury, the political ramifications of his theory of reading remain implicit. But as his commitment to abolitionism intensified, so did the explicitness with which he connected his aesthetics and his politics. As I will soon discuss at length, by the time he met Woodbury, that connection was well theorized and well practiced. Dewey's description of the spectator theory of knowledge suggests to us that given Emerson's disdain for such a theory, his move to reconcile his aesthetic beliefs and his political commitments is in some sense inevitable. For the spectator theory of knowledge, Dewey argues, flows "from the separation (set up in the interest of the quest for absolute certainty) between theory and practice, knowledge and action."[41] Only if the object under scrutiny is believed to be autonomously "true" will it remain unknowable, obscured as Emerson says. Its unknowableness is central to its status as regal; the hierarchy that makes the object of knowledge (a text, for instance) king and the model of practice serf is cemented by the premise that that object is simultaneously a fixed truth and an unattainable one. Remove this premise, as Emerson clearly does in advocating for a model of reading based on the glance, and theory and practice can no longer remain separate. For the philosopher who has reached the conclusion that knowledge and action are co-conspirators, an aristocratic theory of knowledge or of language starts to look a lot like an aristocratic political model. In his discussions with young Charles Woodbury, Emerson was implicitly advocating for a democratic model of reading. And in 1865, the connections between that model and his political commitments were clear enough to Woodbury for the young scholar to note "his [Emerson's] and William Lloyd Garrison's anti-slavery apostleship" and Emerson's "emancipation speeches with their lava fire" as proof that "the man stood behind or abreast of his every statement" (173).

What Emerson's involvement with abolitionism did was effect a change in the scope of his inquiry. It allowed him to see, among other things, that reading was taking place on an incredibly large scale, with an incredibly wide demographic. It allowed him to see that the debate over slavery was a debate highly dependent on theories of reading, on the interpretation of cultural documents and cultural myths. Perhaps most importantly, it allowed him to see the structural impediments that existed to suppress just the model of reading he had for years been promoting. The expansion of Emerson's definition of the reader was coincident with—and partly dependent on—a revised definition of what might be included as "local." This revision, which took place over the course of a decade, ends in an effective explosion of the distinction between the remote and the local, public and private. If readers by the early 1850s had come to include for Emerson "all classes," then, similarly, "locals" had come to include people from all places. Nothing influenced this transition more than the Fugitive Slave Law. Emerson's virulent denunciations of the law are remarkable in and of themselves. A few months after the passage of the law, he addressed an audience by saying, "Against a principle like [freedom], all arguments of Mr. [Daniel] Webster are a child's squirt against a granite wall. . . . As long as men have bowels, they will disobey. You know that the Act of Congress of September 18, 1850 is a law which every one of you will break on the earliest occasion" (CW 11 : 192). The passage of the law caught Emerson by surprise ("I thought none, that was not ready to go on all fours, would back this law," he wrote) and, he said, "had the illuminating power of a sheet of lightning at midnight" (11:184, 182).

The law forced him to address what he had already begun to suspect, that commerce had made personal, local, national, and international politics collaborative. He was confronted with the ripple effect that personal or local ethical decisions now seemed to set inevitably in motion. He begins his 1851 speech "The Fugitive Slave Law" by saying, "The last year has forced us all into politics. . . . I have a new experience. I wake in the morning with a painful sensation" (11:179). His recognition of a wider scope of individual responsibility showed in his growing insistence on the interdependence of theory and practice. One way to follow the growth of this recognition is to mark the change in a key motif of distance from its appearance in "Self-Reliance" in 1841 to its inclusion in "The Fugitive Slave Law" in 1851. The importance of this change has to do with Emerson's revision of what it means to be "a thousand miles off." Early in "Self-Reliance," he writes:

> Every decent and well-spoken individual affects and sways me more than is right. I ought to go upright and vital and speak the rude truth in all ways. If malice and vanity wear the coat of philanthropy, shall that pass? If an angry bigot assumes this bountiful cause of abolition, and comes to me with his last news from Barbadoes, why should I not say to him, 'Go love thy infant; love thy wood chopper: be good natured and modest: have that grace; and never varnish your hard, uncharitable ambition with *this incredible tenderness for black folk a thousand miles off.* Thy love afar is spite at home.' Rough and graceless would be such greeting, but truth is handsomer than the affectation of love. (CW 2:51, emphasis added)

Emerson begins in a familiar vein, extolling the virtues of self-trust over contrasting tendencies to be swayed not only by the ideas of other individuals but by culturally sanctioned standards of decency and well-spokenness generally. That he ought to "speak the rude truth in all ways" is a central tenet of "Self-Reliance," part of his larger argument regarding the interconnectedness of language and selfhood. But the logic of his point

is strained by the example that follows. On the one hand, the hypothetical bigoted abolitionist highlights a contradiction between theory and
practice of which Emerson was increasingly intolerant, the type of contradiction he would lampoon in his discussion of Brook Farm in "Experience."[42] The bigoted abolitionist, moreover, was by no means a fictional
character. Indeed, Gougeon has suggested that the extensive research into
the history of slavery that Emerson began in the early 1840s was partly
in response to a recognition of this contradiction in his own thinking.[43]

On the other hand, the sentences themselves make the hypothesis
seem extremely remote: there is the repetition of "if" followed by a question—"why should I not say to him"—which elevates the rhetorical nature of Emerson's argument. Poirier finds these "imaginary confrontations over terminology" to be self-mocking "arguments with himself over
what to say, and how to say it."[44] In any case, what makes these sentences
so dissonant in an essay like "Self-Reliance" is the impression one gets
that they anticipate acquiescence from the reader. To the first question
one is expected to answer, "No"; to the second, something like, "Why,
indeed?" But while the sentences seem to encourage such tacit agreement, to respond to Emerson's questions in such a way goes directly
against his appeal to the reader in the previous paragraph to "give an independent, genuine verdict" (2:49). That appeal would imply arguing
Emerson's point along two possible lines: the first, a ridiculous one, that
bigoted abolitionism is a thoroughly passable stance; the second, and
more viable, that to seize on the bigoted abolitionist is to dodge what is
really at issue. The central issue, such an argument might go, is whether
"speak[ing] the rude truth in all ways" (the only idea in the passage crucial
to Emerson's concept of self-reliance) would necessarily include speaking out for abolitionism. If the answer is yes—and in 1841 Emerson was
near to concluding that it was—then Emerson's highlighting of the contradiction of bigoted abolitionism seems like little more than an effort to
obscure or varnish the opposite contradiction in his own thinking: the
nonabolitionist believer in liberty and self-reliance. Contrast the hypothetical questions in the passage above to this hypothetical question from
his journals of 1840, written under the heading of "Self-Reliance": "Is it
thought that there is a race of beings in this earth, an exception to all

which we have yet found in nature, one, namely, whose existence cannot be maintained except by another's usurping its independence: except by crime?" (12:153). That this question does not find its way into the essay "Self-Reliance" provides an interesting window into Emerson's conflicted mind during this period.

Emerson's argument depends for its good faith on the insistence that activities that are physically distant lie outside the realm of individual agency; they cannot form part of individual praxis. The manifestation of intellectual life in actual life takes place locally, "at home." The bigoted abolitionist's "tenderness for black folk" is "incredible," Emerson seems to suggest, not because he is a bigot but because those black folk are "a thousand miles off." What takes place "afar" is always subordinate in this scenario. Yet, already, ideas of both travel and news seem to disrupt Emerson's dichotomy; they have the effect of shrinking space and challenging categories that depend on distance for distinction. News, and the newspaper, was something Emerson thought about more and more in the early 1840s. "News from Barbadoes"—and the West Indies generally—was precisely what he would begin to willingly gather at this time in preparation for his address "Emancipation in the British West Indies." And the rise of the newspaper was one of the central facts in his recognition that something like a democratization of readership had taken place in antebellum America. Immediately following the passage on the "bigoted abolitionist," Emerson remarks, "There is a class of persons to whom by all spiritual affinity I am bought and sold." Emerson's metaphor places him in the role of slave—bought and sold to a "class of persons"—and, as such, directs his sentence back precisely to the place from which it intends to depart, the discussion of abolitionism. Rather than dismissing the relationship between abolitionism and self-reliance, it brings it back to the fore. Indeed, the sentence is the first in a series of sentences in which Emerson implicitly compares the self-reliant man to the African American slave.[45] Such sentences seem to predict the impending collapse of his narrow "class of persons." By 1854, in his second major address against the Fugitive Slave Law, Emerson would remark, "When I say the class of scholars or students,—that is a class which comprises in some sort all mankind . . . in these days not only virtually but actually. For who are the readers and thinkers of 1854? Owing to the silent revolution which the newspaper has wrought, this class has come in this country to take in all classes" (11:218). And in 1864, in a letter reprimanding Carlyle for his failure to support the Free States, he concluded, "I hate to write you a newspaper, but, in these times, tis wonderful what sublime lessons I have once & again read on the Bulletin-boards in the streets" (CEC 542).[46] What Emerson recognized was that, as Kenneth Cmiel has argued, "The dramatic expansion of basic schooling and the concurrent breakdown of deference to gentlemen—highly refined—reordered the relationship of education to leadership and pushed the problem of civility to the center of [mid-nineteenth century] society." Far from fretting over this state of affairs (as, for instance, Oliver Wendell Holmes did), Emerson was counting on it.[47] Either the range of his devotion or his sense of the local had expanded considerably.

Again, the change in Emerson's thinking regarding abolitionism is best registered by marking the change in the way distance figures into his arguments. What does the distance of a thousand miles signify? In "Self-Reliance" it signifies an impossible gulf, across which any gesture of tenderness is "incredible." In "The Fugitive Slave Law" address of 1851, it signifies quite differently: "If our resistance to this law is not right, there is no right. . . . This is befriending in our own State, on our own farms, a man who has taken the risk of being shot, or burned alive, or cast into the sea, or starved to death, or suffocated in a wooden box, to get away from his driver: and *this man who has run the gauntlet of a thousand miles for his freedom,* this statute says, you men of Massachusetts shall hunt, and catch, and send back to the dog-hutch he fled from" (11:187–8, emphasis added).

While the passage from "Self-Reliance" begins with Emerson somewhat crabbily clinging to his belief in the rightness of his own self-trust, this passage from "The Fugitive Slave Law" begins with Emerson in a mood to willingly transvalue all definitions of rightness in the name of resistance to slavery.[48] In this latter passage, ironically, his self-reliance, his will to act as nonconformist making "an independent, genuine verdict," is much more pronounced. One sees it in his exasperated redefining of terms: breaking the law becomes "befriending," obeying it be-

comes hunting. Emerson recognized, perhaps more than any other abo-
litionist, that the fight over the direction of the nation was in large part
a fight over vocabulary and grammar. His one critique regarding William
Lloyd Garrison's efforts, which he greatly admired, ran along these lines:
"Garrison accepts in his speech, all the logic and routine of tradition"
(JMN 10:94). Notice how in the passage from "The Fugitive Slave Law"
Emerson hammers down on new possibilities of vocabulary—the repetition of "man" for instance ("a man who has taken the risk," "this man
who has run the gauntlet"), which is then echoed in "you men of Massachusetts" (right down to the phrases' three stressed syllables) as if Emerson means there to be no mistake about his argument for equality.[49]

Emerson's method, then, involved a dialectic of building up and so-
lidifying new vocabularies while deconstructing old ones. The old vocabulary was the subject of bitter sarcasm: "One intellectual benefit we
owe to the late disgraces," he remarks wryly toward the beginning of
"The Fugitive Slave Law." "It ended a good deal of nonsense we had been
wont to hear and to repeat, on the 19th of April, the 17th of June, the
4th of July" (11:182). This is Emerson on the attack, taking aim at outmoded beliefs sanctioned through large-scale rituals of repetition. In the
passage concerning the fugitive slave who has "run the gauntlet of a thousand miles for his freedom," Emerson disrupts and disavows his own previous definition. The thousand miles that in "Self-Reliance" signified the
abstractness of places "afar" becomes in this later instance an area of
travel, a thousand-mile gauntlet of harrowing particulars. It should be
noted that these were particulars of which Emerson now had firsthand
knowledge, having begun a commitment to assisting the Underground
Railroad that would last more than a decade. That commitment was part
of an ongoing, self-imposed directive to school himself in the actual re-
alities of American slavery, a commitment that began with his research
into West Indian emancipation in the late 1830s and early 1840s.

Lastly, one might note Emerson's pun on "gauntlet": it marks a growing insistence on the agency of the fugitive slave. By running the gauntlet,
this man was also throwing down the gauntlet. "The black race can con-
tend with the white," Emerson was increasingly prone to remind his
audiences. "The quality of this race is to be honored for itself" (CW

11:145). In 1864, speaking at a fair in Concord held to raise funds for
Negro orphans, Emerson exclaimed (with the spunk of someone about
to reveal a truth for which he knows his audience is unprepared), "American genius finds its true type—if I dare tell you—in the poor Negro soldier lying in the trenches by the Potomac with his spelling book in one
hand and his musket in the other."[50] The fugitive slave turned poor Negro
soldier, through his own agency, has become the American genius who
reveals the diminishment of the category of distance, the expansion of
the category of readership, and the absolute necessity that the theory and
practice of democracy be made to correspond. "We must realize our
rhetoric and our rituals," Emerson says in "The Fortune of the Republic"
(11:530), making, by then, a familiar point about language and social
practice. Whether the national language would be, structurally, democratic or aristocratic, was, for Emerson, a key indicator of the prospects
of the nation generally.

Emerson's ongoing dialogue with Carlyle during the decades of his
abolitionist commitment provides a helpful venue from which to understand his comparison of democratic and aristocratic linguistic structure.
While Cary Wolfe has used the correspondence of Emerson and Carlyle
to suggest that Emerson "never really found a way to put" the "democratic and aesthetic . . . together in the body politic,"[51] a careful look at
that correspondence reveals quite the opposite. And while Albert von
Frank quite rightly points to Carlyle's goading of Emerson in 1844 for
his lack of activity in the public sphere,[52] I would add this: that when
Emerson does enter the public sphere of abolitionism (as von Frank
points out, the year is 1844), he returns to Carlyle and, armed with a
theory of symbolic action, turns the tables on him. If we recall the example of Emerson's relationship with Charles Woodbury, then the following passage provides an interesting contrast. Newly invigorated by
the controversy over the Fugitive Slave Law, Emerson offers this critique
of Carlyle's role as mentor to English writers: "Espinasse, who is really
a man of wit & capacity, writes unmitigated Carlylese. And when I told
Carlyle, that he ought to interfere, & defend that young man from him,

Carlyle, he appeared piqued, & said, 'he must act as he could, & be thankful'" (JMN 10:540).

Though it might seem a harmless exchange between friends—both well established as mentors to young talent—Emerson's suggestion and Carlyle's rejoinder actually provide a clear window into the philosophical conflict that would strain their friendship during the 1850s and 1860s. The conflict itself had been latent in their philosophies all along. Again, recall the lengths to which Emerson went to provide Woodbury with "no connections" in what were ostensibly words of advice on writing. Emerson suggests that Carlyle's relationship with their mutual friend from Manchester, Francis Espinasse, should function similarly. But it's the *way* in which Emerson offers this suggestion that should hold our interest: Carlyle "should interfere, & defend that young man from him, Carlyle." Carlyle is faced here with a classic Emersonian paradox. How does Carlyle interfere with someone's writing while simultaneously protecting— *defending*—that person from his influence? Clearly, any form of interference resembling the admonition, Don't write like me, won't suffice. That tactic would fail to disrupt the hierarchy that is, after all, the premise for the necessity of interference. Carlyle is privileged—he is one from whom Espinasse needs defense. But he is also, potentially, privileged on a second front—he is one who *provides* defense. This of course is the logical crossroads at which dictatorships are maintained. (Indeed, this crossroads is reminiscent of the one that Burke describes in relation to Hitler's "one voice" rhetorical strategy in *Mein Kampf,* which I discussed in chapter 1.) How to avoid being linguistically or expressively paralyzed by circumstances that make someone else's language both carrot and stick?

Emerson's answer begins with a description of the language itself: Carlylese. The name alone suggests the stability of its source. It is the language of Carlyle, a language, a way of writing that can be learned; it has a vocabulary and a grammar and, to remain identifiable as Carlylese, must be "unmitigated." Note, too, that in order for Carlylese to maintain the illusion of stable signification, Carlyle himself must pose as a stable subject. That he is prepared to defend the structure on which his relationship with Espinasse is built is betrayed by his retort to Emerson:

Espinasse "must write as he could, & be thankful." The element of coercion in the word "must" sets the tone. If we apply Carlyle's logic to Emerson's original complaint then Espinasse *must write Carlylese* by order of Carlyle himself; if he must be thankful that he *can* write Carlylese, it follows that he must be thankful to its maker, Carlyle. And, if we chose, we can draw all of this together in one rather ominous insistence: Espinasse must be thankful to Carlyle for insisting that he imitate Carlyle, that he write Carlylese. To arrive at this final formulation requires that we press down fairly hard on that word "must," but it should be said that adjusting our lens makes the word no less innocuous in this context. If we take "must" as an indicator less of Carlyle's direct insistence on a particular code of behavior (how to write) and more as a general comment on the options open to Espinasse as a writer, the practical consequences remain the same. One way or another, Espinasse is, according to Carlyle, destined to write Carlylese and be thankful for it. Attributing this destiny to a higher power than himself makes no practical difference and in fact is perfectly in line with Carlyle's understanding of the circumstances by which he and Espinasse achieved their separate positions. As he told abolitionist Elizur Wright in 1846, he believed "men ought to be thankful to get themselves governed, if it is only done in a strong and resolute way" (CEC 396).[53] Likewise, Carlyle was governing Espinasse by the strong and resolute dictates of Carlylese, that language and style that Emerson once described as "an enormous trip hammer with an 'Aeolian attachment'" (JMN 10:179).

"Carlyle's projectile style," Emerson wrote, functioned in this way: "He makes an irresistible statement, which stands, and which everybody remembers & repeats" (15:363). For the man who once likened imitation to suicide, Carlyle's methodology was far from ideal. In the 1850s, Emerson saw with increasing clarity that Carlyle's opinions about writing and young writers and his opinions about slavery and democracy were not operating in isolation. In the above advice regarding Espinasse, Emerson suggests a remedy not unlike the one he used in his own relationship with Woodbury, namely, a deconstruction of one's own potentially privileged language via a deconstruction of one's selfhood as represented by authorship. If the problem is that young Espinasse, so full of his own expressive potential in Emerson's mind, writes "unmitigated Carlylese," then one possible solution is for Carlyle to actively mitigate that Carlylese through some sort of paratactic disruption or "antagonized expression" (CW 11:398). Again, this is a favorite tactic of Emerson's that he believed consequently empowered readers, auditors, pupils. The corollary to such a theory of disruption was that it was incompatible with a stable notion of authorship. If in the student's mind there was one categorized Carlyle, then Carlylese would retain its coercive power. Notice how, in his advice to Carlyle, Emerson attempts to disrupt or complicate Carlyle's subjectivity—not only by suggesting that one "Carlyle" defend against another but by wording his advice in such a way that it contains the cluster "him, Carlyle, he," subtly suggesting that Carlyle's selfhood is already contextual and, as a result, multiple.

Taken in isolation, the passage regarding Espinasse might be read as another example of Emerson's early preoccupation with the local relationship between writer and reader, between learned teacher and learned pupil, between, in Carlyle's terms, older and younger "noble-men." But the passage demands also to be contextualized within the network of discussions Emerson was having with and about Carlyle during the 1850s and 1860s. Interestingly, Emerson had made note of his conflict with Carlyle in one of his talks with Woodbury, telling the young man, "A great deep cliff divides us in our ways of practically looking at this world." And Woodbury's extrapolation from Emerson's statement highlights its political character: "They were always at war, their methods transverse, and their separations pronounced. . . . [Emerson] believed in the grandeur of the masses and their self-originated advancement, while Carlyle's sympathies were never democratic" (TE 145).[54] Echoes of Emerson's advice to Carlyle on his relationship with Espinasse can be heard in his 1854 criticisms of Fugitive Slave Law supporters, those who "side with Carolina" and stand "as near to monarchy as they could." Like Carlyle, these supporters have failed to recognize that liberty is dependent on a willingness "to postpone oneself, *to protect another from oneself*" (CW 11:230, emphasis added).[55] Emerson's recognition that power was inscribed in discourse made it necessary for him to work out his republican desires *textually*. A journal entry two years earlier provides another insight into the relations among Carlyle's various roles of writer, mentor, and political voice. Emerson notes: "The young men are eager to see him; but it strikes me like being hot to see the Mathematical or the Greek Professor, before they have got their lesson. . . . I fancy, too, that he does not care to see anybody whom he cannot eat & reproduce tomorrow, in his pamphlet or pillory. Alcott was meat that he could not eat, & Margaret F[uller] likewise, & he rejected them, at once" (10:553).

The young men Emerson mentions are related to Carlyle much as Espinasse is: they arrive to receive and repeat their lesson. More disconcerting to Emerson is Carlyle's inability to engage his friends Alcott and Fuller, and here the critique takes on a markedly political inflection. Fuller had come away unimpressed, to say the least, after a visit to Carlyle in 1846, and she said as much to Emerson, noting in particular Carlyle's "defense of mere force," his belief that "if the people would not behave well, put collars round their necks;—find a hero & let them be his slaves, &c." Emerson called Fuller's description of Carlyle and his discourse "the best I have had" (CEC 412). By the early 1850s Emerson was beginning to relate these distasteful political opinions to Carlyle's aesthetic predilections. That Carlyle did not care to see anyone who might alter those predilections said a lot to Emerson about his politics, his aesthetics, and the relation between the two. For Emerson, both were part of what he referred to as the "covenant" Carlyle had made "with [his] eyes." When one considers this larger conversation, it becomes clear that Emerson's critique of Carlyle's relationship with Espinasse is one element in a broad critique of Carlyle's writing as it relates to his politics.

In a lecture version of "The Fortune of the Republic," delivered several times in 1863, Emerson clearly articulates the distinction he had been describing for over a decade between democratic and aristocratic linguistic structure, using Carlyle's prose as an example. Carlyle—who had infuriated Emerson that year for publishing a brief, racist, and vaguely pro-Southern satirical essay, "Ilias Americana in Nuce," in *MacMillan's Magazine*—is a prime example of the fact that "English nationality is babyish, like the self-esteem of villages, like the nationality of Carolina . . . they are insular and narrow." More to the point, his prose is like "a Venetian aristocracy. . . . The reader is treated as if he were a Prussian adjunct, solely occupied with the army and the campaign. He is ever in the dreamy circle of camp and courts. But of the people you have no glimpse."[56] Here Carlyle's prose mimics his preferred social relations. Rhetorically, it functions in such a way that the reader is placed in a position not unlike that of Espinasse and the other young men eager to see him; that is, the prose is designed to persuade the reader into a subordinate position— that of adjunct—by the promise of connection to Carlyle and separation from the unseen masses, "the people." We should be reminded here of the passage quoted in chapter 1 where Emerson describes how "America is the idea of Emancipation." In that passage, Emerson critiqued Edward Everett for reading Robertson's *History of America* instead of reading America itself, in its currently evolving form, embodied "in the faces of the people" (JMN 11:406). Interestingly, Emerson knew that Robertson's *History of America* was one of Carlyle's first books. Carlyle is making a mistake in his model of writing analogous to the one Everett did in his model of reading. Again, in contrast, reading "in the faces of the people" is an antidote to that view of American culture that would privilege a reified past over evolving possibilities.[57]

Compare Emerson's description of Carlyle's prose to his description, quoted earlier, of the prose of Prescott, Bancroft, and Motley. To say that Motley's prose is "mechanical" leaves the issue in the realm of aesthetic judgment—while such a judgment does have social implications, those implications appear to be local. But the stakes set by *Carlyle's* aesthetic choices are as large as the debate over democracy and aristocracy, slavery and abolition. In joining the abolitionist cause, Emerson had entered into a much wider network of signification. We should contrast abolitionist Theodore Parker's characterization of Emerson's sentences as "an army of all officers" to Carlyle's famous complaint that those sentences "sometimes did not rightly stick to their foregoers and their followers. . . . A beautiful bag of duck shot held together by canvas" (TE 149). Both men are describing Emerson's prose as symbolic action, though Carlyle does so a bit unwittingly. His complaint is that Emerson's sentences have no *rank;* their order seems random (and the word "followers" here certainly would have resonated with Emerson). Parker's metaphor makes this lack of rank both explicit and positive. As both abolitionist and writer, Emer-

son was squarely on Parker's side. In the 1850s and 1860s, Emerson concludes that Carlyle's insistently noncollaborative model of writing ("he
undertook to play all the parts," Emerson wrote) is a kind of aristocratic
symbolic action, and his opinion is encouraged by the fact that he is privy
to the whole range of Carlyle's writings and opinions during this period.
He came to see Carlyle's aesthetic as of a piece with his belief that "there
are about 70,000 of these people who make up what is called 'Society,'"
of which Emerson remarked sardonically, "Of course they do not need
to make any acquaintance with new people like Americans" (JMN 10:249).
As he does in "Fate," Emerson poses human (and communal) liminality
against both historically determined social ossification and the pretensions of an educated, "babyish" Anglo-European elite.

It should be said that Emerson's ongoing critique of Carlyle was not
an easy one for him to make. Emerson had a great affection for Carlyle
and a deep respect for Carlyle's talents, and his criticisms were always
dialectically paired with encouragement toward change.[58] A final example
serves to reveal that dialectic at work. In an 1862 letter to Carlyle noting
that he had received "the 3rd Volume of Friedrich," Emerson notes Carlyle's "imperial scale . . . according to the high Italian rule" and then
goes on to offer this description and plea:

> Tis *sovereignly* written, *above all literature, dictating* to all mortals *what
> they shall accept* as fated & final for their salvation. It is mankind's
> Bill of Rights & *Duties,* the *royal proclamation* of Intellect *ascending
> the throne,* announcing its good pleasure, that hereafter, as hereto-
> fore, & now once for all, the world shall be *governed* by Common-
> sense & law of Morals, or shall go to ruin.
>
> But the manner of it!—*the author sitting as Demiurgus,* trotting out
> his manikins, coaxing and bantering them, amused with their good
> performance, patting them on the back, and *rating* the naughty dolls
> when they misbehave. . . . I find also that you are very willful, &
> *have made a covenant with your eyes* that they shall not see anything
> you do not wish they should. . . . Now that you have *conquered* to
> yourself such a huge *kingdom* among men, can you not give yourself

breath, & chat a little, an Emeritus in the eternal university, and write a gossiping letter to an old American friend or so? (CEC 535, emphasis added)

Emerson's plea is far from subtle. Every sentence is marked by some signifier of aristocracy. Sovereignly written prose poses as royal proclamation qua governing apparatus, dictating to the reader what has in fact, in this conceit, been determined a priori—the criteria by which they shall, or shall not, be saved. (Compare Carlyle's insistence on fated-ness and finality to Emerson's destabilization of fated-ness in "Fate" discussed earlier.) The author is Demiurgus, artificer of this world and its laws, only by remaining "above all literature," and here we should pause to consider precisely what Emerson intends by this phrase. The author who would be god must necessarily move—at least rhetorically—above literature because literature, as Emerson always insisted, was the realm of "mortals"; it existed "among men." As Barbara Packer has shown at length, "Emerson's Fall," the fall into mortality, is the fall into language and the problem of signification. The words "mortals" and "literature" are for Emerson part of a nexus that defines what it means to be human. But Carlyle aspires in his prose to be *above* literature, to *dictate* to mortals, to *conquer* men. The only way he can achieve this is to not engage with those mortals and their "literature," their language, their speech, at all; in their place are the good manikins and naughty dolls, marionettes with which Carlyle puts on a play of rank and rating. The puns on this last word must have amused Emerson to no end, meaning as it does "scolding," "ranking," "enlisted personnel in the British Navy," and, also in England, "apportioning a tax."[59] But the point behind such punning—that Carlyle's vision was dependent in the imaginary world on supreme artifice and in the real world on social coercion—was quite serious. Note, too, Emerson's description of Carlyle's "Bill of Rights & Duties," an obvious joke intended as contrast to the Bill of Rights. If the former was law of an abstract "mankind," the latter, in Emerson's mind, sought to establish rules of commerce "among men." Carlyle's "covenant with his eyes" recalls the fact that he "did not care to see" Margaret Fuller, and both are indicators of Carlyle's failure to achieve a prose style marked by the "antagonized expression" that Emerson himself had adopted as the best hope for a language compatible with the republican aspirations of the abolitionists.

What Emerson sought to do was to take his observation about democratic society—that "contrast, change, interruption, are necessary to new activity and new combinations"—and apply it to the language itself. His plea to Carlyle that he "give himself breath" is interesting in this regard, for as Dewey has written, "breathing is a rhythm of intakings and outgivings," a statement that seems rather matter-of-fact until one considers its consequences to Emerson's hopes for Carlyle. Breath taken in is transformed into breath given out. Or, if we reverse the equation, breath given out is dependent on, and in a sense transformed by, breath taken in. Intakings provoke a series of biological changes and adjustments that result in outgivings. As a metaphor for a potential antidote to Carlyle's sovereign and impregnable voice, it's quite interesting. Likewise Emerson's calls to "chat" and "gossip." To chat is to come down from above into the "low" realm of affectable speech, into dialogue. To gossip has similar implications with an even more pronounced emphasis on the varied and accidental travel of such speech and, interestingly, mediates against Carlyle's masculinist prose—Emerson suggests a kind of role play by which they would act, in the vernacular of the day, as two women friends. The "idle" quality of gossip effects a democratization of speech by calling into question direction and purpose, radically expanding possible vocabularies. In this it is analogous to the willed expansion of his attention and perception that he notes in "Self-Reliance": "My willful actions and acquisitions are but roving;—the idlest reverie, the faintest native emotion, command my curiosity and respect" (CW 2:65). As Robert Duncan has written, Emerson's self-characterization is an argument for "the importance of whatever happens in the course of writing as revelation"—an argument against the a priori ranking of experience and, symbolically, against such ranking in society and culture generally.[60]

Emerson was generally disappointed in his attempts to encourage Carlyle to put his considerable talents to work in the service of re-visioning the relationship between democracy and literature. In 1848, he had mused, "It is a curious working of the English state that Carlyle should in all his lifetime have never had an opportunity to cast a vote," and four years later asked, in a journal entry, "Is Carlyle a voter?" (JMN 10:343, 568). The answer he had hoped for never arrived.

The dialogue itself, however, paid great dividends—it was one of several forums in which Emerson developed and articulated his distinction between democratic and aristocratic symbolic action and his arguments in favor of the former. His growing consciousness of that distinction affected the nature of his experiments with language. I have noted how the scope of Emerson's address expanded as a result of his abolitionism. What is remarkable is that rather than being reined in by a perceived need to "reach" or "makes sense to" the larger public, Emerson continued to experiment with language that was democratically structured. In fact, the imperative to invent a democratic language only became more pronounced in the antislavery essays. The language of Emerson the abolitionist is no less a riddle than the language of Emerson in its earlier manifestations. All the dizzying circularity, the paradoxes and tautologies, the abrupt turns and reversals, remain. But one difference worth noting is the heightened sense of polyvocality in the later work. If Emerson's contradictory prose seems, in the early essays, to be the result of a willed dialogue with the individual reader, the later work seems the result of interruption by and conversation with a multitude of new voices. The manner in which he begins the seminal address "Emancipation in the British West Indies" is to the point:

I might well hesitate, coming from other studies, and without the smallest claim to be a special laborer in this work of humanity, to undertake to set this matter before you; which ought rather to be done by a strict cooperation of many well-advised persons; but I shall not apologize for my weakness. In this cause, no man's weakness is any prejudice: it has a thousand sons; if one man can not speak, ten others can; and, whether, by wisdom of its friends, or by the folly of the adversaries; by speech and by silence; by doing and by omitting to do, it goes forward. Therefore I will speak,—or, not I, but the might of liberty in my weakness. (CW 11:100)

In "Self-Reliance," the fact that Emerson had been "coming from other studies" was a half-hearted excuse for his lack of abolitionist involvement. But in this address three years later, the gesture functions in a quite different manner: far from signifying his distance from the activities at hand (due to his allegiance to a different "class of persons") it actually functions in the service of those activities. Here Emerson notes that he is "coming from other studies" as a way not to separate himself but to designate himself as someone with no "claim to be a special laborer in this work of humanity," that is, to be an everyday laborer.[61] While at first it seems as if he is making a distinction based on expertise, Emerson quickly dispenses with the logic of expertise altogether. He refuses to privilege either strictness or depth of study; he eliminates the discourse of "strengths and weaknesses" as a means for discussing democratic action. When he says "it has a thousand sons," "it" can refer to either "this cause" or to "weakness," but this latter possibility can't be pejorative since "no man's weakness is any prejudice." What Emerson seems to be after, more than anything else, is a sense of large-scale activity and large-scale change; whether you or I speak, he suggests, is of little consequence, since "if one man cannot speak ten others can." "It" has ten thousand sons; "it" goes forward despite wisdom and folly, speech and silence, doing and not doing—or, not despite, but somehow *because of* these things. How? One is tempted to ascribe to Emerson both a Manichean view of the battle between slavery and emancipation and a deterministic belief in the inevitability of the latter. But if that is our reading, how do we explain "therefore"? "Therefore I will speak" is a statement that should follow some argument for the wisdom, efficacy, *necessity* of speaking. The syntactical game Emerson is playing here is one way in which he attempts to get around the contradiction between individual and collective action. The discourse of collective action represented by the "thousand sons" threatens to become a teleological march that would erase any sense of individual agency. Again, this threat is mediated in part by the shifting "it" that leaves open the possibility that these sons are not sons of "this cause" but sons of "weakness." And yet this second possibility does not necessarily disassemble the collective; it simply makes it more flexible. The collective may be based on individual weakness but Emerson has said "no man's weakness is any prejudice." As he does not prejudice weakness, there is the suggestion that weakness has a democratizing effect—an idea driven home by his suggestion that the "might of liberty" resides "in weakness." As he said of "the injured negro" a year later, "in his very wrongs is his strength" (ASW 37).

The collective that Emerson seeks to describe is so contradictory of conventional wisdom as to seem oxymoronic. That collective, however, is grounded in ideas about the individual that he had been developing for decades. "Weakness" comes up three times in this passage. The first time, it is self-directed and stands for a kind of incompleteness: Emerson designates himself as foreign and suggests that he doesn't have either adequate facts or adequate language to say what he wants to say. That state of affairs, we should remember, is one that Emerson insisted was the state of selfhood generally—the truest statement one could make was always some variation on "I am a fragment and this is a fragment of me." The difference here is that Emerson employs his concept of selfhood in the service of the collective "cause" of abolition. He links republicans fighting for "plebeian strength over aristocracy" by their willingness to accept this basic premise about the self. Prejudices are the lifeblood of cultures with "an aristocratic complexion"; they are the sentries that guard "immemorial usage"; and they are ultimately incompatible with a view of the self as incomplete and in transition. In contrast, a view of the self as in the making was not only compatible with but essential to Emerson's conception of a democratic culture. With that conception in mind, the final sentence in the passage above makes a good deal more sense: "Therefore I will speak,—or, not I, but the might of liberty in my weakness." The halting interruption of "I" resembles the way in which the passage begins: "I might well hesitate." Both hesitations are a way to recognize the presence of other voices by employing interruptions followed by silences. When Emerson revises "I"—changes it to "not I"—he purposefully "disowns his former me," as James would say, as a way to suggest not only that his selfhood is evolving but, more specifically, that it is evolving within the context of a republican collective; again, to quote James, his self is the pragmatist self, "including and contemplating its 'me' and its 'not-me' as objects which work out their drama together" (WJ 8:319, 291). By adopting this view of selfhood, Emerson radically complicates both individual and collective, self and other, and puts both in the service of democratic symbolic action. This scheme constitutes the might of liberty in weakness.

———————

It would be impossible (or in any event extremely negligent) to discuss Emerson's connection of democracy and the liminal self without discussing the role played by his growing awareness of African American identity. To this point, I have hinted at two ways in which the actions of African Americans had made an impression on Emerson. First, as fugitives they were running "the gauntlet of a thousand miles for [their] freedom," doing "more for their freedom than ten thousand orations." Emerson's recognition of fugitive slaves was a recognition of the agency of those slaves in the battle for their own emancipation, as well as a recognition of the bankrupt nature of his own earlier tendencies to privilege the local in discussions of freedom. The escape over a thousand miles was itself a symbolic and persuasive act, an argument against using the category of distance to provide cover for empty ethical abstractions. The fugitives' activities were evidence for Emerson that, as Livingston has said, "manual labor is not mindless; mental labor is never disembodied," and this more than anything else was the evidence that enabled Emerson to expand his own definition of what symbolic activity could be. The man who once wrote "Art is the path of the creator to his work" (CW 3:41) was led to recognize new paths, new work, and new creators.[62] That recognition had a deep and lasting impact on his philosophy. At about the time he became aware of the role fugitive slaves were playing in the cultural imagination, Emerson wrote, "I have learned a sordid respect for uses & values: & must have them. . . . Are we to say, a man shall not go out to the shed to bring an armful of wood, lest this violence of action hurt the balance of his mind?" (JMN 11:10–11). By 1862, making sense of mind in terms of "uses and values," in terms of "action," was the cen-

tral imperative of his philosophy. In that year, he posed these questions
to an audience in Washington: "Is [man] not to make his knowledge practical? . . . Is it not for action?" (CW 11:299). It is hard for the contemporary critic to capture these questions under a rubric other than "pragmatism." They might just as easily have come out of the mouths of James
or Dewey—and did, hundreds of times, with minor variations. But the
point I want to make most clearly is that Emerson's development into
what we would now call a pragmatist would have been inconceivable
outside the context of his abolitionist commitments. His many medita-
tions on the activities of fugitive slaves revealed to him how physical actions could be consciously symbolic, and this in turn led to a broad extrapolation: that all symbolism was socially active.

The actions of the fugitive *reader* made perhaps an even more powerful
impression; as I've mentioned, Emerson came to insist that "American
genius finds its true type . . . in the poor Negro soldier lying in the
trenches by the Potomac with his spelling book in one hand and his musket in the other." The fugitive-turned-soldier-turned-reader was the representative American genius because he was fighting for freedom under
a new set of rules, a set of rules that put mental and physical symbolic
activity on the same playing field (or battlefield), a set of rules that made
the liminal self agent in the proposal of a liminal nation. What Emerson
recognized (in part predicted) was a social phenomenon analogous to
those described by Victor Turner, where a particular kind of nonritual-
ized liminality—in individuals or subcommunities—affects the development of a particularly radical state of *communitas* among the larger community. "The detachment of the individual or the group from either an
earlier fixed point in the social structure or from an established set of
cultural conditions," Turner writes, leads to a situation in which the liminal subject "becomes ambiguous, neither here nor there, betwixt and
between all fixed points of classification; he passes through a symbolic
domain that has few or none of the attributes of his past or coming state.
. . . Their liminality is not institutionalized or preordanied. Rather, should
it be viewed as spontaneously generated in a situation of radical structural change . . . when seemingly fundamental social principles lose
their efficacy, their capacity to operate as axioms for social behavior, and

new models of social organization emerge, at first to transect and, later, to replace traditional ones."[63] Emerson believed that what made the African American soldier or the African American reader so important to the prospects of the nation generally was that he or she was uncategorizable in terms of that nation's available vocabulary. When Emerson writes, "the Negro will learn to read and write before the white will,"[64] what he means is that the African American whose reading and writing become public activities changes the significance of reading and writing as such. Reading and writing become essentially new activities that "the white" will subsequently have to learn. Thus the activities of the black reader-writer are central to Emerson's model of social change.

We might think of these activities as essentially poetic in character in that they propose that a new way of speaking (or any new kind of symbolic activity that leads to a new way of speaking) *is a new reality as such;* they dismantle old categories by proposing new ones, just as Emerson says the poem does. "It is not metres, but a metre-making argument, that makes a poem," he writes famously. "It has an architecture of its own, and adorns nature with a new thing" (CW 3:9–10). The poem (a metre-making argument) replaces "the poem" (the logical limit of what could previously be defined as "metres") in the act of writing. Likewise the black soldier, reader, writer, changes the meaning of those terms in the act of self-fashioning—and since those terms causally affect other terms such as "citizen," "nation," and "democracy," these latter terms are inevitably changed as well in the process of accommodation. "He could tell nothing but that all was changed," Emerson writes revealingly in "The Poet." "Society seemed to be compromised" (3:10). If the new black writer was the "true type" of American genius, he was also, it seems, the true type of the new American poet. The poet, who was in 1841 represented as "a youth who sat near me at table," was two decades later the one who would "let old times go & write on . . . Universal suffrage; women's suffrage. . . . The poet shall bring out the blazing truth, that he who kills his brother commits suicide."[65] It is not an exaggeration to say that such a change in focus would have been impossible for Emerson without the example of the black reader, the black writer. As I've suggested, Emerson took the liminal identity of African Americans to be, on the one hand, the most revealing example of liminal selfhood as such and, on the other hand, as emblematic of the possibilities of a liminal nation.

Plenty of critics have noted Emerson's celebration of transitional states, but few have made much of the role "transition" plays in his anti-slavery writings. His most famous aphorism on the subject, from "Self-Reliance" ("Power . . . resides in the moment of transition from a past to a new state" [CW 2:69]), is repeated almost verbatim in the "WO Liberty" notebook: "Man is in transition, that is the attitude of power" (JMN 14:393).[66] The activities of African Americans—as fugitives, readers, writers, soldiers—were the best examples Emerson had of "man in transition." Note that Emerson was not particularly interested in describing this transition as one from a "primitive" to a "civilized" state. Indeed he confounds that model by shifting with great frequency the ways in which he identifies African Americans. Over the course of his antislavery writings, he identifies them not only as "Negro" or "black man" but as "citizens of this our Commonwealth of Massachusetts," "men of African descent," "anti-slave," and simply "man." Such shifting was, again, a way to disrupt the codes of oppression. Emerson understood just how pernicious signifiers could be in relation to black people. As early as 1845 he had noted, "I think there is but one single argument which has any real weight with the bulk of the Northern people, and which lies in one word. . . . That word is *Niggers*! . . . 'Oh, the Niggers!' and the boys straightway sing Jim Crow and jump Jim Crow in the taverns. It is the objection of an inferiority of race" (ASW 36). Emerson understood the symbolic import, the web of arguments behind this single word and was keen to the possibilities inherent in combating it. "Not the least affecting part of this history of abolition," he said in 1844, "is the annihilation of the old indecent nonsense about the nature of the negro. . . . It was the sarcasm of Montesquieu, 'it would not do to suppose that negroes were men, lest it should turn out that whites were not' " (CW 11:140). These words of Montesquieu's were ones that Emerson was fond of quoting (JMN 14:388–89), presumably because they were a wry description of motives, of the anxieties behind rhetorical posturing.

Emerson's answer was equally rhetorical, designed to persuade prejudiced auditors that everything was in fact the opposite of all they had previously assumed: "it now appears that the negro race is, more than any other, susceptible of rapid civilization" (CW 11:140). African Americans were not "niggers" but "forerunners" (ASW 38), prophets of a new social system: "There never was such a combination as this of ours," Emerson wrote in "The Fortune of the Republic," "and the rules to meet it are not set down in any history" (CW 11:536). At an early stage in his abolitionist commitment, Emerson wrote that the arrival of men such as Toussaint L'Ouverture and Frederick Douglass in the arena of symbolic activity suggested that "the black man carries in his bosom an indispensable element of a new and coming civilization." These men, he argued, effectively dismantled the vocabulary on which the logic of slavery in a "democracy" was based. "Here is the Anti-slave," Emerson continues. "Here is man; & if you have man, black or white is an insignificance. Why at night all men are black." Again, it's that power to quickly flip terms that Emerson finds so powerful: if slave is in fact "Anti-slave," what then? One is forced to scramble for new arguments, and in the *gap,* in the space between old argument and new, Emerson shoots first, making a transition, or, a transitional statement: "black and white is an insignificance" (JMN 9:125).[67] It's worth pointing out that Emerson did not base the ability of someone like Douglass to transvalue terms like black and white on Douglass's mere existence. This would have been to uphold him as merely an effective representation of the future state Emerson proposed. Rather, Emerson insisted that African Americans from Douglass to the black soldiers for whom he raised money and to whom he spoke and whose dead he later memorialized (to, for that matter, the black students he spoke to at Howard in 1872) were "strik[ing] for their rights," that is, were *agents.*[68]

Emerson believed that the symbolic activities of African Americans would be a major determining factor in the revelation that "all the facts in history are fables, and untrustworthy." History's fables, he meant to imply, would be exposed as oppressive and coercive discourse and either dismantled or reimagined. Ironically, it was their status as a wronged people that would allow African Americans to play the central role. For they were at once the most keenly aware of the devious workings of cultural forms (as anyone who has read Douglass or Harriet Jacobs on Christianity will recognize) and the farthest outside of the logical space those forms inhabited. Emerson glossed this positionality with the following Persian proverb: "Beware of the orphan; for when the orphan sets a-crying, the throne of the Almighty is shaken from side to side" (ASW 37). Mackey's application of what he calls "the orphan's ordeal" to American literature provides a helpful way to understand why Emerson might be highlighting this proverb. Mackey cites Kaluli, rather than Persian, myth. He notes that "the Kaluli of Papua New Guinea" believe that "music and poetic language . . . arise from a breach in human solidarity, a violation of kinship, community, connection." That violation represents "the orphan's ordeal . . . where in back of 'orphan' one hears echoes of 'orphic,' a music that turns on abandonment." And, most importantly, the music, or poetry, brought about by such abandonment has a specific and far-reaching social function: "The world, music reminds us, inhabits while extending beyond what meets the eye, resides in but rises above what is apprehensible to the senses" (DE 231–32). The poetry of the orphan's ordeal, Mackey suggests, resides in a *liminal space,* somewhere in between the material limits of the present and the possibility of the future, and speaks of the injury of the former and the prospects of the latter. Mackey applies this myth to a wide range of literatures, including slave narratives and spirituals, Ralph Ellison's *Invisible Man,* and the New American Poetry.[69]

My interest in his formulation here involves not only its helpfulness in explaining Emerson's use of the figure of the orphan but also Emerson's use of a key term in his lexicon: *abandonment.* Few words signify more widely and deeply for Emerson than "abandonment." At the end of "Circles," he writes, "The way of life is wonderful: it is by abandonment" (CW 2:321–22). And in notes for his speech to raise funds for the Massachusetts 54th Regiment, he writes, "Negroes good soldiers they love music, dress, order, parade, they have a couth temperament & *abandon,* & Gen[eral] H.'s opinion of their desperate courage" (JMN 15:213). These were notes for a speech meant to persuade a white audience to donate money to a black regiment, and Emerson's list bears some of the markings of that goal. But *abandon* (the emphasis is Emerson's, not mine) is a word he never, in my reading experience, uses lightly—it resonates too deeply with central aspects of his philosophy for him to throw it around. For Emerson, "abandon" or "abandonment" signified the status of being *abandoned* (cut off from others, left on one's own), as well as the possession of *abandon* (freedom from constraint and conventionality and the ability to proceed without them). The pun suggested for Emerson a causality whereby the "abandoned" were the most likely to develop "abandon" and, as such, the most likely to slough off the grammar of the past and enact the grammar of the future.

As he detailed in essays such as "Experience," Emerson believed "abandonment" to be the general, if latent, state of things. Anyone who looked deeply enough at his or her own status would feel a sense of abandonment; for Emerson that is "where we find ourselves" in a contingent universe, and all possibilities of human activity and creation leave off from this point. But he also recognized the unique and deeply ironic position in which African Americans had been placed. Their "abandonment" was, in both senses, much more profoundly sociocultural than his own; thus, for a philosopher who had decided to embrace the social culture, their role in abandoning the grammar of the old republic and inventing the grammar of the new was pivotal. One thinks again of Douglass: the material forces he was forced to confront (the material that made up his "experience") meant that the philosopher, essayist, novelist, and poet was also, inevitably, the sociologist. One way to think about Emerson's transition from "transcendentalist" to "pragmatist" is that he recognized the trend represented by "symbolic activists" like Douglass and was moved to follow suit. Of course it's more complex than this, but the symbolic action of African Americans clearly played a role in the development I've been describing.

Though Emerson didn't recognize it at the time, the call he made in 1841 for new forms of expression unimpeded by the logic of past forms would be answered in large part by black readers, writers, and soldiers. What makes Emerson himself important is that, even in 1841, *he put no limits on who might answer that call:* "It is the vice of our public speaking that it has not abandonment. *Somewhere,* not only *every* orator but *every* man should let out *all* the length of *all* the reins; should find or make a frank and hearty expression of what force and meaning is in him" (CW 2:141–42, emphasis added). What Emerson was employing here in 1841 was something very close to what James would later call "the re-instatement of the vague" (WJ 8:245–46), a linguistic tactic, a mediation of the definitive nature of "grammatical scheme" designed to make signification flexible. As Poirier has argued, "the virtue and necessity of vagueness is brought forward by Emersonian pragmatists as an intellectual and poetic necessity, so that what has always been true of poetry and poetic language is by them made generally so." Upon "re-instating the vague," words "blur and refract," phrases "refuse to surrender [their] vagueness to any one of a variety of competing emphases."[70] One can see how, in Emerson's passage above, that blurring of emphasis has a democratizing effect. The vague conjectural "somewhere" is made even more vague by his re-petitive excess: "every . . . every . . . all . . . all." If *every* orator should let out *all* the reins, then doesn't "somewhere" in fact mean "every-where"? And if that is the case, if we've created a logic in which "some" can, by the associative property, mean "every," then might "every orator" and "every man" be read as "some orator" and "some man"? And, lastly, if we make this leap, changing "every man" to "some man," don't we de-construct the logic by which we made "somewhere" stand for "every-where" in the first place? This dizzying circularity has a point: it makes moot any discussion of who Emerson's implied reader might be. Who is supposed to take up "abandoned" public speech? Who is supposed to speak with reckless and public abandon? Someone, everyone, anyone. As Cavell has said of this passage, "Self-evidently, no one is in a position to know more about this than any other, hence in no position to *tell* anyone of it, to offer information concerning it."[71] Emerson abandons the rhe-torical apparatus by which he might "tell"—by which he might offer de-notative information—as a prerequisite to the community of abandoned public speech he desires and imagines. He would later come to believe that the "abandon," the music, the "desperate courage" of the black sol-diers he met during the Civil War was part of the payoff for that gamble.

Emerson invested in the change brought about by the activities of Af-rican Americans and by the activities of other abolitionists, and he was never afraid to put a fine point on his conviction: "If any cannot speak, or cannot hear the cause of freedom, let them go hence," he once said to what must have been a half-energized, half-horrified audience. "Creep into your grave, the universe has no need of you" (CW 11:100). This was Emerson's way of saying that the immediate re-visioning of the nation had already begun, that radical discontinuity had already set social change in motion. That change, it should be said, was inevitably multicultural in nature. To the abolitionist who was also calling for "doors wide open . . . to every race and skin" (11:541), the American vernacular, culture, and democracy were necessarily a multicultural collaboration: "It is not a question whether we shall be a multitude of people," he said casually. "No, that has been conspicuously decided already" (539). "This continent," he predicted, "asylum of all nations, the energy of Irish, Germans, Swedes, Poles & Cossacks, & of all the Europeans Tribes,—of Africans & of Polynesians, will construct a new race, a new religion, a new state, a new literature" (JMN 9:300). But while this represented a radical new vision of what America would be, it is important to note that Emerson set no limits on the revisability of the body politic, "for liberty," he insisted, "is a short and hasty fruit, and like all power subsists only by new rallyings on the source of inspiration" (539). His most enduring argument is this: that American democracy depends for its existence on a deeply flexible willingness to reinterpret its own vocabulary, its own grammar, and that an American art that exhibits an analogous flexibility on the symbolic level acts "as a function of American democracy." This last phrase is Ralph Ellison's but Ellison realized better than anyone that when he wrote it he was re-visioning "the language of Emerson."

3
Ralph Waldo's Blues, Take 2

Ellison's Changes

Conventional categories and hand-me-down reverence aside, it is only natural for contemporary U.S. writers to proceed as if Ralph Waldo Emerson, for all his New England stiffness, would have been moved by Louis Armstrong and would have acknowledged him as a Representative American Artist, a poet whose melodies "ascend and leap and pierce into the deeps of infinite time."

Albert Murray, *The Blue Devils of Nada*

To fully appreciate the depth and complexity of Ellison's attempt to put democracy into aesthetic action in *Invisible Man,* one must search out, confront, query the role Emerson-as-sign plays in that text. There is no better evidence than Ellison's relationship with Emerson's work of the fact that, as Mackey has written, "Creative kinship and the lines of affinity are much more complex, jagged, and indissociable than the totalizing pretensions of canon formation tend to acknowledge" (DE 3).[1] The critical discourse surrounding the "kinship" of Emerson and Ellison (small as it is) is troubled by a failure to recognize either Emerson's abolitionism or his pragmatism, two aspects of Emerson's intellectual activity of which Ellison was acutely aware.[2] As a consequence, critics who argue for an affinity between the two writers turn them both into caricatured transcendentalists, representative of the man who "glories in the special and soulful nature of his own existence, of which he has finally and totally become aware." Never mind that neither writer's conception of the self allows for "final" or "total" awareness—the most significant drawback of this line of thinking is that it draws our attention away from the sociological aspects of their thought. As a consequence, the critical debate becomes essentially a debate over whether or not Ellison is a transcendentalist. Those who say no find it necessary—because of the way the terms of debate have been set—to argue that Ellison's writings constitute a repudiation of Emerson. In order to do so successfully, they take one of two approaches: they focus on "the applications of Emersonianism" rather than on Emerson's work itself; or, they ludicrously caricature Emerson's work as "basically abstract," "a universal doctrine . . . full of quintessential Emersonian words" that uphold the "patriarchal and aristocratic concept of society."[3] I would suggest that this debate has become immaterial as a result of recent developments in Emerson scholarship that situate Emerson as both pragmatist and abolitionist, as a radically republican thinker. Ellison recognized this all along, but the criticism is just now catching up.

Ellison, as Henry Louis Gates, Jr., has pointed out, is a master signifier, and when Invisible Man leaves Mr. Norton in Raab Hall, politely promising that he "intend[s] to read Emerson" (IM 108), we should recognize in those words Ellison's wink to the reader—his tip that "Emerson," as a sign in the novel, is in play.[4] There are three practical ways to follow this play in an attempt to understand what it has to say and what it is meant to do. The first involves recognizing that in addition to Invisible Man and Mr. Norton, there are a whole range of characters in the novel who are, consciously or unconsciously, claiming Emerson's inheritance by signifying on him. Having recognized that this signifying is occurring seemingly everywhere, one goes about trying to figure out which characters are privileged by Ellison and why and what this has to say about *Ellison's* reading of Emerson. In order to understand the signifying of these characters, one has to be familiar with certain key terms drawn from Emerson's lexicon. I would suggest two primary terms: "names" and "circles." And I should provide at least a brief introduction to how these terms operate in Emerson's work.

Even in his early writings, Emerson believes the perpetually evolving and fractured self to be an "unbounded substance," a "cause which refuses to be named" (CW 3:72). The unnamable self is both a natural state of affairs—"I am a fragment and this is a fragment of me" (3:83)—and the prerequisite to individual agency, that power that "resides in the moment of transition from a past to a new state" (2:69). Ellison is equally interested in the way unnaming is a prerequisite to transition. One always notes the obvious regarding the self-identifying first line of *Invisible Man* ("I am an invisible man")—that it signifies both the blindness of the people with whom he comes into contact as well as a refusal to identify himself visually. But it also—and equally—represents a refusal to identify himself *nominally*. And, as I will discuss in a moment, Ellison's signifying on naming *always* involves signifying on Emerson. First, however, I should point out that neither Emerson's nor Ellison's discussions of naming end with their relevance to private self-realization. As I have discussed in the previous two chapters, over the course of his career Emerson develops what might be called a sociology of naming with which he explains how naming functions to solidify or entrench outmoded structures in American culture. Emerson and Ellison share a "deep" understanding of democracy, to use Judith Green's phrase. They recognize the complex, entangled relationship between the "institutional framework" we call "democracy" and the symbolic activities of individuals and communities that are "of critical significance in determining whether the democratic impulse will achieve its full realization."[5] To repeat: when, in "Self-Reliance," he wrote "I am ashamed to think how easily we capitulate to badges and names, to large societies and dead institutions" (CW 2:51), he meant to suggest not only a list of ills but an equation whereby "badges and names" were the apparatus through which "large societies and dead institutions" sustained their authority and influence. This equation, this description of operations is crucial to Ellison.

"Circles" is Emerson's paean to contingency. In this essay, Emerson begins with a description of nature that we should construe as a desire, as an effort at action. "There are no fixtures in nature," he writes. "The Universe is fluid and volatile. Permanence is but a word of degrees" (CW 2:302). Emerson's insistence on this description of nature is no philosophical abstraction. He means to persuade his reader toward a preference for "truth [over] his past apprehension of truth" (2:309). Emerson's motives are at least as pragmatic as James's were when he said famously, "Truth *happens* to an idea. It *becomes* true, is *made* true by events" (WJ 1:97). And we should be clear about the direction of his persuasion:

Emerson intends to put his theoretical point in the service of a new description of social relations. The pragmatist conception of truth, Emerson suggests, is a tool with which his readers can proceed, under the "intrepid conviction that his laws, his relations to society, his Christianity, his world, may at any time be superseded and decease" (2:309). Remember: when Emerson makes this statement, he is poised to begin a two-decade, blistering critique of American laws, social relations, and religion under the sign of abolitionism. Here as there, he links social change to linguistic change; a belief that social relations and laws are revisable is ultimately indistinguishable from a belief that "the so-called eternal names of fame" can and will be "revised and condemned" (2:308). Emerson himself implies that we should take his descriptions to be efforts at symbolic action. "The use of literature," he writes, "is to *afford us a platform* whence we may command a view of our present life [and] by which we may move it" (2:312, emphasis added). I believe that this sentence marks a seminal moment in the development of pragmatism's methodology. Emerson provides the logic by which a more or less utopian description of democratic symbolic action (one that the realist would say does not and cannot exist) can be seen as having a vital social function. Dewey echoes Emerson's sentence in the following: "The idea becomes a standpoint from which to examine existing occurrences. . . . The suggestion or fancy though still ideal is treated as a possibility capable of realization *in* the concrete natural world, not as a superior reality apart from that world. As such it *becomes a platform* from which to scrutinize natural events."[6]

Dewey understood Emerson's idealism to be a functional strategy; in describing an alternative social and linguistic possibility, Emerson provides a platform from which to scrutinize present social and linguistic systems—that platform is the predicate "by which we may move . . . our present life." The utopian possibility awakens and sustains both dissatisfaction and desire while providing transitional vocabularies with which to inspirit "fledgling social forms and political processes," as Ellison wrote. What is most important in the context of our discussion is that Ellison takes the same position on Emerson that Dewey does and brings that position to bear on discussions of racial inequality. In a 1972 interview, Ellison was asked this question (posed as a statement): "I don't see why—because we live in this myth of democracy—we should assume that we will ever become a true democracy. We have the myth on the one hand and the reality on the other" (CE 229). Ellison answers via a discussion of democratic symbolic action, which implicitly critiques the interviewer's distinction between myth and reality, between symbolic and social action—and his example is Emerson: "You can only [mediate against social inequality] by consciously keeping the ideal alive, by not treating it as a folly, but by treating it as Thoreau and Emerson were treating it, as a conscious discipline which imposed upon you a conscientiousness which made you aware, every hour and every day" (230).

Like Emerson, like Dewey, Ellison treats the democratic ideal "as capable of realization *in* the concrete natural world." His point is not that such an ideal is "real." Rather, his point is twofold: first, that by treating the ideal as a "conscious discipline," one creates a platform from which to examine the real; second, that since language, logical space, is open-ended, the ideal language will seek to make space for itself among those linguistic systems that determine large-scale social practice, and it will often succeed in doing so.

When Ellison signifies on Emerson's "Circles," he is troping on the history of democratic symbolic action. When Emerson characterizes himself as "an experimenter" who "unsettles all things" (CW 2:318), Ellison takes him to be engaged in a rhetorical strategy designed to inspirit a fledgling democracy mocked by the institution of slavery. Likewise with Emerson's most famous statement from the essay: "Our life is an apprenticeship to the truth, that around every circle another can be drawn; that there is no end in nature, but every end is a beginning" (2:301). Ellison of course bookends *Invisible Man* by signifying on this statement of Emerson's,[7] and in doing so he marks both his allegiance with Emerson and his difference from him. He marks, that is, the paradox at the heart of Emersonian pragmatism: that the writer who takes up Emerson's task of putting the liminal self in dialogue with the liminal nation necessarily speaks in a language Emerson would not have—*could* not have—understood. Emerson's end is Ellison's beginning; this is the joke.

To understand how multilayered this joke is, one needs to take a good

look at Ellison's essay "Hidden Name and Complex Fate." The joke begins, Ellison says, as "the joke implicit in such a small brown nubbin of a
boy carrying around such a heavy moniker" (SA 152). That moniker is
"Ralph Waldo," the name given to him by his father, who was an admirer
of Emerson's and a man who "was aware of the suggestive power of
names and the magic involved in naming" (151). The young Ellison won-
dered why he had not been named after Frederick Douglass—and a possible answer comes, interestingly, in *Invisible Man,* in a passage that the
later essay echoes. In a late passage, Invisible Man begins to believe "that
there was a magic in spoken words," and he thinks of Douglass, who "had
taken another name. What had his true name been? Whatever it was, it
was as *Douglass* that he became himself, defined himself. . . . The sense
of magic lay in the unexpected transformations" (151). Douglass stands
as a prime example that "our names, being the gift of others, must be
made our own" (SA 147). Still it's important to keep in mind that Ellison
understands this to be Emerson's message as well as Douglass's. Ellison's
signifying here puts Douglass and Emerson in resonant dialogue; both
were keen observers of the ways in which naming institutionalizes meaning. Ellison recognized in Douglass's activities "a certain triumph of the
spirit, speaking to us of those who rallied, reassembled, and transformed
themselves and who under dismembering pressures refused to die"
(149). And he recognized in Emerson's work a companion piece, an argument for reassembling and transforming the self in the name of one's
republican desires.[8] Both men, Ellison suggests, were manipulating "these
European names" in the hope of discovering variations better suited to
"the egalitarian principles of democracy." And both would have recognized their practice as perpetually extending beyond themselves and
their moment in history: "in following [Emerson's] advice," Ellison writes,
"I reduced the 'Waldo' to a simple and, I hoped, mysterious 'W,' and in
my own reading I avoided his works like the plague" (153).

Ellison understands Emerson's advice to be that one should mystify
his name and avoid his works. He understands Emerson's basic motive
to be *de-authoritative.* Like Whitman, Ellison believes that "the best part
of Emersonianism is, it breeds the giant that destroys itself."[9] And the
signifying joke gets even more complex: how has Ellison "inherited the

provisation that involves the renaming of Norton. In the course of that improvisation, Norton is figured as Thomas Jefferson, John D. Rockefeller, the Messiah, the Creator. Each act of signifying has its own complexity. The joke of Norton-as-Jefferson is perhaps most relevant to our concerns. One of the vets says to another, "Look, Sylvester, it's Thomas Jefferson!" Sylvester responds, "I was just about to say, I've long wanted to discourse with him" (77) and points Norton out to others in the group: "Gentleman, this is my grandfather!" When one of the vets complains, "But he's *white,* his name's Norton," Sylvester answers, "I should know my own grandfather! He's Thomas Jefferson and I'm his grandson—on the 'field-nigger' side" (78). Sylvester's antiphonal improvisation puts to rest any possibility that these vets are merely crazy, that their "game" is a passive manifestation of their insanity. Ellison packs an entire essay on the role of Jefferson-as-signifier in African American culture into these few lines. In Sylvester's expression of long-awaited desire to discourse with Jefferson, one hears the long postponement of the Declaration of Independence's promise, in a tone not unlike that of Jimmy Rushing's "How Long Blues."[19] His insistence that Norton (as Jefferson) is his grandfather comprises a complex joke on ancestry and privilege. When he shouts, "I should know my own grandfather!" he means both "I am sure this is my grandfather, Thomas Jefferson" and "In a just world I would know who my grandfather was." And in between these two options is the bitter irony: that Jefferson, as author of the Declaration of Independence as well as slave owner who fathered slaves, necessarily stands in as grandfather to the institution of slavery and its abolition. Sylvester mends this fissure through joking: he is Jefferson's grandson "on the 'field-nigger side.'" The joke deconstructs the whole idea of lineage as system of privilege by troping on the grammatical pleasantry (on the Rockefeller side, on the Jefferson side) that helps perpetuate it.

The "music" of the vets involves quick changes based on the subversive appropriation of terms. The vets are presented with the Golden Day as if it were the backdrop for all of U.S. history; as one of them recounts, the Golden Day "was a church, then a bank, then it was a restaurant and a fancy gambling house, and now *we* got it" (80). Notice how in its present state, the Golden Day is figured as liminal space—the vet can't say what it is exactly that the Golden Day represents, can't say what precisely "we got." Thus the vets occupy a space that, on the one hand, is laden with historical and cultural memory but, on the other, operates much like a frontier space as Ellison describes it: "Certainly it made for a conflict, but what was good about it was the constant jockeying to assert a different pattern of relationships, and that was very, very important" (CE 256). This, I would say, is what is at stake in the signifying games of the vets in the Golden Day—the games represent an attempt to design what Lyotard would call "flexible networks of language games"[20] that might advance their vision of the "different pattern of relationships" evolving in this barrelhouse. Ellison would say that the vets are engaged in inventing the American vernacular. Note the similarity of their position to the following description of "Americans":

> When Americans set up their own institutions they got locked into the frame projected by those institutions which preceded them, and as you know, it takes a lot of time and consciousness to break the historical precedent and democratize it. . . . I see this as part of a general, eclectic process of culture through which, having started out by imitating British and European models we've improvised our own unique idioms and styles. American vernacular is an amalgamation of prior cultures, including a strong component of the African. . . . Eclecticism is the word. Like a jazz musician who creates his own style out of the styles around him. (CE 357, 364)

Democratizing the historical precedent is precisely the function of the jazzlike cutting of Norton, and that activity leads the vets toward a reconceptualization of history as a term that might better suit their republican desires. Norton's history of "the Great Traditions" is replaced by one vet signifying on Emerson: "I am a student of history, sir," he tells Norton, "The world moves in circles like a roulette wheel" (81). The vet's reference to "Circles" suggests that history is subject to radical reconfigurations since "in the thought of tomorrow," as Emerson wrote in that essay, "there is a power to upheave all thy creed, all the creeds, all the literatures, of the nations" (CW 2:305). Again, the man who claimed to be "like Emerson" is put in the ironic position of having to hear Emerson's words used as tools for the dissolution of his authority. And the vet's metaphor of the roulette wheel leads to a comic prophecy: "soon Ethiopia shall stretch forth her noble wings! Then place your money on the black!" (81). The vet presents his metaphor under the Emersonian presumption that history is a text and that any revision of that text constitutes *a change in history as such.* Emerson believed that the alternative to such "active" reading was "to be bullied by kings and empires" (CW 2:8), those institutions that sought to control historical representation because they understood what a powerfully coercive tool it was.[21]

The vet understands what Invisible Man will only recognize much later: that an unantagonized history is merely the sum total of "lies [that] keepers keep their power by" (439). One begins to disrupt an unantagonized history by asking the question that Invisible Man finally asks toward the end of the novel, "What if history is a gambler?" That is, he asks what if "a firm historicist frame . . . is merely another transitory myth"?[22] Again, the vet is well ahead of the game in his pursuit of an answer. Importantly, his solution is not an appeal to the "real" history but rather a signifying improvisation *on* history, in the course of which he takes up Emerson's call to "transfer the point of view from which history is commonly read" (CW 2:8). Notice how, even in taking what we would call an Emersonian perspective of history, the vet distances himself from Emerson through his metaphor. "The world moves in circles"—on this the vet and Emerson would agree, but the roulette wheel (like the "gambler" as a model for history) is a cultural signifier of the vet's own device. It gestures toward the Golden Day, toward Storyville, toward jazz. It is one of those things that the jazzman might grab on the run, in the moment that it proved itself useful.

This is how we should think of these Emersonian vets: as organic intellectuals improvising off of Emerson's texts the way Charlie Parker improvises off of the accompaniment harmonies to "Cherokee" on his composition "Ko-Ko." Their improvisational signifying, that is, places them in a particular tradition while at the same time foregrounding their difference from that tradition. The vet's reconfiguration of Emerson's circle as "roulette wheel" is akin to Parker mimicking Woody Woodpecker's cackle

over Ray Noble's changes—it marks the paradox by which agreement is
expressed through disagreement.[23] As another vet puts it, "Play the
game, but don't believe in it. . . . Play the game, but play it your own
way. . . . Play the game, but raise the ante. Learn how it operates, learn
how you operate—I wish I had time to tell you only a fragment" (153–
54). This advice comes from perhaps the most important figure in the
Golden Day, the doctor-vet, who reads Norton like a book and first
identifies Invisible Man as both blind and invisible.[24]

Notice the causal relationships suggested by his advice: to "play the
game . . . your own way," you cannot "believe in it." One can best navi-
gate this apparent paradox by recognizing that the doctor-vet has no stable definition of "the game." In fact, playing the game your own way is
predicated on an insistence that the game—the sum total of its rules—is
defined in the playing. The doctor-vet does not imply that the previous
understandings or manifestations of the game are irrelevant. Rather, he
suggests that not-believing is a strategy that allows one to change the
rules of the game *while one is playing it,* according to the demands of one's
experience. Moreover, there is a real usefulness to understanding the
rules of the game as previously manifested; that understanding constitutes one's pragmatic education. "Learn how it operates," the doctor-vet
says. "Learn how *you* operate." And here we have another suggested causality, where learning how you operate follows learning how the game
operates—individual agency begins after one figures out the ways in
which the game has weighed on one's conception of selfhood.[25]

It is impossible to overestimate the importance of this series of equa-
tions to Invisible Man's own self-realization. His relationship with the
doctor-vet recalls Ellison's relationship with Burke: as Ellison put it, after
reading Burke he "began to grasp how language operates" (CE 364). As
such we might think of this moment with the doctor-vet as the beginning
of Invisible Man's development into a symbolic activist. One is also reminded of Ellison's relationship with Emerson. The doctor-vet tells Invisible Man, "I'm nobodies father except my own" and offers this "fatherly advice": "Be your own father, young man. And remember the
world is all possibility if only you'll discover it. Last of all leave the Mr.
Norton's alone" (156). The fatherless and sonless vet who offers fatherly

ELLISON'S CHANGES   111

advice about being fatherless recalls the story of Ellison's "hidden name," where Ellison is left fatherless by the man who named him after a literary "founding father" who advised that one be fatherless. One of Emerson's first memorable bits of advice of course is that we best not "build the sepulchres of the fathers" (CW 1:3). But Ellison links the doctor-vet's "advice" to Emerson's "advice" to Ellison even more explicitly in the following: "Down here they've forgotten to take care of the books and that's your opportunity. You're hidden right out in the open—that is, you would be if you only realized it. They wouldn't see you because they don't expect you to know anything, since they believe they've taken care of that" (154). Here Invisible Man's future recognition of—and use of—his invisibility corresponds with Ellison's "hiding" of his name "Waldo" and his use of this hidden name in the formation of his identity. Both are a consequence of the Emersonian recognition that *no one has taken care of the books,* which is another way of saying that the language on which identity formation and social relations are founded is open-ended and radically malleable despite the best efforts of the power elite. That those in power believe they've "taken care of" the books (codified and institutionalized their meaning) is an opportunity for those on the margins precisely because the powerful are so sadly mistaken on this point.

Invisible Man's education in the Golden Day constitutes an education in how to make sense of the Emersonian and the African American aesthetic traditions as a dialogic continuum functioning to expand democracy. The doctor-vet is a crucial figure in that education because, while he understands the rules that would separate these traditions, he refuses to play by them. His is a mode of symbolic action drawn equally from Emerson and Louis Armstrong. If he begins by offering Emersonian "advice," he's more than flexible enough to change direction by signifying on Armstrong, telling Invisible Man, "I'm really more clown than fool" (154). Like the difference between being crazy and joking, the difference between the clown and the fool is of central importance to Ellison. Put simply, the clown knows the rules of the game; if he plays the fool he does so with hidden motives, out of a desire to manipulate and change the game. The clown makes use of "the joke that always lies between appearance and reality" (53); what Ellison would call the discipline of self-realization is achieved through the manipulation of appearances, particularly when large-scale cultural authority has served only to rigidly codify one's identity.[26] Armstrong is Ellison's prime example; Armstrong is not only a great performing artist but a "clown" whose "clownish license" allows him to subversively "take liberty with kings, queens and Presidents" (239, 52). He knows that "that which cannot gain authority from tradition may borrow it with a mask" (54). His clowning is neither idle play nor passive acceptance of an available role but rather, Ellison insists, is "motivated . . . by a profound rejection of the image created to usurp his identity. Sometimes it is for the sheer joy of the joke; sometimes it is to challenge those who presume, across the psychological distance created by race-manners, to know his identity" (55). The doctor-vet tells Invisible Man that he's "hidden right out in the open" and that this is his "opportunity." Ellison says the same about Armstrong. He also suggests that changing his middle name to "W" was akin to the donning of a mask, a way to hide his name, to hide right out in the open. It occurs to me that this is Ellison's joke: that whoever forgot to take care of the books presented his father with the opportunity to read Emerson; that hiding Ralph Waldo Emerson under a "mysterious W" was Ellison's opportunity to clown all over the powers that be by signifying on Emerson, a signifying they would not see, would not detect, because they "don't expect you to know anything"; and that what the powers that be would understand least of all (what would most disrupt the essentialized version of history and tradition on which their claims to social privilege were based) was the idea that Ellison is advised to "hide" by Emerson and Armstrong alike.[27]

As I have suggested, the events at the Golden Day are prophetic of Invisible Man's eventual development into a pragmatic, jazz-style symbolic activist. I would argue that the pivotal moment in that development comes during his stay in the Liberty Paints factory hospital. Having been informed by Emerson, Jr., that Bledsoe's letters, "addressed to men with impressive names" (150), constitute an act of sabotage, Invisible Man pursues "a possible job at Liberty Paints," "us[ing] Emerson's name without his permission," which "work[s] like magic" (196). Invisible Man's use of Emerson's name here of course recalls "Hidden Name and Complex Fate" and Ellison's description there of "the magic involved in naming." What's important is that here, around the use of Emerson's name, Invisible Man becomes a manipulator of words. By the time he wakes up in the factory hospital, he is unwittingly poised for his first jazzlike improvisation.[28]

The hospital is a classic liminal space, where the past has been momentarily erased by an explosion and the future is radically uncertain. Again, like the liminal subject as described by Turner, Invisible Man's identity has become in this moment "ambiguous, neither here nor there, betwixt and between all fixed points of classification." There is an unrecognized opportunity in the fact that his "liminality is not institutionalized or preordained. Rather, should it be viewed as spontaneously generated in a situation of radical structural change . . . when seemingly fundamental social principles lose their efficacy, their capability to operate as axioms for social behavior, and new models of social organization emerge, at first to transect and, later, to replace traditional ones."[29] The fundamental social principles that have lost their efficacy include the belief that "you have to stick to the plan" (175) and his belief "in the principles of the Founder," a code that has taught him and his fellow students "to be thrifty, decent, upright citizens . . . shunning all but the straight and narrow path" (99). But in the hospital, where these "axioms for social behavior" have suddenly lost their relevance, a new social strategy emerges. The basic tools at Invisible Man's disposal, I would suggest, are his seemingly new understanding of the relationship between naming and Emersonian self-reliance, along with his previously unemployed knowledge of vernacular traditions of nicknaming and "cutting," as in the jazz cutting session. In the course of his improvisation, these tools are brought together in a signifying attack upon the authority of the doctors.

The doctors want the facts. They are like the doctors whom Emerson lampoons in "Experience," the doctors whose incantation is "But, sir, medical history; the report to the Institute; the proven facts!" To this Emerson replies "I distrust the facts and the inferences." He distrusts the facts because he knows that behind the facts are the *motives* that lead to their construction *as facts*. He refuses to accept the doctor's logic because

he believes that once he does, "the doctors shall buy me for a cent" (CW
3:54). Similarly, Invisible Man comes to realize that his doctors' goal—
their game—involves an attempt to impose a single name, a "given"
name, a "real" name on an identity that, in that moment, he can only
make sense of as fractured, fluid, multiple. The contest that ensues represents Invisible Man's real entrance into the jazz-shaped activities of
Harlem:[30]

> "What is your name?" a voice said.
> "My head" I said.
> "Yes, but your name. Address?"
> "My head—that burning eye'" I said. (232)

While the literal situation suggests that the narrator is simply in too
much pain to answer, Ellison allows for a second, more subversive reading—namely, that Invisible Man does in fact answer both questions: that
his name is in fact "my head," that he will identify himself only via this
vague and unsatisfactory signifier of his momentary consciousness. His
"burning eye" is an obvious pun on his burning "I." His half-conscious
evasion is an expression of the desire for "more room" (235) and an antiphonal response to the doctors' insistence on "absolute integrity" (236).
That response grows more conscious and aggressive as the contest pro-
ceeds. When the doctors emphatically thrust a large card in front of him
that reads "WHAT IS YOUR NAME?" he "plung[es] into the blackness
of [his] mind"; this action seems to lead him toward folk materials out
of which he might fashion a new identity. Asked "WHO WAS YOUR
MOTHER?" he responds silently, "And how's *your* old lady today?" in-
stinctually playing the dozens. Asked "WHO WAS BUCKEYE THE RAB-
BIT?" he makes a crucial self-discovery: "I laughed deep, deep inside me,
giddy with the delight of self-discovery and *the desire to hide it.* Somehow
I was Buckeye the Rabbit" (241, emphasis added). The connection of this
"hidden name" to self-discovery of course brings us back to both the
doctor-vet and to Emerson. I would suggest that "Buckeye the Rabbit" is
a kind of *nickname* and that Invisible Man's "desire to hide it" represents
a desire to stamp it as *self*-discovery and also—and of equal importance—

a desire to *continue playing the game*. If he says, "I am Buckeye the Rabbit," the game is over. By concealing that discovery, the contest continues.

In "On Bird, Bird-Watching, and Jazz," Ellison writes that "nicknames are indicative of a change from a given to an achieved identity" and that they "tell us something of the nicknamed individual's interaction with his fellows" (SA 222).[31] Invisible Man's nickname represents an insistence on articulating his newfound self-reliance not as the triumph of the transcendental ego but as something achieved *in the course of interaction*. This distinction is incredibly important. It is the predicate by which the concept of self-reliance connects itself to the concept of self-government. The distinction is at the heart of the insistence (Ellison's and Emerson's alike) that the "free" or "democratic" self, the self given over to "new activity and new combinations" is assisted by whatever "breaks up his torpor . . . contrast, change, interruption" and that a community based on the self-reliant "living soul contending with living souls . . . in every expression, antagonized" constitutes a democratic state (CW 11:533, 398). The nickname "Buckeye the Rabbit" is particularly apropos in this regard given the song in which it appears: "*Buckeye the Rabbit / Shake it, shake it / Buckeye the Rabbit / Break it, break it*" (242). Invisible Man's nickname, I mean to suggest, is not a self-willed gesture toward privacy but a kind of democratic symbolic action that accepts the gray area between self and other as the area in which a momentary version of the self might be worked out and expressed, an area where, in this case, the question "where did my body end and the crystal and white world begin" (238) is necessarily left open.

Aided by a newfound "achieved identity," Invisible Man resumes playing the dozens, responding to the question "BOY, WHO WAS BRER RABBIT?" with "He was your mother's back-door man." At this point he is clearly involved in a game that sounds remarkably like Ellison's description of a jazz "cutting session": "I suspected that I was really playing a game with myself and that they were taking part. A kind of combat. Actually they knew as well as I . . . it made me feel sly and alert" (242). What is happening at this moment in the factory hospital is modeled on the "contest of improvisational skill" of the kind Ellison first witnessed "in such places as Halley Richardson's shoeshine parlor in Oklahoma

City—where I first heard Lester Young jamming in a shine chair . . . as he played *with and against* Lem Johnson, Ben Webster (this was 1929) and other members of the Blue Devils Orchestra" (SA 208, emphasis added). Invisible Man begins to discover "his own unique ideas and his own unique voice . . . his self-determined identity" (209) in the context of his cutting session with the doctors. Having learned "the fundamentals of his instrument" in the Golden Day, and having tested them out with and against the doctors, he begins to improvise. Of one of the doctors he notes, "I thought of asking him about Emerson" and says to him, "I don't suppose we get around in the same circles" (248). This joke on social boundaries (and on the doctor's presumed lack of reading in Emerson's canon) is followed by a new assertion of an identity that is contingent and multiple: "My mind . . . We, he, him—my mind and I—were no longer getting around in the same circles. Nor my body either" (249–50). The activities that close his stay at the factory hospital are worth pausing over: a jazz improvisation on Emerson's "Circles" that crosses social boundaries by troping them, that asserts a self which is manifold and revisable, and that looks back to the vet's "roulette wheel" improvisation in the Golden Day at the same time that it looks ahead to the jazz-style players of Harlem around whom the second half of the novel revolves.[32] These players, of which Invisible Man himself is one, are jazz players and pragmatists alike. In his descriptions of their interactions, Ellison maps out his understanding of jazz as a pragmatic activity, as "a function of American democracy." The following quote might serve as a guide to that activity:

Jazz is an art of individual assertion *within and against the group*. Each true jazz moment (as distinct from the uninspired commercial performance) springs from a contest in which each artist challenges all the rest; each solo flight, or improvisation, represents (like the successive canvases of a painter) a definition of his identity: as individual, as member of the collectivity and as a link in the chain of tradition. Thus, because *jazz finds its very life in an endless improvisation* upon traditional materials, *the jazz-man must lose his identity even as he finds it*—how often do we see even the most famous of jazz artists being devoured alive by their imitators, and, shamelessly, *in the public spotlight*." (SA 234, emphasis added)

If the collective is to allow for the "solo flights" of its members, it must be flexible enough to accommodate (through change) dissonant assertions that gesture outside its own logical space. If the collective is to improvise *its* identity, the individual must cultivate a willingness to lose his identity (as manifested in its most recent "definition") in the course of response to surrounding conditions. I am reminded again of James's description of pragmatism as "a corridor in a hotel." The jazzman, an ensemble player, is by definition *always* in the corridor, always in "the public spotlight"; the consummate pragmatist, he must make sense of his identity in the context of group improvisation and as such must be flexible enough to constantly redefine his identity according to "the collectivity of experience's demands" (WJ 1:32, 44), must be willing, that is, to "lose his identity even as he finds it" (SA 234). I would propose that from the time Invisible Man leaves the factory hospital, he is involved in a collective improvisation, and that the tune called is entitled "History."

———————————

We should set the terms of this improvisation. The soloists to keep an eye on include Invisible Man, Tod Clifton, and Rinehart. The "traditional materials" upon which they are improvising include previous improvisations on "history" in the Golden Day, the activities of jazz figures such as Armstrong and Parker, and Emerson's democratically motivated descriptions of a contingent history, a history in which, to quote Dewey again, "there is real uncertainty and contingency." Why "History"? Because for Ellison history represents textual authority in its most persuasive manifestation. Through its representations of history, the culture expresses what it "would like to have been" as well as what it "hope[s] to be" (SA 199). As a pragmatist, Ellison does not want to apotheosize history since, like Emerson, he believes it to be "a fable" (CW 2:9), in Ellison's words, "ever a tall tale told by inattentive idealists" (SA 199). Nor, however, does he want to merely dismiss it, since this would be to pretend that its coercive power is somehow immaterial, would be to reject the materiality of language as such, to reject "language as symbolic action."

We might think of these two characteristics of history (as fatefully material and structurally malleable) in terms of Brother Tarp's limp and Brother Tarp's link. Tarp's *limp* is a history he literally drags around despite his insistence that it is "not really" there (387). It represents the coercive power of his own history, a history of chains that the body has internalized. The mind, Ellison would say, internalizes patterns similarly. And yet the mind is a metaphor maker. It signifies itself into new logical spaces. Tarp's *link* is a signifying tool that he has used as "a kind of luck piece"; it is the link he "filed to get away," and it signifies for him the difference between "*yes* and *no.*" But he understands that "it's got a heap of signifying wrapped up in it" and "it signifies a heap more." Most importantly, he can "pass it on" to Invisible Man, which is to say, the link is communicative at the same time that its meaning is contingent (388).[33] Tarp's link (and all puns are, I believe, operative here), is the perfect tool for a pragmatist's promotion of the "cross-cultural unity" that Judith Green (following in a long line of pragmatists) has theorized and advocated. The link represents "a fluid and functional unity rather than a fixed and irrevocable one, and its vital norms are equivalence and reciprocity rather than identity or complete agreement."[34] These last words belong to Ellison's predecessor Alain Locke. Both men spent, over the course of their careers, a great amount of intellectual energy to render flexible a "history" that is always ossifying into "fact."

Tarp, I would say, is an old bluesman who couples his "awareness of limitation," his "rock-bottom sense of reality" with "a sense of possibility . . . the possibility of rising above it" (SA 242). Like the jazzman, Tarp is involved in "a struggle which pitted mind against the perversity of circumstance." But unlike the jazzman, the circumstance against which Tarp struggles is largely composed of personal and cultural memory. The jazzman as described by Ellison spatializes time; history, while still deeply relevant and material, reveals itself as rhetoric, as a network of signification. In his confrontations with historical circumstance, the jazzman begins with the premise that, as James said, "the feeling of past time is a present feeling" and insists with Charlie Parker that "the time is now."[35] What I mean to suggest is that the jazzman considers his "context as a space–time continuum," as Albert Murray has put it, and that in such a context, past, present, and future take on "a bottomless or formless quality" that "gives immediacy to all statements and significance to all human endeavor."[36] In spatializing time, the jazzman de-authorizes history while still recognizing the necessity of confronting it, of schooling oneself in its logic and dealing with its influence. Again, recall Ellison's assertion that "it takes a lot of time and consciousness to break the historical precedent and democratize it" (CE 357). Symbol systems are not simply swept away. Their existence means that, in one way or another, for better or worse, they are functioning within the culture. Social change depends on troping, signifying on the symbolic economy and on the invention of new functional vocabularies.

The jazzman's view of history, as exemplified in the signifying riffs of Rinehart and Clifton, initially confuses Invisible Man. He takes Rinehart's improvisation on identity to be a cynical and opportunistic acceptance of chaos, and he takes Clifton's improvisation *on* history to be a "plunge outside *of* history" (447, emphasis added). Invisible Man learns that Clifton's assertion that "sometimes a man has to plunge outside of history" (377) is in effect an assertion that, to paraphrase Ellison, that which cannot gain authority from history may borrow it with a mask (54). Though he first believes Clifton's activities to be a bizarre commercial sellout, he comes to understand that, like the Sambo doll he had been hawking, Clifton had been executing "a dance that was completely detached from the black, mask-like face" (431). Or, put a different way, Clifton is performing a dance that *is made possible by* the mask. The pretense that he has sold out allows him to "hide right out in the open," to signify on his role in the Brotherhood as "an instrument of the committee's authority" (363), on "the twentieth century miracle" that would have one believe that capitalism will "kill your depression and your dispossession," and that the people of Harlem can live "upon the sunshine of [its] lordly smile" (432). Nor should we take Clifton's improvisation to be a self-isolating gesture. I would argue that that moment where Invisible Man says, "our eyes met and he gave me a contemptuous smile" (433) is deliberately provocative, an attempt to "make him speak the unknown tongue, the language of the future" (476), as Invisible Man will later put it. Of course such activity is dangerous and, after Clifton is shot down, Invisible Man despairs that "the cop would be Clifton's historian" (439). But Invisible Man's subsequent actions suggest that Clifton's symbolic action is not so easily contained. Indeed, his own discourses on invisibility seem in part a consequence of his discovery that "Clifton had been making [the doll] dance all the time and the black thread had been invisible" (446). And perhaps his most obvious jazz improvisation is built off of the idea of Clifton's name as mask.

Aroused by the antiphonal exchange between an old man's voice and a horn ("something for which the Brotherhood had given me no name"), Invisible Man delivers a jazz-shaped eulogy around the riff "his name was Clifton." "Jelly Roll" Morton has defined the riff as "a figure, musically speaking . . . what you would call a foundation," "something you could walk on." Gates writes that "the riff is a central component of jazz improvisation and Signifyin[g] and serves as an especially appropriate synonym for troping and for revision."[37] Invisible Man solos from the foundation "his name was Clifton," beginning with the presumption that somehow this riff is an adequate expression of Clifton's identity and gradually improvising an expression of what Clifton's life and death might mean to his community. The movement from the assertion that "all I can tell you is his name" (455) to a consideration of the motives behind his death (because "he was black," because "he thought he was a man," because of a "simple mistake of judgment," because "he forgot his history") is made possible by Invisible Man's (or Ellison's) relation of naming (of language) to jazz improvisation.[38]

What Ellison sets down as Invisible Man's education by Clifton is modeled on Ellison's education by Emerson and Armstrong—Emerson, through whose work Ellison made sense of the idea that "our names, being the gift of others, must be made our own" (SA 147), and Armstrong, who taught him that a name might function as a mask and who shared with him an experiential understanding of the dangers of combating social action with symbolic action ("I don't know if all cops are poets, but I know all cops carry guns with triggers" [459]). Invisible Man comes to believe that Clifton's death is in some sense the consequence of his symbolic activity that is meant "to carry the whole structure with him" (434).

Clifton has not "plunged outside of history," he has plunged out of one history and into another—the cop may even be an unwitting participant in the larger drama unfolding, but he is nonetheless the vehicle through which "the keepers" of the officially sanctioned history "keep their power." Like the doctor-vet, Clifton is a clown who provokes a half-conscious recognition among adherents to the dominant ideology that "a Negro like that should be under lock and key" (140). That Ellison signifies on Emerson and Armstrong through Clifton is worth keeping in mind when one turns to a consideration of what he has in mind with Rinehart, since Invisible Man's manipulation of Rinehart's name, hat, and sunglasses as masks seems largely a consequence of what he has learned from Clifton's signifying.

One way to think about Invisible Man's entrance into Rinehart's world is as Ellison's consideration of "bebop's politics of style," to use Eric Lott's phrase. Like Ellison's hiding of Emerson's name, like invisibility as described by the doctor-vet, "there is a magic in" Invisible Man's donning of Rinehart's hat: "It hides me right in front of their eyes" (485). And through Rinehart's sunglasses he sees "the merging fluidity of forms" (491). These masks allow him a "new freedom of movement," and in the context of that freedom he ponders the significance of Rinehart:

> Could he be all of them: Rine the Runner and Rine the Gambler
> and Rine the briber and Rine the lover and Rinehart the Reverend?
> Could he himself be both rind and heart. . . . He was a broad man,
> a man of parts who got around. Rinehart the rounder. It was true
> as I was true. His world was possibility and he knew it. He was
> years ahead of me and I was a fool. I must have been crazy and blind.
> The world in which he lived was without boundaries. A vast seeth-
> ing, hot world of fluidity, and Rine the rascal was at home. Perhaps
> only Rine the rascal was at home in it. . . . Sitting there trembling
> I caught a brief glimpse of the possibilities posed by Rinehart's mul-
> tiple personalities and turned away. It was too vast and confusing to
> contemplate. Then I looked at the polished lenses of the glasses and
> laughed. I had been trying to simply turn them into a disguise but

they had become a political instrument instead; for if Rinehart
could use them in his work, no doubt I could use them in mine.
(498–499)

As a "rounder," Rinehart, too, gestures, despite all historical logic, toward
Emerson's "Circles," and the world he proposes is a signifying gesture on
the world Emerson proposes.[39] Rinehart's world is a "vast, seething hot
world of fluidity . . . without boundaries"; Emerson's, as described in
"Circles," is "fluid and volatile" with "no inclosing wall" (CW 2:302,
304). Both are symbolic activists who aim to "unsettle all things" (2:318).
Why? To answer this question we need to make sense of Invisible Man's
stipulation that a Rinehartian model of identity and social space might be
used as a "political instrument."

Recall that the Brotherhood uses Clifton and Invisible Man as "instrument[s] of the committee's authority" (363) and that Ellison describes
the American vernacular as "a flexible instrument" (GT 317). Ellison's
whole conception of symbolic action revolves around these two characterizations of the "instrument." (To remind us that we are talking about
symbolic action, there is also the echo of Ellison's assertion that Burke
gave him "the first instrument with which I could orient myself.") They
represent a tale of opponents: the "authorized" instrument of the one
voice versus the flexible, democratic instrument. And they represent the
diverse nature of symbolic action itself, where "language as symbolic action" is in dialogue with other "cultural forms." What I would suggest is
that Invisible Man comes to terms with his ambivalence about Rinehart
—learns to "accept it . . . rine and heart" (508)—through his recognition of Rinehart as symbolic activist. Ultimately, he decides that the
question of whether Rinehart is "really" a confidence man, whether he is
"devoid of a human center" (SA 230) relies on an ontological fallacy not
worth pursuing. He moves on to a different question, a pragmatic question; namely, what does Rinehart do and how do his actions operate symbolically in the community? What he discovers is that Rinehart is taken
to be "a principle of hope" (510). Ellison explains that while Rinehart is
"the personification of chaos [he] is also intended to represent America
and change" (SA 181). Remember that in writing Invisible Man, Ellison

aimed "to dream of a prose which was flexible, and swift as American change is swift" and that he saw such change as the predicate of "individual self-realization" (105). In addition, recall how Ellison describes the operations of the American vernacular as symbolic action: one of its central functions is to create "confusion out of no longer tenable forms of order."[40] When Invisible Man says that Rinehart's "world of fluidity," his "multiple personalities" are "too confusing to contemplate," he is in effect describing the importance of Rinehart's role as symbolic activist.

As a liminal operator in a liminal space, Rinehart makes room for "new models of social organization [to] emerge, at first to transect and, later, to replace traditional ones."[41] Both Ellison and Emerson have a soft spot for "criminals" like Rinehart because both perceived there to be "always an element of crime in freedom," as the doctor-vet put it to Invisible Man (155). Emerson and Ellison perceive the productive role of the criminal to be his interrogation of the culture's absolutist logic. By his symbolic actions the criminal notes with Emerson that "All stealing is comparative. If you come to absolutes, pray who does not steal?" (CW 3:79). The value of his actions lies in the fact that they entice the culture into asking pragmatic questions, Why is one form of stealing criminalized and not another? Who polices such designations? Of course no community understands the importance of such questions better than the African American community, whose very existence *as African Americans* began with a decriminalized and murderous form of stealing by a culture who refused to ask—who systematically *repressed*—all such pragmatic questions.

As both criminal and minister (the two poles represented by the title "Rine the rounder"), Rinehart is developing the vocabulary of an emergent democracy. If, in doing so, he is participating in the continuum of Emersonian pragmatism, he *resembles* no one so much as Charlie Parker, who, Ellison says, was "in many ways criminal." Like Rinehart, Parker "operated in the underworld of American culture, on that turbulent level where human instincts conflict with social institutions" (SA 227). And like Rinehart, who "has lived so long with chaos that he knows how to manipulate it," Parker and his fellow bop musicians are in some sense "dedicated to chaos" (202). Or, put in Ellison's pragmatic terms, they are dedicated to making chaos out of no longer tenable forms of order, a dedication born of a need "to bring social reality and our social pretensions into a more meaningful balance" (228). For these reasons—because they throw into stark relief the revisability of social and symbolic systems alike, because they offer up a transitional language that gestures toward new logical spaces—Harlem accepts "Rever'n Rinehart" as "a principle of hope for which they gladly paid" (510), just as Parker's "friends paid willingly for the delight and frustration which Parker brought into their lives" (224). We need to understand that Ellison places no a priori limits on the form that democratic symbolic action will take and that, despite his hesitancies regarding Parker in particular and bop generally, he himself is a bop stylist.

Remember that in suggesting that "Parker was poor robin come to New York here to be sacrificed . . . for the creation of a new jazz style" (SA 231–32), Ellison connects him to Invisible Man, who comes to New York and sings in self-recognition, "they picked poor robin clean" (IM 193). Ellison's relationship with bop is commonly misunderstood.[42] Ellison saw bop as representative of "the folk personality . . . caught in a process of chaotic change," and while he harbored anxiety over the fact that the "technical virtuosity of bebop" was indicative of "a further triumph of technology over humanism" (SA 300), he nonetheless understood its vital significance. Bop affirmed jazz's commitment to a pragmatic method, whereby "the masters of jazz came to either observe or participate and be influenced and listen to their own discoveries transformed" (210), and where the "continuing symposium of jazz" was marked by an insistence that its logic and grammar had "not been rigidly codified" (209). Ellison's anxiety over Parker is largely the consequence of his observation that Parker was in some sense complicit in his own reification by the white middle class as the "world's greatest junky" and the "supreme hipster" (227) and that this phenomenon rendered Parker's "studied ignoring of the audience" ironic and hollow. But that observation should not obscure the fact that Ellison was a careful student of bop and that his critique is not unlike many of the critiques that were eventually worked out from within bop itself. The bop musicians Ellison admires most include Sarah Vaughn, Tadd Dameron, Fats Navarro, and Clark

Terry, all of whom made major contributions to bop (CE 313). Ellison's interest in Terry may stem from the fact that he occupies a position between swing and bop as trumpeter for both Duke Ellington and Milt Jackson. Vaughn's premier position as a bop vocalist is obvious. Dameron and Navarro are as important and virtuosic as any figures in bop. Dizzy Gillespie notes that "Fats probably had the best attack of all of us," and Jimmy Heath remembers less kindly that at the seminal bop sessions at Minton's, "Fats ate Miles [Davis] up every night. Miles couldn't outswing him, he couldn't outpower him, he couldn't outsweet him, he couldn't do anything except take that whipping on *every* tune." Crouch notes that "through Clifford Brown, [Navarro] became probably the most influential of all the bebop trumpeters, Dizzy Gillespie and Miles Davis included" and that Dameron "was the most influential arranger of the bebop era." Kenny Clarke "recalls hearing [him] . . . at Minton's in 1940 using eighth notes in what would become the new bebop style."[43] I go to such length here to highlight the importance of recognizing that bebop was an ongoing conversation rather than a military coup, that some of its originators shared Ellison's interest in the role of dance in jazz and in the possibilities of larger ensembles, and that Ellison's criticisms of bop are criticisms *from within the jazz community* and do not necessarily represent wholesale criticisms of "bebop's politics of style" as such. This is more than incidental since it affects how we read his portrayal of Rinehart and his "boys."

The bop-style activities of "Rine the gambler" lead directly to one of the most important moments in the novel, that moment when Invisible Man asks himself, "What if History was a gambler, instead of a force in a laboratory experiment, and the boys his ace in the hole? What if history was not a reasonable citizen, but a madman full of paranoid guile and these boys his agents, his big surprise!" (441). The history proposed by Invisible Man's question is one that reveals itself as "mysterious and uncertain [in] its raw violence and capriciousness" (SA 104). And, again, we should understand this question as literally rhetorical, as an effort at action. As Ellison put it, "Our task then is always to challenge the apparent forms of reality—that is, the fixed manners and values of the few, and to struggle with it until it reveals its mad, vari-implicated chaos, its false faces, and on until it surrenders its insight, its truth" (106). In Ellison's pragmatist model of social change, one makes chaos out of no longer tenable forms of order while providing a new vocabulary of "truth" that has the "capacity for creating order out of chaos." Note, too, that the word "always" marks this process as perpetual. Like James, Ellison insists that truth is always "happening" to ideas, to language. The boys living in Rinehartian historical space are bop stylists par excellence; they are "men of transition" who "speak a jived-up transitional language full of country glamour, speak transitional thoughts" (441).[44] Like Clifton, they are not so much "outside the groove of history" (443) as they are in a different groove; like Parker they are "birds of passage who were too obscure for learned classification" (439). Their role as "saviors" depends on the gamble that in speaking "the unknown tongue," they may be designing the "language of the future" (441, 476). In recognizing these men of transition and likening himself to them ("men like them, like me"), Invisible Man rewrites himself as a jazz musician and democratic symbolic activist. He marvels at the possibility that such activity might still be operative in the culture, that he and these men are "an accident, like Douglass" who "by all historical logic . . . should have disappeared around the first part of the nineteenth century, rationalized out of existence" (442). Ellison of course marvels similarly at the fact that by all historical logic he should have been neither named after Emerson nor attempted "to achieve some of the things which he asked of the American writer" (SA 166). And yet a rejection of historical logic is precisely what makes way for a collective improvisation that might include—impossibly!—Emerson, Parker, Burke, and Armstrong.

The improvisation that Ellison describes, and in which these artists are all soloists, is the improvisation of American democracy. Emerson described it as a "mood, and some vague guess at a new fact [that] is nowise to be trusted as the lasting relation between that intellect and that thing" (CW 3:56). In Harlem, Ellison insists that "the only true history of the times [is] a mood blared by trumpets, trombones, saxophones and drums, a song with turgid, inadequate words" (IM 443). In describing the history of the times as a jazz mood, Invisible Man is proposing a version of Harlem as liminal space where the improvisers are attempting to make good

on the promise of a democratic republic. As Ellison writes of the improvising going on at Minton's Playhouse, "what we know is that which was
then becoming" (203). As critics, Ellison says, we tell "the tall tales told
as history . . . feed on the results of their efforts" (212).

Likewise, we tell tales and feed on Ellison's efforts when we attempt
to articulate the consequences of Ellison's own symbolic action. Yet this
is what we do, and at its most useful, perhaps it amounts to a necessary
"capacity for making order out of chaos." So, here is an attempt to voice
the upshot: Ellison describes democratic symbolic action as a jazz-shaped
collective improvisation in which the soloists pursue individual self-realization via the integrative mind that, in James's words, "includ[es] and
contemplat[es] its 'me' and its 'not-me' as objects which work out their
drama together" (WJ 8:290–91). Democracy, then, is a *process* that shamelessly—and necessarily—transgresses the boundaries of time and text.
This process is Emerson's territory as it is the territory of jazz. And its
survival depends upon the rhetorical game that makes players out of
audiences. Invisible Man plays this game underground, in a liminal state
of hibernation, where it must necessarily be played, where audience
might transform author "into something else, someone else" (336) and
vice versa. Hence his final "jiving" question, "Who knows but that, on the
lower frequencies, I speak for you" (581), which blends the gesture of
"telling it like it is" with halting modifiers and a diametrical gesture toward the inaudible, toward interference or noise. Noise, writes Mackey,
voices "reminders of the axiomatic exclusions upon which postings of
identity and meaning depend" and is thus a gesture in the direction of
open form (DE 19–20).[45] Ellison brings himself and his reader to the
lower frequencies where he might enact an Emersonian de-authorization, might speak for you by not speaking for you. That is his contribution
to the vernacular improvisation of a democratic culture.

I would also suggest that we pay attention to the manner in which
Ellison's symbolic activities shed light on their immediate local context—the New York of Ellison's most productive period, that of the
1950s and 1960s—a time when, as LeRoi Jones described it in 1963,
"scores of young Negroes and, of course, young Negro musicians, began
to address themselves to the formal canons of Western nonconformity,

as formally understood refusals of the hollowness of American life, especially in its address to the Negro."[46] Here we might keep our eye on an artist such as Ellison's fellow southwesterner Ornette Coleman, who was specifically describing his "free jazz" as a "democratic experience."[47] If Jones was king of Greenwich Village in 1963, then, despite scholarly commonplaces to the contrary, Ellison was its hidden prophet.

4

Tribes of New York

Frank O'Hara, Amiri Baraka, and the Poetics of the Five Spot

No poetry has come out of England of major importance for forty years, yet there are would-be Negro poets who reject the gaudy excellence of 20th century American poetry in favor of disemboweled Academic models of second-rate English poetry. . . . It would be better if such a poet . . . listened to the tragic verse of Billie Holliday than be content to imperfectly imitate the bad poetry of the ruined minds of Europe.

LeRoi Jones (Amiri Baraka), *Blues People*

Proof? "Oh it's a mighty poor theory
that can't abide a couple of facts
to the contrary," said William James.
. . . .
                    still I throw
myself away by the handfuls
on you who still repay me

with looks of love so burning
from your wintry pallor
I am confounded, but
speechless I am not

to whom is given to declare
among the Americans
just how a thing is,
and what I say I do.

Paul Goodman, "A Pragmatic Love Song"

Frank O'Hara moved to New York at about the time Ralph Ellison was finishing *Invisible Man*. I note this fact to suggest an analogy. Ellison was a one-time jazz musician who found in the work of pragmatists from Emerson to Kenneth Burke an analogy for the symbolic action of jazz performance, a discovery that helped to produce his great first novel. Similarly, O'Hara was a poet (and trained pianist) who came to find, in the late 1950s, a style of jazz analogous to the work of the pragmatists with whom he was familiar: Emerson and Paul Goodman as well as Gertrude Stein and William Carlos Williams (poets who were steeped in the work of William James and John Dewey, respectively). Both Ellison and O'Hara were interested in art that, in Ellison's words, "inspirited . . . fledgling social forms and political processes with the egalitarian principles of democracy," art that functioned as *democratic symbolic action*.[1] In the late 1950s, O'Hara was introduced to the Five Spot, a downtown club that featured the live music of the new jazz avant-garde, music characterized by "its heavy emphasis on individual freedom within a collectively improvised context," as Mackey has put it (DE 34). He would come to associate this music and the social milieu in which it was performed with other forms of egalitarian desire, including his own poetry and the Civil Rights movement. Over the course of this chapter, I will argue that our recognition of O'Hara's concern with the politics of poetic form and his engagement with the downtown jazz culture of the late 1950s and early 1960s provides the groundwork for a new understanding of O'Hara as, among other things, a consciously political writer. O'Hara learned what Ellison had known for two decades: that jazz was the most effective, the most persuasive, form of democratic symbolic action and that American writers would do well to consider both its formal and social implications.

As in the case of Ellison, to designate O'Hara a pragmatist (let alone a leading figure in an "alternative" pragmatism) is to flout conventional wisdom. While O'Hara's affinity for a particularly Emersonian line in American poetry (for instance, his claim that "only Whitman and Crane and Williams . . . are better than the movies"[2]) is not disputed, critics are at least as likely to contextualize his work in relation to the European avant-garde (French surrealism, dada, Russian futurism) or to the abstract expressionism of Jackson Pollock and Willem de Kooning. Only recently has the idea of pragmatism's relevance to O'Hara's poetry been broached by critics, most notably in a brief review by Richard Poirier that argues that O'Hara's central poetic concerns are "found everywhere in the work of the great American predecessors whom he read and admired, Emerson and Whitman, and their successors Crane, Stevens and (of particular interest to O'Hara) Gertrude Stein."[3] While Poirier glances in the direction of this nexus he calls "poetry and pragmatism," I intend to make the case that O'Hara draws much of his aesthetic disposition from pragmatism, sometimes directly, sometimes through the work of other poets.

But, to quote Emerson, "I know better than to claim any completeness for my picture." O'Hara's corpus simply defies broad generalization—one never talks about *O'Hara* as a single, stable entity, or at least one never should. The poet who wrote "In Memory of My Feelings," who spoke of the "scenes of my selves," and who insisted that "a 'poetics' based on one of my poems . . . any other poem of mine would completely contradict" (CP 510), is a difficult poet to describe with any sense of completeness or closure. Instead, one talks, as Emerson and James do, of moods, of tendencies. My hope is that my version of O'Hara will supplement, rather than supplant, other versions. I will focus on what O'Hara called "personism," a basic approach to the poem that increasingly shaped his work beginning about 1957. The roots of personism, I'll argue, can be found in American pragmatism and in the African American cultural expression to which O'Hara was exposed after his 1957 move to Greenwich Village. "The tendency toward a pragmatic view of the poem as a kind of democratic symbolic action" is to my mind the best way to read "Personism" and the poems associated with it. O'Hara's pragmatism found its inspiring counterpart in the avant-garde jazz of late 1950s Greenwich Village.

O'Hara's intense devotion to the poetry of William Carlos Williams and Gertrude Stein places him just a step away from the classical pragmatists on whose work I have been drawing: James, Dewey, and Burke.[4] Stein (as a student of James's) and Williams (as a friend of Burke's and also influenced by James and Dewey) were an important source of pragmatist theory for the generation of American poets who succeeded them, a group that included O'Hara, John Ashbery, Allen Ginsburg, Charles Olson, Robert Creeley, Denise Levertov, Robert Duncan, Amiri Baraka, and others. As Ginsberg has said of this loosely associated group of "New American Poets," "the common ground seemed to be admiration building on William Carlos Williams's American vernacular idiomatic diction and rhythm and the spontaneous writing of Gertrude Stein. So this was quite a phalanx of poets who liked each other to some extent."[5] At age twenty, O'Hara described Stein's *The Autobiography of Alice B. Toklas* as "one of the most interesting things I've ever read by anyone." In his homage to modernism, "Memorial Day, 1950," O'Hara claims to have "named several last things / Gertrude Stein hadn't had time for" (CP 17). O'Hara seems to have responded powerfully to Stein's sense of how American English called into question the motives of conventional grammar. In a letter to Vincent Warren, he glossed Stein's *The Making of Americans* with an idiomatic assertion of Mae West's: "I ain't afraid of pushin' grammar around so long as it sounds good" (CPT 99). West's "style," O'Hara joked, was "a lot like Stein." The two women "were not too unlike each other, especially in their attitude towards parents and forbears in general."[6] Of course, when one gets down to particulars, Stein and West are infinitely more different than they are alike. But O'Hara employs the unlikely analogy, I think, in order to connect Stein's symbolic activities to the American vernacular as symbolic action—much as Ginsberg does when he groups Stein's "spontaneous writing" and Williams's "American vernacular idiomatic diction and rhythm." In elevating West's gab to the level of Stein's experiments, O'Hara relies on a pragmatic assumption about language that Paul Goodman states in this way: "speakers and hearers are active and shaping. They intervene in the world . . . and what they primarily act on and shape is the inherited code that they have learned in their speech community—in order to say what needs to be said."[7] O'Hara implies that when West and Stein "push grammar around," they do so with the conviction that their spontaneous, nongrammatical sentences—and not the inherited code that is "English"—*are the American language.* Though this "interpretation" of Stein's work by no means closes the book on O'Hara's view of her, neither is it incidental that she be situated in this instance in the familiar territory in which I have placed Ellison (himself an admirer of Stein's work): as another in that line of American pragmatists whose vernacular inventions "inspirited . . . fledgling social forms and political processes with the egalitarian principles of democracy."[8]

If we take these various references to Stein as indications of O'Hara's debt to her view of speech and language, then we should also recognize Stein's debt to William James along the same lines. As a student of James's while at Radcliffe, Stein participated in his automatic writing experiments. In *The Autobiography of Alice B. Toklas,* she describes James as "the important person in [her] life" during those formative years and remembers in particular his admonition to students: Keep your mind open. When a student would protest, "but Professor James, this that I say is true," James would reply, "Yes, it is abjectly true." Stein, then, was getting an education in what James called his "genetic theory of what is meant by truth" (WJ 1:37). Truth insisted upon is truth grown slavish and, in all likelihood, not truth at all. "Truth," James said, "*happens* to an idea. It *becomes* true, is *made* true by events" (WJ 1:97).[9] Likewise with the "meaning" of language: "The 'meaning' of a word taken thus dynamically in a sentence may be quite different from its meaning when taken statically or without context" (WJ 8:255). One need only have the most basic familiarity with Stein's concerns to understand how important such a statement must have been to her when she read it;[10] and the sentiment —that meaning in language is dynamic and contextual—would become equally important to O'Hara. When O'Hara writes that "the only truth is face to face, the poem whose words *become*" (CP 305, emphasis added), he is expressing perhaps his most basic assumptions—pragmatic assumptions—about the nature of truth and language: words become true in the course and context of their face-to-face confrontations. The poem is "a form of communication actively mediating—and mediated by—social forces."[11]

William Carlos Williams was also of central importance to O'Hara. He, too, is referenced in "Memorial Day, 1950," and he is given a particularly pragmatic shading: "Poetry is as useful as a machine!" O'Hara writes in that poem (18), an allusion to Williams's assertion that "A poem is a small (or large) machine made of words." Williams's statement (which O'Hara, like so many other avant-garde poets of his generation, internalized) has remained a deeply resonant metaphor for the pragmatic belief that, in Rorty's words, "language is a set of tools rather than a set of representations." Indeed, both Williams's and Rorty's statements take their cue from Dewey's statement in *Art as Experience* that "the intelligent mechanic caring for his materials and tools . . . is artistically engaged." As I argue in chapter 1, Dewey's view of language as a set of tools whose significance was determined in the course of their "operations in experience" (in the course of their *use*) made a deep impression on Williams —and O'Hara, in turn, was the beneficiary of Dewey's premise.[12] Nor was this the only instance in which Williams acted as a conduit for pragmatism. The close attention that O'Hara paid to Williams's *Paterson* had a significant affect on what Gooch has quite rightly called O'Hara's "pragmatic American feeling for the solidity of objects" (CPT 146).[13] In *Paterson,* the focal point of this "pragmatic American feeling" is the mantra, "Say it, no ideas but in things." Commonly considered Williams's most memorable aesthetic pronouncement, it has its origin in a statement of James's from *The Principles of Psychology:* "*it is* THINGS, *not ideas, which are associated in the mind. We ought to talk of the association of objects, not of the association of ideas.*" For James, the *idea*—"the conception with which we handle a bit of sensible experience"—has no significance apart from its use as a tool in the environment on which it acts (WJ 8:522, 455–56). The idea is a thing, an object that is associated with and agent among other objects. Williams adapts James's notion for use in his poetic method. Thinking of both James and Williams, Paul Goodman provides a useful description of the assumptions behind Williams's phrase "no ideas but in things": "When speaking intervenes in the world and shapes experience," Goodman says, "it often is, or is taken as, a direct action in the environment, an energy or even a physical thing." Likewise, "poetic speech [is] a physical thing, a direct action on the audience."[14] Williams's decisively anti-metaphysical, pragmatic approach to language and poetry had a deep and lasting impact on O'Hara's own poetic predilections. When we talk about O'Hara's poetry as being "full of objects," when we talk of it as part of his everyday experience, as something he considered a useful form of communication with real agency, we are necessarily talking about O'Hara as an American pragmatist—and we are doing so neither casually nor idly.

Goodman stands alongside Stein and Williams as one of the most pervasive influences on O'Hara's poetic method—indeed Goodman's role in O'Hara's development as a pragmatist may be paramount. Before detailing the nature of that influence, we should simply note the following statement by Goodman: "I grew up breathing the air of Jamesian pragmatism, which has seemed to me to be politically right and, if I may say so, in the American grain." Goodman's aesthetic philosophy is centered around an insistence that speech "is itself a practical event," a position closely allied to Burke's descriptions of "language as symbolic action": "we must ask," Goodman writes, "what the speakers and hearers of language are *doing,* because this will influence the forms."[15] O'Hara was more than amenable to Goodman's position that the poem was an act, an event, that should be considered according to one's sense of what it was meant to *do* for the poet and his or her readers. At a pivotal moment in his development as a poet—coincident with his move to New York— one finds O'Hara hyperbolically praising Goodman as "master of the English language," comparing him to Shakespeare and telling Jane Freilicher that Goodman "is really the only one we have to look to now." He saved his greatest praise for Goodman's essay "Advance-Guard Writing, 1900–1950," which appeared in the *Kenyon Review* in the summer of 1951. "If you haven't devoured its delicious message," O'Hara told Freilicher, "rush to your nearest newsstand."[16]

Goodman's essay is worth looking at in some detail. At heart it is an attempt to explain American advance-guard writing via the lexicon of pragmatism. The twin emphases of such writing, Goodman argues, are "a rhetorical attitude toward the audience" and "an experimental handling of the medium" (AW 359). In saying so, Goodman is on the familiar ground of Dewey and Burke; he is building on their descriptions of the poet who "operates experimentally" (LW 10:149) and of "the poem [that] is designed to 'do something' for the poet and his readers."[17] Here is what O'Hara was garnering from Goodman and the other sources of pragmatism available to him: that the advance-guard or experimental artist was

to set forth a version of himself as evolving within the context of a democratic collective. "His audience and his relation to his audience," Goodman told him, "are his essential plastic medium. . . . Throughout there
is the attractive and repulsive tampering of the artist and the audience
with each other" (378). Again, such "tampering" was most likely to occur
between an artist and an audience whose respective identities were liminal and whose socially symbolic actions functioned like *original composition*. "*All* original composition," Goodman writes in his essay, "occurs at
the limits of one's knowledge, feeling and technique; being a spontaneous act, it risks, supported by what one has already grown up to, something unknown" (357). Goodman's descriptions of self and community
as they relate to the individual artist recall both Emerson's descriptions
of "conversation and action" that "come from a spontaneity which forgets
usages" (CW 3:68) as well as Ellison's descriptions of the jazzman who
improvises an identity by acting both "within and against the group." And
indeed Goodman *should* recall these two writers; he and Ellison are
drawing from a set of terms and concepts either directly attributable to
or given stimulus by Emerson.[18] O'Hara embraces these terms and concepts as he finds them in Goodman, just as he had embraced Emerson's
essays five years before, using them to bolster his conviction regarding
the unpredictability of the self: "Emerson says something to the effect
that 'I have no patience with consistency. Only a stupid man is consistent!'" This is of course a paraphrase of lines from "Self-Reliance," where
O'Hara would also have read, no doubt approvingly, "whoso would be a
man must be a non-conformist" (CW 2:50, 57).[19] The trajectory from
Emerson to Goodman provided O'Hara with a succinct lesson in pragmatism's take on the politics of form.

At this point it might be worthwhile to summarize just what O'Hara
took away from his reading in and around the lineup of pragmatists I have
assembled. I would list O'Hara's basic premises as follows: first, that Williams's "American vernacular idiomatic diction and rhythm" and Stein's
"spontaneous writing" were paramount examples of the American artist
operating experimentally; second, that their writing was "active and
shaping" in relation to the inherited code and was in fact designed to "do
something" for these poets and their readers; and lastly, that O'Hara's

own work would be novel insofar as the *context* of that work was novel, and that new contexts were dependent upon a maximum amount of "attractive and repulsive tampering of the artist and the audience with each other."[20] In regard to this last insight, O'Hara took from Goodman a very specific, very practical piece of advice. "In literary terms," Goodman explained, "this means: to write for [the audience] about them personally . . . personal writing about the audience . . . where everybody knows everybody and understands what is at stake" (AW 375). I would argue that *here,* in Goodman's advice, is an important catalyst for O'Hara's pivotal essay "Personism: A Manifesto" (CP 498–99).[21] In saying so, I intend to make a claim for something much larger than Goodman's influence on O'Hara. Written in 1959, "Personism: A Manifesto" is an unrecognized "classic" of American pragmatism whose significance is by no means limited to O'Hara's own artistic production; the "manifesto" is a site of confluence for O'Hara's pragmatic orientation and his interest in African American culture, owing equal debts to Goodman and Baraka (known as LeRoi Jones during the time of his friendship with O'Hara, though I'll refer to him as Baraka over the course of this chapter). In addition, it was an important touchstone for contemporaries of O'Hara's such as Ginsberg, Creeley, Duncan, and Baraka, and its pervasive influence is manifest and ongoing in American experimental writing.

One conversation in particular surrounding "Personism" suggests its importance both to the contemporary poetry of the time and as a gauge of pragmatism's influence on that poetry. This conversation, between Robert Duncan and Robert Creeley, involved contextualizing O'Hara's work vis-à-vis the more general attempt "to transform American literature into a viable *language.*" This attempt, it should be said, was a kind of pedagogical imperative behind the curriculum at Black Mountain College, where Duncan and Creeley taught along with Charles Olson and, briefly, Paul Goodman. The course catalog of 1954 includes the statement that "the 4-year discipline is organized on the premise that the American language and culture are departures from the Western norm, and that both the use of language and the position of man as individual and in society is undergoing change." A "premise" like this should give us pause; it is uncannily similar to the motivating premise behind Ellison's

Invisible Man as well as the bulk of his essays.[22] Like Ellison, Duncan was theorizing "pragmatic literary agency," the attempt "to transform American literature into a viable *language*—that's what we were trying to do." And, it should be said, Duncan saw this attempt as the explicit mandate of Emerson and Dewey. As both critic and practitioner of "the New American Poetry," Duncan provides a more explicit map of its sources in pragmatism than any of his contemporaries. It is Duncan who notes, "I point to Emerson, or to Dewey to show that in American philosophy there are foreshadowings or forelightings of [Olson's] *Maximus.*"[23] It is Duncan who argues that Emerson speaks "directly for the poetic practice of open form, for the importance of whatever happens in the course of writing as revelation," calling both himself and Creeley "Emersonian." It is Duncan who, perhaps most significantly, groups Emerson, Whitman, and William James as "men who have prepared our way" by insisting that "*democracy must strike out for itself new forms.*" In short, Duncan reads pragmatism as a kind of democratic symbolic action and reads the New American Poetry as a kind of pragmatism. Into this nexus of signification Duncan inserts O'Hara. Creeley recalls their conversation in this way:

> Speaking of Frank O'Hara, [Duncan] noted that extraordinary poet's attempt "to keep the *demand* on the language as *operative,* so that something was at issue all the time, and, at the same time, to make it almost like chatter on the telephone that nobody was going to pay attention to before . . . that the language gain what was assumed before to be its *trivial* uses. . . . So I think one can build a picture, that in all the arts, especially in America, they are *operative.* We think of art as *doing something,* taking hold of it as a *process.*" At Black Mountain these preoccupations were insistent.[24]

In the course of his conversation with Creeley, Duncan is not merely sharing his opinion of O'Hara's poetry. Rather, he is explicitly describing O'Hara's poetry in terms of Dewey's *Art as Experience.* On the opening page of that book (deeply important to Duncan), Dewey sets down the following problem and proposed solution: "When artistic objects are separated from both conditions of origins and *operations in experience,* a wall is built around them that renders almost opaque their general significance" (LW 10:9). Dewey's "task," then, "is to restore continuity between the refined and intensified forms of experience that are works of art and the *everyday events, doings.*" If on the one hand the poem *separated* from "operations in experience" is rendered opaque, then, conversely, the poem *grounded* in such operations (as "event," as "doing") is endlessly significant; it is set in unanticipated motion as a process that is "doing something" for the poet and his readers. This latter possibility is what Duncan means when he discusses O'Hara's "demand" that the language be "operative."[25] "Instead of signifying being shut up with one's own private feelings and sensations," Dewey writes, "it signifies active and alert commerce with the world" (LW 10:25).[26]

In connecting O'Hara to Dewey and the pragmatist tradition, Duncan was also suggesting the specific motives behind O'Hara's poetic acts. As he said to Creeley, Duncan believed that the function of O'Hara's poems was to make poetic speech "almost like chatter on the telephone that nobody was going to pay attention to before [so] that the language gain what was assumed before to be its *trivial* uses." Why? O'Hara's motives seem to be twofold. First, rendering the poem "like chatter on the telephone" blurs the distinctions between high and low speech by designating *all* speech as fundamentally *colloquial*—whether O'Hara is talking about Rachmaninoff or about dropping his sunglasses in the toilet, one is always aware of the fact that he is *talking;* this has the affect of exploding poetic regimentation (as Goodman notes, "there are too many immediate occasions, face-to-face meetings, eye-witnessings, common sense problems, for common speech to be regimented"[27]). Second, the very nature of the telephone, as instrument, suggests that the poem is *dialogic.* What O'Hara had done was invent a rhetoric that navigated the pragmatist's paradox of individual and collective and bore witness to the fact that "individuality itself is originally a potentiality and is realized only in interaction with surrounding conditions" (LW 10:286). Duncan understood O'Hara's "chatter" as an example of "democracy striking out for itself new forms," the manifestation of his recognition that "one is obliged, as William James was always saying, to get down from noble aloofness into the muddy stream of concrete things." Like philosophy, poetic speech had "become unconsciously an apologetic for the established order, because it had tried to show the rationality of this or that existent hierarchical grading of values and schemes of life" (MW 11:52). O'Hara's "chatter on the telephone" acted as a corrective. And his reference to the telephone leads us to the touchstone for O'Hara's invention, "Personism: A Manifesto." In "Personism" the telephone serves as that thing that makes manifest Goodman's concept of "personal writing," writing for the audience about them personally. As O'Hara tells it: "One of [Personism's] minimal aspects is to address itself to one person. . . . It was founded by me after lunch with LeRoi Jones on August 27, 1959, a day in which I was in love with someone (not Roi, by the way, a blonde). I went back to work and wrote a poem for this person. While I was writing it I was realizing that if I wanted to I could use the telephone instead of writing the poem, and so Personism was born. . . . It puts the poem squarely between the poet and the person. . . . The poem is at last between two persons instead of two pages" (CP 499).

Personism, then, is not a theory ("there's nothing metaphysical about it," says O'Hara) but a *method* by which the poem might encourage a particular kind of linguistic and social relation—like pragmatism as James described it, "it stands in the midst of our theories like a corridor in a hotel" (WJ 1:32). What personism is designed to do is to prompt the sort of poem that lives as a set of uncertain terms "between two persons." The poem is *between* two persons; the word suggests, on the one hand, that the poem is in an intermediate state, a state of between-ness, its position, the meanings of its various signifiers, unfixed, undecided. On the other hand, the word gestures toward confidentiality: "between you and me," "between you, me, and the lamppost." A good pragmatist, O'Hara wants both: the contingency of the poem and its communicative agency, so that at any moment what *stands* between you and me might *be* between you and me.

O'Hara's sense of audience functions similarly; though the poem which engenders personism ("Personal Poem") is ostensibly addressed to one person (Vincent Warren, "a blonde"), O'Hara understands that its potential address is much wider. The poem itself recounts the conversation between O'Hara and Baraka, so it is in some sense already "between" them

as much as it is "between" O'Hara and Warren. Perhaps most importantly, it is "between" O'Hara and his various, unpredictable readership, a possibility about which O'Hara is purposefully coy; he knows
well that the flirtatiousness of a line such as "I wonder if one person out
of 8,000,000 is / thinking of me" simply won't stay put as a private matter between him and Warren—hence his own intentionally vague answer: "possibly so" (CP 336). One finds the same rhetorical strategy at
work in "Personism," where O'Hara describes it as "a movement I recently founded and which nobody knows about [which] interests me a
great deal." Of course, "nobody knows about" the personism movement
because it's not a movement in any traditional sense; O'Hara gives the
impression that its "rules" are in the process of being constructed as one
reads, and in a way that is the case. Simply put, personism is what happens when one reads personism; it is the "attractive and repulsive tampering of the artist and the audience with each other" engendered by
O'Hara's style.

O'Hara will give you only "a vague idea," only a "part of Personism,"
because this is all he admits to have. When he says personism "interests
me a great deal," he is saying it as if he has learned of its existence rather
than invented it. At the same time, the sense we have as readers that we
not only can but *should* tamper with personism is bolstered by O'Hara's
insistence that its meaning will not be decided by any previous configu-
rations: "You just go on your nerve," he writes. "If someone's chasing you
down the street with a knife you just run, you don't turn around and
shout, 'Give it up! I was a track star at Mineola Prep.'" In O'Hara's comic
metaphor, identity is determined by what one *does* rather than what one
was, and the two are not necessarily related. Here he is truly the inheritor
of that Emerson who wrote, "I simply experiment, an endless seeker,
with no Past at my back" (CW 2:318). And he shares, too, the corollary
to Emerson's statement: that the experimenter, having abandoned consistency and precedent, adopts *usefulness* as the test of value. O'Hara's
joke is to the point: the track star's technique may be entirely inadequate
to running while chased in the streets (track stars, after all, never train
to, say, dodge down an alley and up a fire escape), or, he may simply have
lost all of that technique, being a different person now than he was when

he "was a track star." In any event—and this is the point—he had better figure out *something,* something that works. O'Hara's emphasis on usefulness is at the heart of personism—it explains such statements as "If they don't need poetry bully for them." The poem exists at any given moment as a set of tools for the poet and his or her readers, tools whose usefulness is a matter of collective decision. Our reading is a conversation. The poem is a telephone call.

The poems O'Hara most closely associated with personism were the ones he called his " 'I do this I do that' poems" (CP 341). This designation may be characteristically leisured and funny, but we should not leave it at that; it is also an important clue to O'Hara's pragmatist inheritance. O'Hara's "I do this I do that" poems, in their personal address and emphasis on *doing,* are analogous to what Goodman called "a pragmatic love song," written by the poet "to whom is given to declare / among the Americans / just how a thing is, / and what I say I do."[28] It is the emphasis on doing that sets the writer/reader dynamic in motion. The writer cultivates an experimental or improvisational attitude toward the writing of poems (the poem as a kind of doing without a priori notions of what it will become); the reader is encouraged by the perceived lack of closure toward a participative model of reading.[29] What Spahr has said of Harryette Mullen's work is clearly true of O'Hara's as well: "This work urges that readers abandon that feeling of cleverness, of being well-trained, of successfully penetrating a work to an exhaustiveness, and instead recognize reading as connective."[30] I am struck by that common opening question in telephone conversation, "What are you doing?" The question is aimless (it may have nothing to do with the primary purpose of the call) except insofar as it sets a particular tone; it leaves open the possibility that the person one has called might be doing something worth knowing about, something that will affect how they present themselves (and in that sense affect their identity *as such*), something that, in turn, might shape the conversation in a manner heretofore unexpected. That O'Hara says what it is he does as if he were on the telephone, then, is relevant to his motives for saying it. Like Emerson, his writing strategies are largely an attempt to persuade the reader that "the ear and the tongue are two organs of one nature" (CW 2:84). Or, as O'Hara puts it in "St. Paul and All That," "I read simply because I am a writer" (CP 406).

O'Hara invokes telephone conversation to elucidate his poetic method because he sees that conversation as a kind of democratic symbolic action. Like Ellison, though perhaps not as consciously, O'Hara saw writing "as a function of American democracy"—in his own words, writing was a way to both test and revitalize "Democracy's ultimate and penultimate validity."[31] The telephone facilitated a kind of collective improvisation that represented for O'Hara democracy in aesthetic action. The best example of this is an actual telephone conversation between O'Hara and poet Jim Brodey, caught on film for the "USA: Poetry" series in 1966. As O'Hara and Alfred Leslie are collaborating on dialogue for a film script, the telephone rings. O'Hara picks up the phone and describes the drama unfolding to Brodey, saying, "This is a very peculiar situation because while I'm talking to you, I'm typing and also being filmed for educational TV. Can you imagine that? Yeah. Alfred Leslie is holding my hand while its happening. It's known as performance. What? Yeah, all right! Flash and bolt. What does that mean? Flashing bolt, you mean. Oh, good, flashing bolt. [types] A flashing bolt. Is that art or what is it? I just laid it on to the paper."[32] Here (where "performance" is a "happening," where O'Hara's analogy of writing to telephone conversation has become startlingly literal), O'Hara's "personal writing," characterized by a maximum amount of "attractive and repulsive tampering of the artist and the audience with each other," comes to full flower. The transcript is evidence of O'Hara's eagerness to place himself in precisely the type of environment that Dewey described in *Art as Experience*—that is, an environment that allows for "more comprehensive and exact relationships among the constituents of his being . . . more opportunities for resistance and tension, more drafts upon experience and invention, and therefore more novelty in action, greater range and depth of insight and increased poignancy of feeling" (LW 10:29). What O'Hara calls his "peculiar situation" is the situation a pragmatist finds most suitable to the creation of art as a function of democracy. As the performance develops, we are encouraged to embrace and participate in "the idea," in James's words, "of a world growing not integrally but piecemeal by the contributions of its several parts a social scheme of cooperative work genuinely to be done" (WJ 1:140). Each action in the performance is mediating *and being mediated by* each other action—the performance of the entire scene; the film being made of that performance; the actions of O'Hara and Leslie as "players" conscious of the fact that they're performing; the telephone conversation between O'Hara and Brodey that leads to the semantic pull-and-tug of "flash and bolt" versus "flashing bolt"; the film that Leslie is making and that O'Hara is helping him write; and of course whatever O'Hara gets onto paper. "Can you imagine that? . . . What? . . . What does that mean? . . . Is that art or what is it?"—these questions accrue in rhetorical importance. They challenge the distinction between great utterances and small ones; they challenge the boundaries between the individual and the collaborative (as Ellison's conception of the jazz performance does). In short, they democratize the notion of what art, and poetry in particular, is. The answer to "Is that art or what is it?" is "I just laid it onto the paper." "Poetry," O'Hara believed, "liberates certain forces in language" (CPT 217), and, we can conclude, democratic improvisation begins with the liberation of "art" as a signifier. That gesture—utopian to be sure—is the platform from which such improvisation "is treated," in Dewey's words, "as a possibility capable of realization in the concrete natural world."[33]

Though it may seem at first far-fetched to compare O'Hara's collective improvisation on the telephone (and thus his concept of personism) to Ellison's descriptions of collective jazz improvisation, there are good reasons for doing so. In fact, if we follow O'Hara's various telephone references, we end up, interestingly, in a discussion about jazz. I would like to draw this connection before moving on to a broader discussion of O'Hara's relationship with jazz and African American culture. In connecting the telephone to jazz, I am thinking especially of several references O'Hara makes to painter Larry Rivers. In "Larry Rivers: A Memoir," O'Hara describes Rivers as coming into his world "like a demented telephone. Nobody knew whether they wanted it in the library, the kitchen or the toilet, but it was electric. Nor did he" (SS 170). That nobody knows what to do with Rivers, that he doesn't quite know himself, makes him the ideal telephone collaborator and, in this case, the ideal *telephone* (which I take to mean the ideally unpredictable conduit through which the various players in O'Hara's circle might converse). Rivers, O'Hara understood, was improvising his identity (how else does one become a telephone?), giving testimony to the pragmatist claim that "the divisions and dislocations of the discursive self cannot be constructed as deviations from the truth of selfhood, and thus as falsehood. . . . They become not the proximate cause but the enduring conditions of identity in every sense."[34]

What the telephone image demands is that we understand Rivers's improvisation as occurring in connection with other mediating voices. In "Sonnet for Larry Rivers and His Sister," O'Hara characterizes Rivers's "talking to his sister on / the telephone" as "diametric." This last word is an elaborately complex signifier, where *dia* is a pun on "two" (di) as well as an etymological play on "opposed," "between," "passing through"; *metric* is a play on "distance," "measurement," and, significantly, "poetic measure." As with his characterization of the poem as "between two persons" in "Personism: A Manifesto," O'Hara sees Rivers's telephone as the method by which he might pass from one state of "between-ness" to another, by which he might orchestrate or prompt an antiphonal improvisation on his identity. The poem ends with a further complication: O'Hara, characteristically discontent with only two voices, adds a third, "the operator," who "interrupted, / 'Your bagatelle has been accepted.'" In thinking of this telephone conversation as "bagatelle," one can't help but be reminded of Duncan's claim that O'Hara wrote poems so "that the language gain what was assumed before to be its *trivial* uses." In that light, we might read the conclusion of "Sonnet for Larry Rivers and His Sister" as an invitation to join the interaction between O'Hara, Rivers, and his sister by "accepting" the "bagatelle." Thinking of Rivers, O'Hara was inspired to invent such games.

Of course Rivers was not by trade a telephone conversationalist—he was a painter, and painting was the act in which he most significantly performed his identity. And, as O'Hara well knew, he was also a jazz musician, a sax player whose name had been invented (changed from Yizroch

Loiza Grossberg to Larry Rivers) as a result of a misintroduction at a nightclub, and whose painting was deeply informed by jazz.[35] O'Hara takes both Rivers's painting and jazz into account in describing Rivers's identity in the following passage:

> Its name is not so simply sociological as "identity." It might more clearly and less lazily be called risk. It is comfortable to ask yourself to risk, but it is more serious when the request comes from outside yourself. . . . Here an analogy to jazz can be justified: his hundreds of drawings are each like a separate performance, with its own occasion and subject, and what has been "learned" from the performance is not just the technical facility of the classical pianists' octaves or the studies in a Grand Chaumiere class, but the ability to deal with the increased skills that deepening of subject matter and the risks of anxiety dictated variety demand for clear expression. (SS 95, 173)[36]

We ought to spell out the logic of O'Hara's concept of "risked identity." Rivers's identity "might more clearly and less lazily be called *risk*" *because* the request for risk *comes from outside;* to accept this request is to accept, necessarily, the risks of "variety" and the consequent "deepening of subject matter." What one learns from each "separate performance" of one's identity is "the ability to deal with . . . increased skills," but in learning to deal with increased skills, one has necessarily "risked" one's identity to such an extent that it has changed. In this stream of causalities, O'Hara suggests, there is an analogy to jazz. Whether any other form of art is "truly" analogous to jazz is of course a matter of endless debate, but one thing seems, to me, quite certain: that O'Hara's description of how Rivers risks and performs his identity is analogous to jazz *as Ralph Ellison understood it.* As evidence I would return to Ellison's most famous description of jazz performance:

> Jazz is an art of individual assertion *within and against the group.* Each true jazz moment (as distinct from the uninspired commercial per-

formance) springs from a contest in which each artist challenges all the rest; each solo flight, or improvisation, represents (*like the successive canvases of a painter*) a *definition of his identity:* as individual, as member of the collectivity and as a link in the chain of tradition. Thus, because jazz finds its very life in an endless improvisation upon traditional materials, *the jazz-man must lose his identity even as he finds it.* (SA 234, emphasis added)

Not to put too fine a point on it, Ellison's jazzman, being a "member of a collectivity," improvises an identity in response to input *from outside;* this "contest of improvisational skill," as Ellison calls it elsewhere, implies a constantly risked, constantly changing "definition of his identity" (finding one identity, losing it, finding another), a process which is "like the successive canvases of a painter." O'Hara's and Ellison's analogies are mirror images of each other, and they are of course implicitly including themselves in their analogies. Ellison's description appeared in the *Saturday Review* on May 17, 1958, and again in 1964 as part of *Shadow and Act.* O'Hara's descriptions of Rivers are from 1959 and 1965. The comparison is so similar it seems likely that Ellison's piece influenced O'Hara's (indeed O'Hara's close friend poet Bill Berkson has remarked to me that "it's not unlikely that Frank knew the Ellison text").[37] In any event, we should summarize the implications: that O'Hara's personism, a pragmatic method that increasingly informs his poems in the late fifties and early sixties, is "born" out of his realization of the broader significance of telephone conversation; that when we follow O'Hara's signifying acts involving telephones, we become aware that he is using personism as a kind of democratic symbolic action in which, as with Rivers's painting, "an analogy to jazz can be justified." If this is the case, then, returning to personism, Baraka's role in the development of O'Hara's method begins to seem more significant, as do the concluding lines of O'Hara's manifesto: "What can we expect of Personism? (This is getting good, isn't it?) Everything, but we won't get it. It is too new, too vital a movement to promise anything. But it, like Africa, is on the way." This concluding nod to liminality, like Ellison's conclusion to *Invisible Man,* speaks for us, for our expectations, by not speaking for us, and the analogy of personism and Africa ought to lead us, at the very least, to an examination of O'Hara's Ellisonian strategies in light of his contact with African American culture.

O'Hara's introduction to Baraka coincided with his move to 90 University Place—in what he called "the free, glamorous Village"—in early 1957. If the intellectual milieu of "Personism: A Manifesto" is, as I have argued, chiefly that of pragmatism, its social milieu is that of Greenwich Village. This is not to say that O'Hara's social conscience was merely the product of a change in address. As Gooch has pointed out, O'Hara "never swayed in his condemnation" of racism. He was, in his longtime friend and roommate Joe LeSueur's words, "a liberal who supported civil rights early on, and he had a special interest in anything involving blacks—their culture, their music, their history." His interest in African American culture had been impressing upon his writing at least since, as a nineteen-year old sailor, he began writing "Tribute to African Americans" shortly after having "enjoyed Duke Ellington at the Golden State Theater more than the San Carlo Opera Company's production of Lucia di Lammermoor" (CPT 75, 84).[38] But it was in the Village of 1957 that he came into contact with a culture dominated by African American expression, a culture that was self-evidently "jazz-shaped" in Ellison's meaning of that term and that—again in Ellison's sense—was uniquely "American." "I recognize no American style," Ellison says, "which does not bear the mark of the American Negro" (CE 174). In O'Hara's Greenwich Village, this statement was true on its face. It was here that O'Hara was introduced to Baraka—first, in late 1958, through his fledgling poetry journal Yugen and later, in early 1959, in person. Baraka, O'Hara wrote in 1959, was "a saint."

The association of personism with Baraka goes well beyond the fact that "it was founded by [O'Hara] after lunch with LeRoi Jones on August 27, 1959." Both "Personal Poem" and "Personism: A Manifesto" first appear as public documents in Yugen, numbers 6 (1960) and 7 (1961) respectively. By this time Baraka and O'Hara had become close friends, and O'Hara was involved in Baraka's other publishing projects, the journals The Floating Bear and Kulchur, as frequent contributor to the first and contributing editor to the second. Though Olson, Creeley, Duncan, and Ginsberg were all frequent contributors to these ventures, O'Hara singled out Baraka and African American poet A. B. Spellman for praise, telling Vincent Warren that Baraka's *The System of Dante's Hell* was "one of the best and most important works of our time." By 1963 Baraka was comfortable enough with O'Hara to ask him for comments on a draft of his play *The Toilet,* and the two of them were soliciting work for a special civil rights issue of the journal *Kulchur.* Baraka's essay "Expressive Language" appeared in that issue. Among his many insights was a sentence whose basic premise echoed Emerson's statement on emancipation in the British West Indies ("the negro has saved himself, and the white man very patronizingly says, I have saved you" [JMN 9:126]), as well as Ellison's many declarations regarding the centrality of African American culture to the evolution of American democracy. Baraka put it this way: "Very soon after the first generations of Afro-Americans mastered this language they invented white people called Abolitionists."[39]

A statement such as Baraka's here provides an interesting—and I think proper—context for the sentiments expressed by O'Hara in his 1963 poem "Answer to Voznesensky and Evtushenko" (CP 468). Directed toward "two Russian poets he felt had drawn overly simplistic political cartoons of the American race situation in their poetry" (CPT 426), O'Hara's poem announces, "we are tired / of your dreary tourist ideas of our Negro selves," asserting, "you shall not take my friends away from me / because they live in Harlem." O'Hara's conflation of "we poets of America" with "our Negro selves" should not be taken as casual. Indeed, as a pragmatist immersed in the culture surrounding *Yugen, The Floating Bear,* and *Kulchur,* insisting that the self be mediated by social forces, aspiring toward art that functioned like an ideal democracy, what else would he have concluded? In the same year, Creeley said (thinking specifically of Baraka) that "the Negro consciousness" was the "reality, which has become *the* dominant reality in the States today."[40] I would say that, like Ellison, O'Hara and Creeley made African American cultural expression the prime mover behind the "experimental attitude" of the American avant-garde—not only because they believed that it was in fact the impetus behind much advance-guard art but because doing so kept the connection between that art and social activity like the civil rights movement

operative and in the foreground. One's "experimental attitude," as Ellison insisted, was the method by which one "return[ed] to the mood of
personal moral responsibility for democracy" (SA 102). O'Hara more
clearly makes this connection between one's aesthetics and one's politics
in the conclusion to "Answer to Voznesensky and Evtushenko":

> I consider myself to be black and you not even part
> where you see death
> you see a dance of death
> which is
> imperialist, implies training, requires techniques
> our ballet does not employ

O'Hara's critique here of European conventions such as "danse macabre"
and of the notoriously strict, grand, rigid Imperial Ballet mode of Russia
recalls, in both rhetorical strategy and motive, Emerson's critique of
Carlyle's *History of Friedrich II of Prussia, called Frederick the Great.* Like
Emerson, O'Hara was objecting to an art that emphasized "the author
sitting as Demiurgus . . . dictating to all mortals what they shall accept
as fated," codifying the rules by which "the world shall be governed," and
then "trotting out his manikins" (CEC 535). Like Emerson, his alternative was a "ballet" operating under the sign of an ideal democracy that
"does not employ" such "imperialist" strategies. And we should not lose
sight of the fact that in "Answer to Voznesensky and Evtushenko," this
juxtaposition between the democratic and the imperial is syntactically an
explanation of and an elaboration on the juxtaposition that precedes it:
"I consider myself to be black and you not even part." Insofar as American
art was democratic in form and content, it was "black art."[41]

One source for O'Hara's juxtaposition of race, ballet, and democracy
was George Balanchine's production of Stravinsky's *Agon,* which debuted
with the New York City Ballet the year O'Hara moved to the Village.
There was much in the structure of both the score and choreography that
facilitated O'Hara's contrast to the Imperial Ballet mode. His friend Edwin Denby had reviewed *Agon* in *Evergreen Review,* noting that "the general
effect is an amusing deformation of classic shapes due to an unclassic

drive or attack," emphasizing and analogizing "the atonal harmonies of the score" and the "dissonant harmony" of the dancing. In his poem, O'Hara (who Denby quotes in the conclusion to his article) implicitly likens these paradoxical qualities in "our ballet" to the paradoxical "antagonistic cooperation" of American democracy. He also seizes on the social subtext of Balanchine's choice of dancers: the pas de deux in *Agon* is performed by black dancer Arthur Mitchell and white dancer Diana Adams. This integrationist gesture, the first of its kind, performed on opening night (by pure coincidence?) exactly two years to the day after Rosa Parks was arrested for violating the segregated seating ordinance on a Montgomery city bus, was synthesized with choreography that, in Denby's words, "turned pas de deux conventions upside down"; "classic movements turned inside out" and "a pose forced way beyond its classic ending reveal[ed] a novel harmony." The pas de deux between Mitchell and Adams, as Burke would put it, "promptly integrates considerations of 'form' and 'content.' "[42] In saying so, I don't mean to suggest that such was Balanchine's intention (a stickier issue on which I'll defer to critics of the ballet proper[43]) but rather that such seems to have been O'Hara's conclusion as it found its way into "Answer to Voznesensky and Evtushenko." And, in truth, it seems to me that Balanchine's New York City Ballet was a reference point more useful for its relevance to O'Hara's debate with the Russian poets than to his description of a model of democratic symbolic action. If O'Hara, by 1963, saw *Agon* as "a function of American democracy," he was able to do so because of the other models—poetic and musical—at his disposal.

The pas de deux of *Agon* was only one of several implied reference points for O'Hara's "ballet." The poem asks us to treat "our Negro selves" as the basic fact (one might even say cause) behind "we poets of America" and "our ballet." If we accept this proposition, then the term "ballet" begins to lose its Eurocentric specificity; it blurs and refracts until it is something more like a vague metaphor for collective performance, which might be directed this way or that depending on its context. And in the context of "our Negro selves," in the context of a collectivity that "considers itself to be black" by birth or culture, collective performance circa 1963 gestures toward one thing: "our ballet" is jazz. (Thinking of O'Hara's

critique of an imperialist ballet, I note a recent comment of Baraka's, that
"Bourgeois European music, as Max Roach says, has the score as the law,
the composer as God, the conductor as the jailer."[44]) To understand how
O'Hara might casually transgress the boundaries between ballet and jazz
on his way to an argument about art and democracy, we need to understand that at the time of *Agon's* opening, there was another gig in town
that O'Hara attended, most likely several times: the storied, six-month
run by Thelonious Monk and John Coltrane at the Five Spot.[45]

Monk's and Coltrane's performances drew the best jazz musicians in
New York and the artists and the poets of the downtown scene into the
Five Spot—and into close proximity with one another. Bop trombonist
J. J. Johnson called it "the most electrifying sound I've heard since Bird
and Diz [Charlie Parker and Dizzy Gillespie]."[46] Thinking of this ex-
tended gig, Coltrane would later note two things about Monk that perfectly illustrate the "between-ness" I have discussed in relation to O'Hara's
Personism. On the one hand, Coltrane says, "I always had to be alert with
Monk, because if you didn't keep aware all the time of what was going
on you'd suddenly feel as if you'd stepped into an empty elevator shaft."
On the other hand, the sense of connectedness between the two musicians was intense: "Monk just looked at my horn and 'felt' the mechan-
ics."[47] I will have more to say about Monk in particular later in this chapter. Suffice it to say for now that O'Hara was witnessing the interplay
between contingency and communicative agency in the Thelonious Monk
Quartet two years before he made that interplay the catalyst of his personism.[48]

To be convincing regarding the influence of jazz on O'Hara's "personal
poetry," one must survey O'Hara's Village landscape with a good deal of
care. Two facts have generally discouraged poets and critics from considering what jazz might have meant to O'Hara's poetics. First, O'Hara
seemingly had as many selves as he did friends, and with the great majority of them (particularly those uninterested in jazz) he seems not to
have discussed it at all. Second, O'Hara never approached jazz fawningly.
We need to keep in mind that the beat movement, which most freely
associated jazz with poetry during this period, was, as Mackey has pointed
out, burdened with a tendency toward "romanticization of 'the Negro,'

with the inaccuracy of labels, with the popularization that eventually co-opted their stance of revolt" (DE 63). Throughout his friendship with Baraka, O'Hara remained keenly aware of their differences and, at the same time, remained willing to let Baraka's influence impress upon and shape his identity and aesthetic. It should be obvious that this was a rather thin tightrope O'Hara was attempting to walk, but I would argue that the attempt is a successful one. In "A True Account of Talking to the Sun at Fire Island," O'Hara writes, "always embrace things, people earth / sky stars, as I do, freely and with / the appropriate sense of space" (CP 307). In "Bathroom," he writes "So that the pliant / and persuadable map / will appeal to you I'll / imagine that my skin / is infinitely ex-tensible" (473). The first is a formula for ensuring that difference is not swallowed by "freedom." The second is a formula for permitting differ-ence to shape the "pliant and persuadable map" of one's identity. Together they represent the dialectic of O'Hara's approach to African American culture.[49] In regard to jazz, we might say that what begins as a decision to maintain "the appropriate sense of space" develops under Baraka's in-fluence into a nuanced relationship to jazz that is itself "jazz-shaped."

In 1957, poetry readings performed to jazz were in vogue and O'Hara began to receive invitations to participate in them himself, invitations that he always turned down. Early on, his rationale was that jazz simply didn't "go with" the poems he had written to that point—and his confu-sion over those who *were* reading to jazz is telling. Of Howard Hart and Philip Lamantia—who were reading at the time "with a French hornist as the Jazz Poetry Trio"—O'Hara wrote to Gregory Corso, "I don't re-ally get their jazz stimulus" and then embarked on a lengthy analogy to his interest in abstract expressionism based on the premise that "where jazz is fleeting (in time) and therefor poignant, de K[ooning] is final and therefor tragic." Two things should be highlighted regarding O'Hara's ex-planation to Corso. First, by 1959, O'Hara had abandoned the idea that his own writing was tragic, switching gears in the casual style of person-ism: "it used to be that I could only write when I was miserable; now I can only write when I'm happy." Second, the explanation itself casts doubt on O'Hara's own commitment to it: "This may not be too inter-esting," he says, "and I don't know whether I really believe it or not—but

I do." He muses about reading in front of a painting by Pollock or de Kooning and ends with a befuddled last attempt at explanation: "I guess my point is that painting doesn't intrude upon poetry. What got me off on this?"[50] Again, as O'Hara's interest in collective improvisation evolves, the sensitivity here—regarding what intrudes upon what—goes by the wayside.

At some point in 1958, it seems, O'Hara began to make useful, useable, connections between what was going on in jazz and Goodman's idea of "attractive and repulsive tampering of the artist and the audience with each other." What remained constant, however, was his aversion to striking any sort of jazz-poetry pose that might devolve into cliché. His highest compliment for Corso, for instance, was that he was "the only poet who, to my taste, has adopted successfully the rhythms and figures of speech of the jazz musician's world without embarrassment" (SS 83). The "embarrassment" O'Hara speaks of is *the embarrassment of appropriation,* the kind that would go along with the self-discovery that one's writing was replaying the motif of jazz's "cooptation by white 'swing' bandleaders like the aptly named Paul Whiteman."[51] This was a very productive kind of embarrassment indeed. It was the corrective that kept O'Hara from merely writing *about* jazz (as Creeley put it, "trying to be some curious social edge of that imagined permission"[52]) and that eventually assisted him in developing an aesthetic that was *analogous to jazz.* Two months after his letter to Corso about the Jazz Poetry Trio ("I don't get their jazz stimulus"), O'Hara wrote "Elegy on Causality in the Five Spot Café" (which would later become the first seven lines of "Ode on Causality"). The poem began with the sentence, "There is a sense of neurotic coherence" (CP 302). Here perhaps was a first stab at defining the "antagonistic cooperation" of jazz.[53] And in July 1958, O'Hara dealt head-on with the issue of collaboration across racial lines in "Ode: Salute to the French Negro Poets," announcing, "like Whitman my great predecessor, I call / to the spirits of other lands to make fecund my existence."

In his ode, O'Hara brought his pragmatic belief that "the only truth is face to face" into contact with questions of racial difference, addressing Aime Cesaire by saying, "if there is fortuity it's in the love we bear each other's differences / in race which is the poetic ground on which we rear our smiles." "Dying in black and white," O'Hara wrote, "we fight for what we love, not are." O'Hara's repetition of "love" is crucial to both his navigation of questions of race and identity as well as to his growing interest in the collective improvisation characteristic of jazz. O'Hara was putting love in the service of his pragmatism, drawing on that aspect of pragmatism that, as James Livingston has written, "foregrounds the sensational, desiring body as the necessary and enduring condition of self-consciousness and selfhood." As a pragmatist, O'Hara understood that the "notion of selfhood as the effect of entanglement in externality enables a new, discursive model of personality." Selfhood is the doings and operations of O'Hara's lover-on-the-telephone. As he says in his ode, "we fight for what we love, not are." A model of selfhood based on what we "are" implies a self utterly unchanged by "the love we bear each other's differences in race." In contrast, a model of selfhood based on "what we love" holds out the possibility of an active self approaching racial difference in such a way that "the distinction between knower and known, self and other . . . must be recreated and embodied in time in new social forms, not assumed to be fixed or given by the past." In short, O'Hara was coming to terms with the role race played in his pragmatic vision of the self as "personality as the consequence of 'reciprocal exteriority.' "[54]

Again, the line O'Hara was trying to walk between "entanglement" and appropriation was a fine one. But the conclusion of his ode suggests that he was well aware of the distinction. "The beauty of America," he writes, is "neither cool jazz nor devoured Egyptian heroes," and in these lines there is evidence that O'Hara was becoming aware of debates within the jazz community itself, debates that were insistent for someone like Baraka. Miles Davis (who appears in O'Hara's "Personal Poem" being "clubbed 12 / times last night outside BIRDLAND by a cop" [335]) recalls the subtext of "cool jazz" during this period in the following: "A lot of white musicians like Stan Getz, Chet Baker, and Dave Brubeck—who had been influenced by my records—were recording all over the place. Now they were calling the kind of music they were playing 'cool jazz.' I guess it was supposed to be some kind of alternative to bebop, or black music, or 'hot jazz,' which in white people's minds, meant black. But it was the same old story, black shit was being ripped off all over again."[55]

Baraka, following Davis's lead, compared "cool jazz" to "arranged big-band swing . . . the tepid new popular music of the white middle-brow middle class."[56] O'Hara was at pains not to follow the "cool jazz" model ("black shit . . . being ripped off all over again") and thus was insistent that it was not part of the "beauty of America." The reference to "devoured Egyptian heroes" is also interesting in relation to black and white conflict, black and white dichotomies. It seems to be O'Hara's joke on the Judgment of the Deceased in Egyptian mythology. The deceased come to the Hall of Judgment to convince Osiris that they are pure and worthy. If they are judged impure and unworthy, then they are thrown to "Amemait the devourer," a hybrid monster—part lion, part hippo, part crocodile. In pairing and dismissing "cool jazz" and "devoured Egyptian heroes," O'Hara seemed to be attempting to do away with judgments based on the purity of distinctions. But in emphasizing "the love we bear each other's differences," he was also underscoring that one *loves* (becomes entangled with) what one does not *know*. O'Hara's "love" was a rejection of the "spectator theory of knowledge." If jazz (or the jazz musician) was treated as an object "fixed in its regal aloofness," he or she might be gazed at romantically in a dreamed moment of transcendental "knowing" or imitated as in photorealistic portraiture, but what *wouldn't* be happening is anything akin to the activity of jazz itself.

Romanticization, O'Hara understood, was merely the flip side of negation, and so most of his poetic engagements with jazz and African American culture are marked by, on the one hand, a mix of purposefully clumsy, intentionally awkward boundary crossings ("attractive and repulsive tampering") and, on the other hand, moments of hesitancy, of communicative impediment, of not-knowing. The stress is on the incompleteness or instability of any single description. Again, O'Hara's strategy helps him to avoid a lot of pitfalls. In late 1962, he explained to Rivers, "I didn't read in the Five Spot because the idea made me nervous and I thought I'd be no good at it."[57] Out of context this statement might be taken as a nervousness about jazz *as such,* but in fact it is quite the opposite. As Rivers knew, the kind of reading he was asking O'Hara to do had long since regressed into parody, the best example being a performance in which Rivers and Kenneth Koch parodied poetry/jazz improvisation at the Five Spot, "Koch reading from the phone book." Billie Holliday (who O'Hara had once called "better than Picasso") was in attendance and afterward she smiled at Koch, commenting, "Man, your poetry is weird."[58] Holliday's comment to Koch most likely preceded her impromptu concert at the Five Spot, the one recorded by O'Hara in "The Day Lady Died." In any event it seems clear that O'Hara's nervousness about the appropriative and/or parodic dangers of "jazz-poetry nights" is one resonant subtext for that poem.

"The Day Lady Died" (CP 325) is one of the "I do this I do that poems" where the notion that words *do* supplants the notion that words *mean* and where truth happens to one's words in the course of their reception and re-direction. O'Hara clearly wants to celebrate Holliday (much as Baraka would do in juxtaposing her to "disemboweled Academic models of second-rate English poetry"[59]), but, contrary to most critical views of the poem, he is well aware of the hazards involved in his undertaking, and the poem is designed so that it might avoid descending into either "traditional elegy" or clichéd rendition of the "white intellectual worshipping a black jazz performer."[60] The title itself is one aspect of O'Hara's strategy: the elegiac, transcedent bearing of the syntax ("The Day Lady Died," accenting "Day" so as to remove it from the continuum of days, as in "The Day the Earth Stood Still") is undercut by O'Hara's play on Holliday's nickname, "Lady Day." A second possibility arises, that the title is a plain statement of fact: "The Day Lady" (Lady Day, Billie Holliday) died. Keeping in mind that the poem is contemporaneous with O'Hara's invention of personism, we should recognize the importance of O'Hara's play, the way he figures Holliday's death as one in a series of everyday events.

I can think of no better answer to Dewey's call "to restore continuity between the refined and intensified forms of experience which are works of art and the everyday events, doings," and I am reminded of how Dewey's panegyric on "operations in experience" is based on his sense of how such operations are anathema to all processes of objectification. The first four stanzas of O'Hara's poem are built on a series of the most plain, present-tense declarative statements: "I go . . . I walk . . . I go . . . I get . . . I do think . . . I stick with . . . I just stroll . . . I go." The sense of rapid movement is enhanced by his use of specific times (12:20, 4:19, 7:15), and the whole passage is a model of what James called "reactive spontaneity" (WJ 8:380).[61] "I don't know the people who will feed me," O'Hara insists, and each encounter is an entanglement in externality, a literal modification in his discursive self, the complexity of which is registered in his vernacular expressions. He buys "an ugly NEW WORLD WRITING to see what the poets in Ghana are doing these days," as if reading across boundaries of race and culture were as casual and egalitarian as knocking on your neighbor's door or calling her on the telephone, and in that way the antithesis of the romantic act of "discovery" (in which the operative question is not "what are you doing?" but "who are you, what do you represent?"). He signifies on the name of his bank teller, Miss Stillwagon, who would ordinarily stop him in his tracks by looking up his balance (and here his joke is relevant to the improvisational aesthetic of those New American Poets interested in jazz: as Creeley explains it, "verse turns, and takes turns in turning—which are called *verses* in my book, like changes [in jazz]—and not those *stanzas* or stops, standstills"[62]). Lastly, he turns around. In describing that turning, he reveals just how actively the social text is mediating the poetic text: "then I go back where I came from to 6th Avenue." This is of course a joke on the racist question, Why don't you go back where you came from? and O'Hara's answer renders the question absurd—where he came from isn't Africa or Mississippi or Massachusetts or China, Mexico, Ireland; it's "6th Avenue." Just as "the only truth is face to face," O'Hara measures origins in blocks. The joke is a gesture in the direction of his vision of New York as a multiethnic radical democracy. Notice that with more than 80 percent of the poem gone, Holliday hasn't even been mentioned. And yet we can read O'Hara's personism-style games as prelude to the final stanza or as a return to where the games "came from."

I have mentioned how Holliday's performance at the Five Spot and O'Hara's nervousness over the jazz-poetry events held there are relevant subtexts for the poem, but there is another generally neglected subtext for the poem that I believe needs to be reinstated—namely, the music most associated with the Five Spot itself, the music of the new jazz avant-garde characterized by "its heavy emphasis on individual freedom within a collectively improvised context." That music, as Mackey has argued, "proposed a model social order, an ideal, even utopic balance between personal impulse and group demands" (DE 34). I noted earlier how O'Hara's move to the "free, glamorous village" coincided with Thelonious Monk's famous run with John Coltrane at the Five Spot. Monk's influence on the young jazz avant-garde that congregated at the Five Spot (Coltrane, Davis, Cecil Taylor, Ornette Coleman, and others) was profound. Stanley Crouch explains that "the Five Spot had begun its music policy in 1956 with the band of Cecil Taylor . . . [whose] style can be almost totally traced to *Work,* a composition performed by Monk in the early fifties."[63] Monk himself was something of a "new thing" at this moment since, as Orrin Keepnews points out, "in 1957, for the first time in many years, Thelonious became regularly available to New York nightclub audiences." (In fact, Monk's run that year at the Five Spot was booked at the suggestion of O'Hara's good friend Rivers.)[64] Moreover, Monk's influence extended beyond young jazz musicians to include young poets such as Baraka, Spellman, and Creeley. O'Hara, I think, belongs in this mix; the kinds of associations that Mackey makes between Creeley or Baraka and Monk, Taylor, and Coleman might just as valuably be made between these latter musicians and O'Hara.

Mackey's associations are strengthened by the fact that these musicians and poets were actually in dialogue with one another, largely through Baraka's initiative. If Taylor, for instance, was reading the work of Duncan, Baraka, Olson, and Creeley, which became "absorbed in his music" (DE 32), then surely Baraka, Creeley, and, I would say, O'Hara, would have been influenced by Taylor's descriptions of jazz improvisation: "Each ensemble member as an active / community agent attempting a special / social function (human)" (34). (Berkson notes that Taylor helped to run off copies of *The Floating Bear* in the early sixties, and O'Hara, as a highly skilled pianist, would no doubt have been interested in Taylor's combination of, in his words, "European technical facility" and the "uninhibited collective improvisation" of avant-garde jazz.)[65] As Baraka explains in *Blues People:* "The reciprocity of this relationship became actively decisive during the fifties when scores of young Negroes and, of course, Negro musicians, began to address themselves to the formal canons of Western non-conformity, as formally understood refusals of the hollowness of American life, especially in its address to the Negro" (BP 231). I can't pass by Jones's characterizations of the times without noting that the most obvious "canon of Western non-conformity" is Emerson's: "whoso would be a man must be a non-conformist . . . for non-conformity the world whips you with its displeasure" (CW 2:51, 57). These were prescriptions and warnings for the writer who would use language as democratic symbolic action. And what we have in the milieu of the Five Spot is an instance where artists involved in different mediums were consciously tampering with each other—consciously transgressing the law of genre —in order to invent new forms of democratic symbolic action. Insofar as O'Hara's "The Day Lady Died" represents activity in the Five Spot, it is one of these new forms.

The strategy at work in the last stanza of "The Day Lady Died," which I would like to highlight, is one that Mackey calls "a heterogeneous inclusiveness evoked in terms of non-availability" (DE 254). "Heterogeneous inclusiveness" is one of those oxymoronic phrases—like Ellison's "antagonistic cooperation"—that gestures toward the workings of an ideal democracy. A tactical emphasis on nonavailability, on the disruption of signifying systems, on the *between-ness* of all communicative gestures, serves to voice "reminders of the axiomatic exclusions upon which positings of identity and meaning depend" (DE 19). James called this "the re-instatement of the vague" (WJ 8:246). To admit the inaudible message is to acknowledge that the source of that message is resistant to all fixed classification; it is to circumvent the issues of objectification and romanticization without precluding the possibilities of extemporaneous dialogue. The poem that foregrounds nonavailability is "at odds with hypostasis, the reification of fixed identities that has been the bane of socially marginalized groups . . . with taxonomies and categorizations that obscure the fact of heterogeneity and mix" (DE 20). Like identity itself, words and sentences are rendered transitional—on the fly that is open, so to speak. Always mediating against fixity, the poem is *not* at odds with the idea of language as *evocative*. Recall that O'Hara quite literally plays the evocator in "Ode: Salute to the French Negro Poets" (calling to spirits of other lands to make fecund his existence) and that any sense of "heterogeneous inclusiveness" in that poem—between O'Hara and Cesaire for instance—is predicated on O'Hara's insistence *that he does not know who Cesaire is* or who the two of them are as a fixed "we." O'Hara banks on a refusal to posit "our desires and allegiances" as reified, rational entities. "That's not why you fell in love in the first place," as he says in "Personism: A Manifesto," "so you have to take your chances and avoid being logical." O'Hara's critique of the logical is, more specifically, a critique of *logocentrism:* of the reasonable, proportionate, referential word.

As I have already argued, personism is a catalyst for poems that live as a set of uncertain terms between people, poems that encourage a particularly democratic social relationship. What is most interesting to me about the conclusion to "The Day Lady Died" is that it is a practical application of personism:

> and I am sweating a lot by now and thinking of
> leaning on the john door in the 5 SPOT
> while she whispered a song along the keyboard
> to Mal Waldron and everyone and I stopped breathing

To whom did Holliday whisper, and who stopped breathing? The absence of punctuation is an impediment; it precludes a definitive answer. Did she whisper "to Mal Waldron and everyone" or only to "Mal Waldron," her fellow black jazz musician, and to no one else? And what of "I," which, in such a chatty, vernacular poem, seems to want to be an indirect object despite the rules of grammar? Then, if "everyone" and "I" are separate objects, did Holliday whisper "to Mal Waldron and everyone" or "to Mal Waldron and everyone and I"—meaning, has O'Hara been left somehow out of the communicative loop? *Whether* O'Hara heard and *how* he heard are only tentatively defined. What we have as evidence of his reception are a physiological response ("stopped breathing") and the writing of a poem called "The Day Lady Died." What we do not have is anything we might confidently call "understanding" or "knowing." The fact that we cannot decide whether the members of this collective are subjects or objects has the uncanny effect of obscuring their position in space. Much is dependent on whether Waldron and O'Hara can both be included in "everyone"—the only noun that, in true grammatical fashion, occupies the position of both subject and object. And here is the genius of O'Hara's invention: Waldron and O'Hara are irreconcilable subjects mediated by a collective "everyone" which creates the potential position between subject and object, though neither of them occupies it alone, and their inclusion is dependent on dispensing with the grammatical laws that would separate them.

The scene bears the markings of what Mackey calls "the obliquity of a utopian aspiration": "the accent that falls upon the insufficiency of the visual image," he explains, "is consistent with an anesthetic-synesthetic enablement that displaces the privileged eye" (DE 255). To observe is to be overcome with, first, a sense of *anesthesia* (blurring to the point of blindness) and, second, the need for a *synesthetic* leap of faith; the "privileged eye" ("I") is supplanted by an unnamed actor who chooses verse (versatility) over verity (verisimilitude). Faced with the irresolvable tangle of subjects and objects, the operative metaphor becomes not the eye but the keyboard: "she whispered *along* the keyboard." O'Hara's choice of prepositions has the effect of emphasizing just how *long* the keyboard is, to the exclusion of several common definitions of "key": "something that secures or controls entrance to a place," "a systematic explanation of symbols." The multiplicity of interpretive possibilities implied by the keyboard puts to rest these more confining definitions of key. Even the common musical definition—"the relationship perceived between all tones in a given unit of music and a single tone or key note"—won't accommodate O'Hara's verbal play. For Holliday does not *sing in* a key but, rather, *whispers along* a key*board*. In doing so, she gestures outside the realm of Western musical notation. (We might also note how the action O'Hara ascribes to Holliday mediates against the sort of masculinist version of jazz that Williams and Miller adopt for the composition of *Man Orchid*. I think of one of Miller's phallic metaphors: "They had the right keyhole, those guys, but the wrong key" [81].)

Holliday's whisper is a symbolic action of the kind Mackey refers to as "noise": "a resonance that interferes with the audition of a message in the process of emission." Keep in mind that the question of who "re-

ceives" Holliday's whisper is an open question. "Noise is whatever the
signifying system, in a particular situation, is not intended to transmit,
be the system a poem, a piece of music, a novel, or an entire society,"
Mackey says. "Open form is a gesture in the direction of noise" (DE 19–
20). In relation to a strict sense of "key," jazz musicians have always employed noise (Ellington called it "the dirt") in the form of manipulations
of timbre, all sorts of tonal inflections via pitch bending, muting, the blu-
ing of notes, even Louis Armstrong's characteristic rips (his quick rises
in pitch directly preceding a tone). In keeping with O'Hara's keyboard
metaphor we might cite Monk's "voicing" of chords: the unpredictable
ways in which he pulls notes away from the position they hold within a
single octave, spreading the chord over the range of the keyboard (or,
conversely, compacting chords by using "diads"—that is, striking two
notes only one whole step or half-step apart, with his fourth and fifth
fingers, at once). In his improvisations, Monk is always omitting typical
notes and adding atypical ones to the chord (his voicing, it was said,
"could make an in tune piano sound out of tune"). As Mackey points out,
Monk described his voicing strategies simply as "how to use notes differently. That's it. Just how to use notes differently" (DE 275). But we should
also understand that using notes differently was (is) a response to the fact
that "no written notes sounded right."[66] In the late 1950s Monk more
than anyone else represented the eccentric individual jazz musician employing noise as a way to gesture outside of the *already inscribed.*

Still, if Monk represents some culminating moment in the use of noise
within the jazz idiom, this should not preclude one from recognizing
similar gestures among his predecessors. Holliday's vocal inflections
might be included along with examples in the work of an Armstrong or
an Ellington. A year after writing "The Day Lady Died," O'Hara explicitly connects Holliday and Monk in "Tonight at the Versailles, Or Another
Card Another Cabaret"—a poem of scorching irony that recognizes how
the "cabaret card" system was used to harass and oppress black musicians
and that makes O'Hara's allegiance and identification clear. In the poem,
the police commissioner says to O'Hara, "try not to spread the infection
/ like Billie and Monk and the others / be a good whatever-you-are"
(375). Holliday and Monk are aligned politically and aesthetically in

O'Hara's imagination; like O'Hara himself (and O'Hara foregrounds this by discussing his "sexual offenses" in the poem) they are among "the others," among the "whatever-you-are's," classified by their "criminal record[s]" (note the pun) but nonetheless unclassifiable in their artful living and living art. The poem suggests that O'Hara's commitment to gay rights—the attempt "to win for fairies equal rights" as he once put it— was in his own mind related to the African American civil rights movement, and that advance-guard creative expression might function in service to both. "Tonight at the Versailles" also gestures toward the Five Spot since Monk's and Holliday's cabaret-card troubles both resulted in performances there—Monk, triumphantly, his card restored; Holliday, surreptitiously, as recounted in "The Day Lady Died."

Moreover, "The Day Lady Died" erects an important generational bridge when it introduces Mal Waldron. It is clear enough that as the final scene of "The Day Lady Died" takes place in the Five Spot, one would have to at least loosely associate it with the aesthetic environment of that venue. But the fact that Waldron is one of the players should provoke further scrutiny. Gooch identifies Waldron as "a black pianist who usually accompanied Holliday" (328), but this is misleading in that it suggests that Waldron would have been identified by the Five Spot community simply as Holliday's pianist. In fact, Waldron was an important member of the jazz avant-garde who figured prominently in groups led by Charles Mingus and Eric Dolphy among others and who was heavily influenced by Monk. In October 1958 (while Monk was still holding forth at the Five Spot), Waldron played on Steve Lacy's *Reflections: Steve Lacy Plays Thelonious Monk,* along with Elvin Jones (soon to become Coltrane's legendary drummer). A few months later he played on Mingus's famous *Blues and Roots* recording. The point is that by the time O'Hara composed "The Day Lady Died," Waldron's significance as a player lay much more clearly with the jazz musicians being touted by Baraka than with Billie Holliday (though, as I've said, both Baraka and O'Hara would not have hesitated to include Holliday among those jazz musicians whose music was a "formally understood refusal of the hollowness of American life"). Our reading of the "whisper along the keyboard" should take into account the fact that O'Hara—as an accomplished pianist familiar with

Monk, Cecil Taylor, and Waldron and conversing with (and reading) Baraka—was aware of the imminent jazz experiments in liberating "key" from even its flexible meaning as defined in bop improvisation.

For the Five Spot community, this liberation of key would culminate in the arrival of Ornette Coleman, who debuted at the Five Spot in late 1959, the exact same time that O'Hara was developing "ideas about suitable prosody for musical setting of American diction."[67] Spellman described Coleman's arrival as "the greatest furor jazz had seen in fifteen years."[68] In *Blues People,* Baraka quotes George Russell on Coleman's impact: "[H]is pieces don't really infer key. They could be in any key or no key. . . . [T]his approach liberates the improviser to sing his own song really, without having to meet the deadline of any particular chord." "The implications of this music," Baraka writes, "are extraordinarily profound" (BP 227). Baraka's pragmatic view of Coleman's music (its structure is designed to liberate the improviser) is informative.[69] While Russell takes some musicological liberties (Coleman's music is never precisely in "no key" but, more accurately, employs shifting tone centers), his and Baraka's reading of the music's mood is quite accurate. That Baraka and Coleman were friends is also significant; as he did with Cecil Taylor, Baraka was exchanging aesthetic notions, his metaphors one half of a synesthetic two-way street. Other close friends of O'Hara's such as Berkson were analogizing just as freely. Berkson writes, "Monk and Coleman were instructive about tone, [about] what a structure or syntax might accommodate, what the ear could not just tolerate but actually enjoy."[70] Notice how Berkson moves liberally from discussing musical tonality to discussing syntax. Again, the context of Greenwich Village seems to have validated such gestures, just as it validated Cecil Taylor's liberal application of Black Mountain, "open field" poetics to his own musical experimentation.[71]

Frank O'Hara was an active participant in the scene I have been describing. Though, as I have suggested, the very multiplicity of O'Hara's personae precludes one from arguing for the centrality of any scene vis-à-vis his artistic production, this milieu is at least supplemental to the others in which he involved himself. In the summer of 1960 (when "Personal Poem" appeared in *Yugen* 6 and "The Day Lady Died" and "Ode:

Salute to the French Negro Poets" appeared in print for the first time in *The New American Poetry*), O'Hara was very excited about Ornette Coleman. Part of the occasion for that excitement was the affair going on between Coleman and O'Hara's friend Diana Powell. In a letter telling Don Allen about the affair, O'Hara underscores Coleman's name as "<u>*ORNETTE COLEMAN*</u>!!!" and in a contemporaneous letter to Vincent Warren, he notes seeing Coleman at the Five Spot, prompting Warren's memory by describing the group as "the one with the little trumpet [Don Cherry's pocket trumpet] and sax." While the references are typically gossipy, and while O'Hara's interest in Coleman included his usual lack of distinction between the artistic, the personal, and the sexual,[72] they lead in the direction of a provocatively different version of O'Hara than the one commonly invoked. As Baraka has recently explained: "Frank dug the music, went to the 5 Spot often. We were all hit with the heavy impact in G[reenwich] V[illage] of Ornette C[oleman]. He was a New Thing, in that era of new things. . . . Jazz was New York! It was urban, new, hot, revelatory, &c, it was the anthemic back and foreground of the art denizens of the then and there. Like language and city sounds . . . Frank was always looking for inspiration. The music inspired him."

Baraka goes on to suggest what it was about Coleman that would have inspired O'Hara: "Jazz is Democratic in form, it basically is collective improvisation. It is about singular and collective spontaneity, and composition, both formal and mise en scene."[73] In this instance—thinking about Coleman, thinking about O'Hara—Baraka's view is remarkably close to Ellison's: the jazz band puts democracy into aesthetic action. Coleman's music, as released on a series of Atlantic LPs between 1959 and 1962 and as played at the Five Spot and the Jazz Gallery during this time, sent jazz musicians and poets alike scrambling for phrases equivalent to Ellison's "antagonistic cooperation." Mingus called it "organized disorganization, or playing wrong right." Spellman said Coleman was "changing the relationships within the group until the gap between soloist and rhythm accompanist diminished to the disappearing point," a point on which Gunther Schuller concurred: "Although everyone is a soloist in [Coleman's] *Free Jazz*—relatively independent and equal with the seven others—the word solo has to be reinterpreted from its conven-

tional meaning. There is no one soloist, and there are no merely supporting accompanists. Everyone is equal, and in a sense everyone is at all times
simultaneously leading (soloing) and supporting (complementing)."[74]

What Spellman and Schuller were suggesting, in effect, was that Coleman was conceiving anew the relationship at the heart of jazz improvisation whereby each musician is always playing both "within and against the
group" (Coleman would sometimes remind members of his group to
"play against the piece"[75]). For Ellison, this "contest," as he calls it, is the
predicate by which jazz becomes "a function of American democracy."
Here, then, was a highly cathectic counterpart to O'Hara's personism,
staring him in the face. Recall that Ellison (in 1958) analogized jazz improvisation to "the successive canvases of a painter" and that O'Hara saw
Rivers's canvases as akin to jazz performances. We ought to consider both
in relation to the following fact: that less than a month before he begins
turning up in O'Hara's letters, Coleman described in print (the liner
notes to his *Change of the Century*) "certain continually evolving strands of
thought that link all my compositions together" and provided his own
analogy: "Maybe it's like the paintings of Jackson Pollock." Baraka considered Coleman's suggestion reasonable enough to include it in *Blues
People* (BP 234). The relevant authority on Pollock at this moment was of
course O'Hara, whose monograph, *Jackson Pollock,* had been published
just nine months previous to Coleman's statement.[76]

O'Hara's personism, his "personal pragmatism," evolves in the context of his relationship with Baraka and his response to the "new thing"
jazz of the period. The connection Ellison draws between "the American
vernacular as symbolic action" and *jazz* as symbolic action (namely, that
they are both forms of *democratic symbolic action*) is a connection O'Hara
makes as well, almost inevitably. The poet who has embraced pragmatism
will, given the chance, recognize the most pragmatic American art form
(jazz) as collateral to (and *catalyst* to) his own project. In Baraka's journals, the ones that most frequently published O'Hara, pragmatism and
jazz were constant bedfellows. I have already given some of the context
surrounding O'Hara's references to Coleman, but there is more worth
mentioning. Alongside "Personal Poem" in *Yugen* 6, for instance, were poems by Olson, Creeley, and Baraka. In that same summer of 1960, *Kul-*

chur 2 published Martin Williams's "Ornette Coleman: First Impressions" (in which the author concludes, "somehow, one has the feeling hearing him play or talk that *he will simply do what he must do*"), as well as an essay by Paul Goodman that begins, "The relation of theory and practice . . . is a thorny one; but it *must* in every case be decided in the direction of absolute freedom of speculation and publication, otherwise it is impossible to live and breathe." For Baraka, for O'Hara, it would not have been much of a leap to read Goodman's prescription as relevant to Coleman's project and vice versa. When one steps back to see the big picture surrounding Baraka's publishing projects of 1959–62, one gets the impression that his most frequent contributors—Spellman, O'Hara, Martin Williams, Creeley—were in the process of putting two and two together. The year 1961 is particularly interesting in this regard. It is the year O'Hara participated in the *Floating Bear* benefit readings, praising Baraka and Spellman, the year in which he again saw Coleman perform (at least once, on opening night at the Jazz Gallery, and probably several times). *Floating Bear* 2 included four of his poems alongside an essay by Creeley on William Carlos Williams's "The American Idiom." Williams's most cogent—and unlikely!—statement on the American idiom had appeared in *Paterson,* book 5, in 1958 (a text dear not only to Creeley but to O'Hara): "We poets have to talk in a language which is not English. It is the American Idiom. Rhythmically [the poem is] organized as a sample of the American idiom. It has as much originality as jazz." Williams's point about the American vernacular is almost identical to Ellison's (remember Ellison's statement, "we forget, conveniently sometimes, that the language which we speak is not English" but rather a jazz-shaped "flexible instrument" predicated on "dissonances"?), and it was readymade for reception by the writers involved with *Yugen, Floating Bear,* and *Kulchur.*[77] *Floating Bear* 6 included letters to the editor regarding Coleman, Coltrane, Cecil Taylor, and Larry Rivers. That same year, Coleman released *Free Jazz* with liner notes by Martin Williams. Williams concludes those notes by invoking the American vernacular: "The man who isn't bothered about 'newness' or 'difference,' but says only that, '[Coleman] sounds like someone crying, talking, laughing,' is having the soundest sort of response to Ornette Coleman's music." Martin Williams—

who Baraka says "hipped [him] to Ornette Coleman"[78]—was linking Coleman's music as symbolic action to the American idiom as symbolic action and thus was providing *Kulchur's* readership with what I have discussed in chapters 1 and 3 as Ellisonian pragmatism.

In simply piling up these related strands coming out of Baraka's initiatives in the early 1960s, I am trying to provide some of the feel of the "heterogeneity and mix" to which O'Hara was privy at this moment. At the same time, I want to argue that there is a logic to this mix, a logic that Ellison was already theorizing across town, from his spot in Harlem. Ellison contended that the artist looking to make good on pragmatism's celebration of democratic symbolic action would do well to rediscover its roots in Emerson's engagement with African American culture, but that, for a practical application of what he or she was looking for, that artist need look no further than jazz music and the jazz-shaped American vernacular. As he put it in his review of Baraka's *Blues People,* "American culture was, even before the official founding of the nation, pluralistic; and it was the African's origin in cultures in which art was highly functional which gave him an edge in shaping the music and dance of this nation" (SA 255). In positing this nexus of jazz and pragmatism, he helps explain the logic and energy behind projects such as *Yugen, Floating Bear,* and *Kulchur.* There is a reason that Ellison is so valuable as a theorist when one is trying to make sense of O'Hara's personism and his "personal poems." Simply put, Ellison somewhat unwittingly theorizes this culture that so inspirits O'Hara's personal writing from roughly 1957 to 1965.

The skeptic will note that Ellison found Greenwich Village culture somewhat dubious, that he was ultimately dedicated to Armstrong and Basie and not to the "new thing" jazz being played at the Five Spot, and that he and Baraka had an adversarial relationship. These facts are all true, as far as they go, but they are also misleading. They stack the deck in favor of generational discrepancies in taste to the neglect of commonalities in both theory and practice. They also ignore the fact that Baraka circa 1963 had an adversarial relationship *with himself.* As Mackey has written, "*Consistency* is one of the last words one would use in characterizing Baraka's thinking during the first two decades of his career" (DE 22). In his review of *Blues People,* Ellison seizes on a central irony in Baraka's argument regarding black authenticity, that is, regarding "the impression that there [is] a rigid correlation between color, education, income, and the Negro's preference in music." He gives the example of a father of a racially, educationally, and economically heterodox black family who is also "a walking depository of blues tradition" and then remarks, "Jones's theory no more allows for the existence of such a Negro than it allows for himself." Personal motivations aside, Ellison has his thumb on an interesting aspect of *Blues People:* that, particularly when he begins toward the end of his book to describe the "reciprocal" Greenwich Village culture where jazz is in dialogue with "the formal canons of Western non-conformity," Baraka's examples actually run *counter to* the overarching premise of his book. It is simply impossible to square the fledgling black nationalist impulse with celebratory descriptions such as the following: "The feeling of rapport between the jazz of the forties, fifties and sixties with the rest of contemporary American art is not confined merely to social areas. There are aesthetic analogies, persistent similarities of stance that also create identifiable relationships. And these relationships seem valid whether they are found in the most vital contemporary American poetry or the best new American painting. The younger musicians sense this as much as, say, the younger writers."

Chief among Baraka's examples of "younger musicians" and "younger writers" were Coleman and O'Hara. As Baraka begins to break with the culture he describes above, he must necessarily rewrite these "aesthetic analogies, persistent similarities," and "identifiable relationships," reinterpreting the poetry as "a cloud of abstraction and disjointedness, that was just whiteness"[79] and the music as, in Mackey's words, "a return to the African ethic," the "communalist impulse" whereby "the black-musician-as-saboteur" targets "the Western cult of individualism" (DE 23, 35–36). But if, as Mackey argues, "these notions of black communality carry the weight of a wished-for release from egocentricity" (DE 36), they are not precisely a repudiation of pragmatism. Pragmatism has always included a critique of egocentricity, as exemplified by James's critique of Kant's concept of the transcendental ego; for Kant, James said, what is outside is "a mere empty locus," a premise James flatly rejected. Kant's "ego," he scoffed, is "as ineffectual and windy an abortion as Philosophy can show." O'Hara's "personal poems" are nothing if not attacks on the concept of *self* as "presupposition and 'transcendental' condition," on "the bare transcendental Subject" as "*conditio sine qua non* of experience" (WJ 8:341–52). Those poems bear constant witness to the fact that, as Dewey says, "prejudice blinds us; conceit looks through the wrong end of a telescope and minimizes the significance possessed by objects in favor of the alleged importance of the self" (LW 10:110). Baraka himself understands this, which is why he will to this day note that O'Hara's "emphasis on the everyday, the commonly dug occurrence rendered revelatory by the poem" was his strategy "to eschew the imbecile profile of the evil that proliferated throughout the world" and that personism was "good for [him, Baraka]."[80]

Seeing O'Hara's "personal pragmatism" as a jazz-influenced critique of the egocentric self helps to shed light on the otherwise enigmatic facts of his relationship with Baraka. As examples, I would note that it is *after* Baraka publishes "The Politics of Rich Painters" in *Floating Bear* 22 (with its excoriation of "some up and coming queer [who] explain[s] cinema and politics while drowning a cigarette") and *after* he publishes "Tokenism: 300 Years for Five Cents" in *Kulchur* 5 (lambasting white intellectuals for their "malevolent liberalism") that he appoints O'Hara art editor of *Kulchur*. These events took place within months of each other in mid-1962. As I have noted, in mid- to late 1963, O'Hara read a draft of *The Toilet* at Baraka's behest, and the two of them began working on a special civil rights issue of *Kulchur*. By 1964 they were even closer—close enough for O'Hara to worry (pleasantly) that they were "getting to be like the Bobsy Twins" (CPT 426). Mackey maintains that what Baraka is in the process of rejecting during this period "is an alleged failure of the Beat and Black Mountain writers to live up to the extra-literary (especially political) implications of their poetics" (DE 25). It appears that Baraka saw O'Hara as living up to the implications of his poetics in more convincing fashion. He himself has suggested as much: "Frank at least had a political sense. Kenneth Koch and Kenward Elmslie and all those people were always highly anti-political, which is why I couldn't get along with them longer than two minutes" (CPT 425). We ought to see O'Hara's "political sense" as one of the natural implications of his more overarching pragmatist sensibility. Like Ellison, he saw his writing as a socially symbolic act and social action as having a symbolic economy. His castigation of "imperialist" ballet in "Answer to Voznesensky and Evtushenko," for instance, foregrounds the political implications of his aesthetic choices, which he would have seen as of a piece with his contemporaneous work on the civil rights issue of *Kulchur.* Both, we should understand, were forms of democratic action, and though O'Hara didn't employ this term, he nonetheless understood them as such.

During the month in which O'Hara told Rivers that he and Jones were "getting to be like the Bobsy Twins," he also suggested to the artist Jan Cremer that they collaborate on drawings and poems to be called "THE NEW YORK AMSTERDAM SET (set as in 'jazz set')." His alternative title, interestingly, was "THE END OF THE FAR WEST . . . the far west being western civilization" (CP 556). In one of the poems for this proposed collaboration, "Here in New York We Are Having A Lot of Trouble with the World's Fair" (CP 480–81), O'Hara writes,

> If every Negro in New York
> > > cruised over the Fair
> > in his fan-jet plane
> > > and ran out of fuel
> > > > the World
> > would really learn something about the affluent
> > > > > society.

The poem ends with the wry observation, "We pay a lot for our entertainment. All right, / roll over." In fact, the poems O'Hara sent to Cremer are full of biting commentary on the state of Western culture ("The Shakespeare Gardens in / Central Park / glisten with blood," "You can't have much of a / revolution on three dollars," "I'm going to plant some corpses"). The implied alternative to a bankrupt Western tradition was the improvised collaboration itself, a kind of collective improvisation that O'Hara increasingly sought out in the early 1960s and that he saw as analogous to the "jazz set." O'Hara's collaborative form was the imminent ideology proposed as corrective to that which he critiqued. Just as Rivers's drawings were, in O'Hara's view, each like a separate jazz performance, so with O'Hara's poems—and *more so,* if they could be produced under the peculiar demands of collective, as opposed to individual, improvisation. By 1964, O'Hara's pragmatic inheritance finds itself *here,* in his self-consciously jazz-shaped collaborations.

———————

I would say that Baraka's *cleanest* break with O'Hara comes quite late, after O'Hara's death, in the 1969 poem "Three Modes of History and Culture," not as a break with O'Hara per se but as a repudiation of pragmatism in the form of Dewey:

> The Party of Insane
> Hope. I've come from there too. Where the dead told lies
> about clever social justice. Burning coffins voted
> and staggered through cold white streets listening
> to Wilkie or Wallace or Dewey through the dead face
> of Lincoln. Come from there and belched it out.[81]

Baraka knew that a repudiation of Dewey was implicitly a repudiation of, at the very least, Black Mountain poetics. He had published an interview with Robert Creeley in *Kulchur* 16 where Creeley admitted as much to Charles Tomlinson:

CT: The intellectual force behind Black Mountain would be John Dewey, then?
RC: Yes, the influence was John Dewey.

. . . .

CT: And how would you evaluate this concept of "energy," as it keeps appearing in any discussion of American art?
RC: Well, one could use Robert Duncan's too little known essay on Olson's work. In Olson's aesthetic—and Duncan sees this as having "forelightings," as he calls it, in Emerson and Dewey—in Olson's aesthetic, "conception cannot be abstracted from doing."[82]

In "Three Modes of History and Culture," Baraka was rejecting "the intellectual force behind Black Mountain," rejecting what he called in another poem of this period "the bitter bullshit rotten white parts" of himself. Yet the ironies are thick. Ellison would insist that the "Party of Insane Hope" was specifically African American in character and that jazz was its most successful artistic manifestation. To see pragmatism as the "white parts" is to ignore its sources in, for instance, Emerson's and Douglass's abolitionist writings, its development via the relationship between James and DuBois as well as Locke, its consummate articulation in Ellison's work, and its recent expression in the work of Cornel West. The pragmatism West has inherited "consists of a future oriented instrumentalism that tries to deploy thought as a weapon to enable more effective action. Its basic impulse," West argues, "is a plebeian radicalism that fuels an antipatrician rebelliousness for the moral aim of enriching individuals and expanding democracy."[83] *This* pragmatism also informs Mackey's work. Most importantly, it is shadowed, from its inception, by black music. As such, Baraka never rejects it outright, coming closest only when, in his most vehemently black nationalist or Maoist phases, he seems to reject democracy as a possibility capable of realization. His dedication to jazz—"Democratic," as he says, "both formal[ly] and mise en scene"— occasionally amounts to a contradiction but more often is the expression of his fundamental allegiance with what might be called radical (African)- American pragmatism. When Baraka notes that O'Hara "dug [Ornette Coleman's] music" and "had a political sense," he provides us with a small window into a heterodox version of pragmatism to which all three artists might belong—a pragmatism whose mood and motives are suggested by Coleman's recent preface to his recordings of the late 1950s and early 1960s, a little Steinian classic in which he talks democracy while refusing to say it (or play it) straight: "Communism, socialism, capitalism, and monarchy in the world (have) & are changing for a truer relationship of the democracy of the individual. Every person who has had a democratic experience by birth or by passport knows there are no hatred or enemies in democracy, because everyone is an individual. Learning, doing, being, are the conversationship for perfecting, protecting and caring of the belief existence as an individual in relationship to everyone, physically, mentally, spiritually—the concept of self."[84] Notice the manner of address: like Ellison's projection of liminal space at the end of *Invisible Man,* like O'Hara's personism that, "like Africa, is on the way," Coleman's grammar of democratic goals and motives ("the belief existence as an individual in relationship to everyone") is in the process of "changing." Their work is democratic symbolic action, antidotes to unjust asymmetries of power, unperfected in the social sphere—"deferred action," as Burke sometimes called it—platforms from which we might critique and change present circumstance in favor of democratic vistas, pragmatic visions of what is imminent.

Epilogue

And then I thought, okay, well, I'm going to need to do something to
integrate this audience.

> Harryette Mullen, on why she wrote Muse & Drudge,
> "A Conversation with Harryette Mullen," *Combo* 1

Emerson's dirge for the black and white soldiers of the 54th Massachusetts Volunteer Infantry (written in the immediate aftermath of Gettysburg; the massacre of the 54th at Fort Wagner; the New York City con-
scription riots in which dozens of black citizens including many children
were murdered and which only subsided when troops returning from
Gettysburg intervened, all during a two-week span in July; and Frederick
Douglass's meeting with Lincoln on August 10, 1863) begins with an
homage to black music.

> Low and mournful be the strain,
> Haughty thought be far from me;
> Tones of penitence and pain,
> Moanings of the Tropic sea;
> Low and tender in the cell
> Where a captive sits in chains,
> Crooning ditties treasured well
> From his Afric's torrid plains.
> Sole estate his sire bequeathed—
> Hapless sire to hapless son—

Was the wailing song he breathed,
And his chain when life was done.

(CW 9:205)

Glancing between the poem and my Webster's Dictionary,[1] Emerson's words somehow seem to have included both their rich and troubled history and their most resonant future meanings.

strain[2] **1.** the body of descendants of a common ancestry. **8.** a streak or trace.

strain[1] **3.** to impair, injure or weaken by stretching or overexertion. **5.** to stretch beyond the proper point or limit. **4.** to cause a mechanical deformation in (a body or structure) as the result of stress. **2.** to exert to the utmost: *to strain one's ears to catch a sound.* **29.** a passage of music. **31.** a passage or piece of poetry. **28.** a flow or burst of language, eloquence.

haughty 1. disdainfully proud; snobbish; arrogant; supercilious; *haughty aristocrats.* **2.** *Archaic.* exalted; lofty or noble.

croon. [late ME *croyn* (to) murmur]

ditty 1. a poem intended to be sung. [ME *dite* < OF *dit(i)e* poem, n. use of ptp. of *ditier* to compose < L *dictare,* freq. Of *dicere* to say]

estate 2. *Law* **b.** The legal position or status of an owner, considered with respect to his property in land or other things. **8.** *Obs.* High social status or rank.

sire 3. *Archaic.* a father or forefather. **4.** *Archaic.* a person of importance or in a position of authority.

bequeath 1. *Law.* to dispose of (personal property, esp. money) by last will. [OE *becwethan* (*be-* BE- + *cwethan* to say)]

hap[1] *Arachaic.* **1.** One's luck or lot. **2.** An occurrence, happening or accident.

hap[2] *Dial.* **1.** to cover with or as with a fabric, esp. with a cloak or bedclothes. **2.** a covering, esp. one of fabric for warmth.

wail 1. to utter a prolonged, inarticulate, mournful cry as in grief or suffering. **2.** *Jazz.* to perform exceptionally well. **3.** *Slang.* to express emotion musically or verbally in a satisfying way. [c.f. OE *wælan* to torment]

DOUGLASS: In hottest summer and coldest winter, I was kept almost naked—no shoes, no stockings, no jacket, no trousers, nothing on but a coarse tow linen shirt, reaching only to my knees. I had no bed. I must have perished with cold, but that, the coldest nights, I used to steal a bag which was used for carrying corn to the mill. I would crawl into this bag, and there sleep on the cold, damp, clay floor, with my head in and feet out. My feet have been so cracked with the frost, that the pen with which I am writing might be laid in the gashes.[2]

DUBOIS: The songs are indeed the siftings of centuries; the music is far more ancient than the words, and in it we can trace here and there signs of development. My grandfather's grandmother was seized by an evil Dutch trader two centuries ago; and coming to the valleys of the Hudson and Housatonic, black, little, and lithe, she shivered and shrank in the harsh north winds, looked longingly at the hills, and often crooned a heathen melody to the child between her knees, thus:

> Do ba—na co—ba, ge—ne me, ge—ne me!
> Do ba—na co—ba, ge—ne me, ge—ne me!
> Ben d' nu—li, nu—li, nu—li, nu—li, ben d' le.

The child sang it to his children and they to their children's children, and so two hundred years it has travelled down to us and we sing it to our children, knowing as little as our fathers what its words may mean, but knowing well the meaning of its music.[3]

———————

In the spirit of emancipation I would lobby for an open-ended definition of what pragmatism means—asking not merely what is its definition but what does it, and what should it, do. In my experience, the history of pragmatism survives most unexpectedly, and therefore most startlingly, in black music and contemporary experimental poetry. In the wake of the 2000 presidential election and the myriad subsequent signs that, as Emerson put it, "Representative Government is really misrepresentative," I am also struck by how badly the moment calls for a pragmatist critique and pragmatist solutions. "Nothing remains but to begin at the beginning to call every man in America to counsel, Representatives do not represent, we must take new order & see how to make representatives represent us," Emerson calls out from history. What Emerson and what pragmatism have to say about an era in which "strict constructionist" judges decide elections against the will of the people, I hope I have made clear over the course of this study. As one radical democrat recently reminded, "Chief Justice William Rehnquist's definition of a 'strict constructionist' jurist when he was President Nixon's assistant attorney general in charge of vetting judicial candidates was one who would be 'not favorably inclined toward claims of either criminal defendants or civil rights plaintiffs.'"[4] I can not spell it out any clearer.

Nor can I extend my own study into the present moment with the kind of care and rigor I have tried to bring to that period whose bookends were civil war and civil rights, my own immersion in contemporary poetry and current events notwithstanding. I approach the arbitrary margin. Moreover the contemporary writing that most interests me is at this very moment risking something unknown, is still becoming. At the very least it demands its own book. But in the few steps I have left, perhaps it would be of use to propose further study. As I suggested earlier, the tradition of "collective reading and connective identity" that Juliana Spahr maps in *Everybody's Autonomy* is directly related to Emerson's "emancipated prose." Spahr's study begins with William James's student Stein, whose "American English is not made by 'them' but by 'everybody,'" and goes on to discuss at length language writers Bruce Andrews and Lyn Hejinian as well as Harryette Mullen and Teresa Hak Kyung Cha, locating in their work "a collective attention to the multiple, an attention to the diversity of response in the name of individual rights."[5] Spahr's criticism suggests that one does not necessarily have to be responding to the writings of pragmatism, narrowly defined, to be doing pragmatist work. Contemporary experimental poetry, then (particularly in the case of someone like Cha), provides an important test case for the flexibility of pragmatism as a defining term. A recent issue of the poetics journal *Tripwire* was devoted to African American writers who "advance content outside the prescribed or expected limits and/or [are] formally innovative or experimental," including Renee Gladman, Giovanni Singleton, Mackey, Mullen, Wanda Coleman, Erica Hunt, Mark McMorris, Lorenzo Thomas, Will Alexander, C. S. Giscombe, and Julie Patton.[6] These writers proceed on the premise that "experimental writing," far from being a departure from African American cultural traditions, is born out of those traditions. Indeed, the writing in *Tripwire* suggests that they share many of the political and aesthetic concerns of the African American pragmatists whom Posnock champions in *Color and Culture*.

I myself would begin by suggesting that Susan Howe and Harryette Mullen are important American pragmatists who speak through their work to each other and to us. I see these two poet-critics as sharing many of the philosophic, social, and aesthetic concerns of the Black Mountain poets[7] but, as Ellison did with Emerson, disrupting the whole notion of lineage in the process by reconfiguring Black Mountain's own ancestry. Reading their work I am again reminded of this previously quoted statement of Creeley's and of a companion statement by Olson on the "Black Mountain" philosophy and aesthetic:

CREELEY: Yes, the influence was John Dewey. . . . One could use Robert Duncan's too little known essay on Olson's work. In Olson's aesthetic—and Duncan sees this as having "forelightings," as he calls it, in Emerson and Dewey—in Olson's aesthetic, "conception cannot be abstracted from doing."[8]

OLSON: And that there was a poetics? Ha ha. Boy, there was no poetic. It was Charlie Parker. Literally it was Charlie Parker.[9]

One contention of my book is that Creeley and Olson are both right, that Dewey and Parker should not be seen as alternatives but rather as collaborators. But Mullen and Howe open the field even more widely. To read Mullen and Creeley, Howe and Olson, side by side provokes a similar series of recalculations, rearticulations, as reading Emerson's antislavery writings or Douglass's "What to the Slave Is the Fourth of July?" alongside James and Dewey. Rather than an implied narrative of Howe descending from Olson like the precocious daughter in a father's vast library, or a description of Mullen writing "Creeleyesque" quatrains, we wake to and confront a new truth, namely, that Olson and Creeley are in debt to black expressivity and women's writing, to Mary Rowlandson, to Douglass, to Dickinson, to Stein, Armstrong, Holliday, Parker, and Monk, among many others.

This is something Creeley readily admits (more readily than Olson, his comment on Parker above notwithstanding), as in the following:

> I feel a rhythmic possibility, an inherent periodicity in the weights and durations of words, to occur in the first few words, or first line, of what it is I am writing. . . . I tend to posit intuitively a balance of four, a foursquare circumstance . . . as in the music of Charlie Parker—an intensive variation on "foursquare" patterns such as "I've Got Rhythm." Listening to him play, I found he lengthened the experience of time, or shortened it, gained a very subtle experience of "weight," all by some decision made within the context of what was called "improvisation"—but what I should rather call the experience of possibility within the limits of his materials (sounds and durations) and their environment. . . . There is an interview with Dizzy Gillespie (in the *Paris Review* No. 35) in which he speaks of rhythm particularly in a way I very much respect. If *time* is measure of change, our sense of it becomes what we can apprehend as significant condition of change—in poetry as well as in music.[10]

Creeley makes the connection of poetry to jazz more explicit when he writes, "Verse turns, and takes turns in turning—which are called verses, in my book, like changes—and not those stanzas or stops, standstills"

(576). This formulation takes us clearly toward both pragmatist and jazz practice. Creeley betrays a characteristically pragmatist distrust of what James called the "substantive parts" or "resting places" as they are manifested in language in favor of what James again called "our acts, our turning-places, where we seem to ourselves to make ourselves and grow" (WJ 1:138). Likewise, Creeley's poem is analogous to the Deweyan self that courts "continuous interchange and blending" and that "comes to include within its balanced movement a greater variety of changes" (LW 10:29). But it is the jazz improviser Parker who comes most immediately to Creeley's mind, Parker who, like his fellow bop composers Gillespie and Monk, would literally lose fellow musicians in their effort to include a greater variety of changes (take Monk's "Brilliant Corners," for instance, which was patched together in the studio from several failed attempts to play it all the way through). A vision of the self-as-jazzman, constantly obliged to incorporate change, is analogous to a pragmatist self that, as Giles Gunn has written, "insists that we abandon the attempt to compensate for the continual disintegration of [the self's] unity and coherence by absolutizing some version of it as a suitable model for the construction of selfhood."[11]

Mullen's *Muse & Drudge*[12] posits a foursquare pattern, four quatrains to a page, unpunctuated, unnumbered for eighty pages. As Creeley does, Mullen articulates "the experience of possibility within the limits of [her] materials." In doing so, both poets raise questions that Howe has attributed to the work of Gertrude Stein (herself crucial to the projects of Creeley, Mullen, and Howe): "Who polices questions of grammar, parts of speech, connection, and connotation? Whose order is shut inside the structure of a sentence?"[13] Mullen constantly tests the boundaries of her stanzas:

> occult iconic crow
> solo mysterioso
> flying way out
> on the other side of far (40)

When I interviewed Mullen with Farah Griffin and Kristen Gallagher, she said of these lines, "I am thinking of someone like a Thelonious Monk, you know, who could just be out, and people just said, 'Well, that's where he is.' "[14] Reading the stanza, I think of Ellison, who, having read "Self-Reliance," flies solo by changing his Waldo to a "mysterious W," and also of Creeley, who, like Monk, positions his signs on the side of the other.

MACKEY: [Creeley] registers the impact of those thoughts of his apprehension on the other inhabitants of the field or space in which this articulation takes place. The allowance he makes for the sensibility of his audience exemplifies a decentralizing impulse, a field approach, his admission that not only other things but also other minds exist. This making evident of the impingement and impact of otherness upon consciousness, of a space occupied by other people, other things, even other places and other times, is what Warren Tallman means when he says of Creeley that "rather than think thoughts he thinks the world." (DE 119–20)

Creeley's "field approach" involves "the acknowledgement of obduracy as a component of experience, an otherness unamenable to appropriation." This, Mackey says, is "the admission that opens the field." When otherness impinges on consciousness, in Creeley as in Monk, the result is often a stutter. Mackey calls this stutter Monk's "troubled eloquence, othered eloquence" (DE 43). Duncan calls it Creeley's "practiced stumbling." I hear it too in Mullen's "occult iconic crow" (the iambs halting at the repeating hard C as in "I cant, I cant, I cant"). Mullen's stutterer plays the "Star Spangled Banner" on a "stark strangled banjo" (18), opening the field to new instruments and vocabularies. The abandoned make way for abandonment.

HOWE: There you have Olson at his wisest. "The stutter is the plot." It's the stutter in American literature that interests me. I hear the stutter as a sounding of uncertainty. What is silenced or not quite silenced. All the broken dreams. . . . We have come onto the stage stammering.[15]

The notion of the "not quite silenced" provides the logic for both Howe's and Mullen's critical excursions back into history—Howe most notably in *My Emily Dickinson* and *The Birth-Mark,* Mullen in *Freeing the Soul: Race, Subjectivity and Difference in the Slave Narratives,* as well as their historicized poetry. Susan Schultz has written, "The more I read and teach [Howe's] work, the more forcefully I am struck by the essential conservatism of her poetics. . . . Howe believes in history and furthermore she believes, unfashionably, in the possibility that history (and gender) can be transcended through art."[16] But Schultz is engaged in an epistemological debate with Howe that seems to me somewhat beside the point. As a reader of Howe's work I would give Schultz's formulation a more pragmatist shading:[17] Howe *chooses* to believe in *a* history *because* of the possibility that history (and gender) can be *transformed* through art. Her history is a half-legible palimpsest masquerading as an official edition. She encourages her readers to consider that history might have been (written) otherwise by proposing that it *was* otherwise. Nor does she set any limits on how we, her readers, might interpret history, her own enthusiastic exegesis notwithstanding. (As she puts it in "The Nonconformist's Memorial," "*We* plural are the speaker."[18]) The prevailing address of her poems and essays is an invitation, ushering us into the library stacks and archives. "Of course I know that history can be falsified, has been falsified," she says. "Still, there are archives and new ways of interpreting their uncompromising details. I am naïve enough to hope the truth will out. . . . If you are a woman, archives hold perpetual ironies. Because the gaps and ironies are where you find yourself" (BM 158). In this fascinating answer to Emerson's question from "Experience" ("Where do we find ourselves," the essay begins), Howe blurs the distinction between a truth that "outs" and a truth that *happens*. Her most Emersonian observation is that one locates *oneself* in history not in spite of but because of its ironies and gaps, because it is, to use James's word, vague.

It is the unsettled quality of history that allows Howe to make her most audacious and valuable assertions: "I think [Mary] Rowlandson is the mother of us all. American writers I mean. Already in 1681, the first narrative written by a white Anglo-American woman is alive with rage and contradiction. She is a prophet. She speaks for us now, in the same way that the slave narratives do" (BM 167). And like Emerson's, Howe's own work provides spaces for readers to insert themselves ("I wanted to write something filled with gaps and words tossed, and words touching, words crowding each other, letters mixing and falling away from each other, commands and dreams, verticals and circles," [BM 175]). Here she is truly Mullen's co-operator. Mullen and Howe share a pragmatist's desire to interrogate and revise history, the heretofore agreed-upon fable, to "unsettle the wilderness," and as Mullen puts it (in the most Emersonian terms), to

> proceed with abandon
> finding yourself where you are
> and who you're playing for
> what stray companion (80)

An emancipated pragmatism happens whenever and wherever a creative mind or community of creative minds engages in democratic symbolic action. While I am writing these last pages, I come upon a special section of new writing from South Africa and Zimbabwe in *Tripwire* 6. There I read poems by South African poet Victor Khulile Nxumalo, along with his explanation of "psycho-narration," a term I have never heard for a method that seems intimately companionable.

KHULILE NXUMALO: psycho-narration is a narrative form, whereby we can discard the idea that a speaker is speaking inside their own head only, as if there is a clear line of distinction between "the inside of their own head" and the "objective world" that receives or upon which the narration falls. . . . i only discovered the theoretical term of what i thought would be a fresh way of taking forward the tradition of mongane serote when i went to academia. but if you look closely at poems in "tsetlo" and "no baby must weep" you cannot miss the jazz based rhythms, the amazing spaces where improvisation happens. . . . one can think of psycho-narration as a multi-vocal way of writing or telling stories that happens not so much like free-style talking/writing/making poems. but as a less authoritative voice, democracy in the poem.[19]

When judges presume to read our constitutions as a set piece, when language itself functions as a setup, democracy must necessarily begin with new words between us.

Notes

CHAPTER 1

1. Gougeon, *Virtue's Hero: Emerson, Antislavery, and Reform* (Athens: University of Georgia Press, 1990), 4. Some of the details in the following paragraph I have gathered from Gougeon's book and I will have more to say about its importance in chapter 2.

2. *The Complete Works of Ralph Waldo Emerson,* centenary edition, vol. 2, ed. E. W. Emerson (Boston: Houghton Mifflin, 1903–4), 9–10. Hereafter cited as CW with volume and page number.

3. John Dewey, *The Middle Works, 1899–1924,* ed. Jo Ann Boydston, 15 vols. (Carbondale: Southern Illinois University Press, 1984), 11:43. Hereafter cited as MW with volume and page number.

4. *The Journals and Miscellaneous Notebooks of Ralph Waldo Emerson,* ed. William H. Gilman and others, 16 vols. (Cambridge: Harvard University Press, Belknap Press, 1960–82), 11:351. Hereafter cited as JMN with volume and page number.

5. Emerson's proposed remedy for the Church was, interestingly, the same as his remedy for the government: "the church should always be new and extemporized" (CW 11:478).

6. In form, this strategy recalls the one that Kenneth Burke makes note of in Hitler's *Mein Kampf:* Of "Hitlerism," Burke notes, "irrational it is, but it is carried on under the slogan of 'Reason' . . . the rationalized family tree for this hate situates it in 'Aryan love.'" See Kenneth Burke, *The Philosophy of Literary Form: Studies in Symbolic Action* (Berkeley: University of California Press, 1973), 199.

7. Richard Rorty, *Essays on Heidegger and Others* (New York: Cambridge University Press, 1991), 13.

8. Clifford Geertz, *The Interpretation of Cultures: Selected Essays* (New York: Basic Books, 1973), 169, 144, 168. For an enlightening example of how an incongruency between cultural structure and social structure actually gives rise to social conflict and change, see Geertz's chapter "Ritual and Social Change: A Javanese Example," pages 142–69.

9. "I hope in these days we have heard the last of conformity and consistency," Emerson says in "Self-Reliance." "Let the words be gazetted and ridiculous henceforward" (CW 2:61). And in a journal entry from 1844, he wrote playfully, "If I made laws for Shakers or a School, I should gazette every Saturday all the words they were wont to use in reporting religious experience as 'Spiritual Life,' 'God,' 'soul,' 'cross,' &c. and if they could not find new ones next week they might remain silent" (JMN 9:117). I should note that as early as 1835 one does find Emerson engaged in a similar and highly suggestive critique of political speech: "Even Everett has come to speak in stereotyped phrase & scarcely originates one expression to a speech. I hope the time will come when phrases will be gazetted as no longer current and it will be unpardonable to say 'the times that tried men's souls' or anything about 'a Cause' & so forth" (JMN 5:92). Even Thomas Paine, it seems, was not exempt from the necessity of reimagining the rhetoric of democracy.

10. *The Letters of Ralph Waldo Emerson,* ed. Ralph L. Rusk and Eleanor Tilton, 10 vols. (New York: Columbia University Press, 1939–96), 5:18. Hereafter cited as L with volume and page number. As I will explain further in chapter 2, the fact that Holmes paid little to no attention to Emerson's abolitionist activities in his biography has had major ramifications for Emerson scholarship. Emerson's full chastisement of Holmes's Southern sympathies is worth quoting:

> The cant of union like the cant of extending the area of liberty by annexing Texas & Mexico is too transparent for its most impudent repeater to hope to deceive you. And for the Union with Slavery no manly person will suffer a day to go by without discrediting disintegrating & finally exploding it. The "union" they talk of is dead and rotten, the real union, that is, the will to keep & renew union, is like the will to keep & renew life, & this alone gives any tension to the dead letter & if we have broken every several inch of the old wooden hoop will still hold us staunch
>
> You see I am not giving weight to your disgust at the narrowness & ferocity of [the abolitionists'] virtue for they know that the side is right & it is leading them out of low estate into manhood & culture.

Attacking the narrowness of philanthropy is something for which Emerson himself is often accused in contemporary criticism but his own critique of Holmes reveals how limiting such criticisms of Emerson actually are.

11. James Livingston, *Pragmatism and the Political Economy of Cultural Revolution, 1850–1940* (Chapel Hill: University of North Carolina Press, 1994), 288.

12. Maryemma Graham and Amritjit Singh, eds., *Conversations with Ralph Ellison* (Jackson: University Press of Mississippi, 1995), 83. Hereafter cited as CE. The full quote reads, "Culturally speaking I inherited the language of Twain, Melville, and Emerson, after whom I'm named."

13. Cornel West, *The American Evasion of Philosophy: A Genealogy of Pragmatism* (Madison: University of Wisconsin Press, 1989).

14. See especially Leonard Harris, ed., *The Critical Pragmatism of Alain Locke: A Reader on Value Theory, Aesthetics, Community, Culture, Race, and Education* (Lanham, Md.: Rowman and Littlefield, 1999). The book contains three essays by the other philosophers significant to my own inquiry: Nancy Fraser, "Another Pragmatism: Alain Locke, Critical Race Theory and the Politics of Culture," 3–20; Judith M. Green, "Alain Locke's Multicultural Philosophy of Value: A Transformative Guide for the Twenty First Century," 85–94; and Richard Shusterman, "Pragmatist Aesthetics: Roots and Radicalism," 97–110. See also Judith M. Green, *Deep Democracy: Community, Diversity and Transformation* (Lanham, Md.: Rowman and Littlefield, 1999).

15. James Livingston calls this process "the morality of form." See Livingston, *Pragmatism and the Political Economy*, 343.

16. Ross Posnock, *Color and Culture: Black Writers and the Making of the Modern Intellectual* (Cambridge: Harvard University Press, 1998). See especially pages 191–92, where Posnock discusses Kallen's and Locke's conversations in relation to their interest in James. Posnock also sees Ellison as a central figure in the pragmatist landscape, but his emphases are quite different than mine, as he focuses on neither Ellison's interest in Emerson nor jazz. I am in obvious agreement with Posnock regarding Jerry Watts's recent critique of Ellison's "social and political disengagement." See Jerry Gafio Watts, *Heroism and the Black Intellectual: Ralph Ellison, Politics, and Afro-American Intellectual Life* (Chapel Hill: University of North Carolina Press, 1994), 116. Posnock asks, "Why does Ellison's protection of black intellectual freedom not count as a profoundly important political achievement?" and determines that "Watts's moralism leaves him with no cogent answer" (300). I will argue in effect that Watts never comes to terms with Ellison's insistence on, to use Jameson's Burkean phrase, "narrative as socially symbolic act."

17. Posnock, *Color and Culture*, 208.

18. *The Works of William James*, ed. Fredson Bowers, 16 vols. (Cambridge: Harvard University Press, 1981), 1:116. Hereafter cited as WJ with volume and page number.

19. Rorty, *Essays on Heidegger*, 13. Rorty's centrality among pragmatists is thrown into doubt once one considers Ellison's alternate "inheritance." Among other things, Ellison's emphasis on the polyvocal character of the American vernacular and the role that vernacular tradition plays in the development and sustenance of American democracy is in dissonant juxtaposition to Rorty's "ethnocentrism," which depends on a more or less homogenized view of American, and even Western, language.

20. These are definitions 1, 2, and 3 of "idiom" from *Webster's New Universal Un-abridged Dictionary* (New York: Barnes and Noble, 1992), 707.

21. Ralph Ellison, Description entitled "Schweitzer Program in the Humanities," 3–4, in "Schweitzer Chair Files," Connor Cruise O'Brien Files, Box 3. New York University Administrative Archive.

22. I am in basic agreement with David L. Hildebrand's essay "Was Kenneth Burke a Pragmatist?" *Transactions of the Charles S. Peirce Society,* 31, no. 3 (summer 1995), 632–58. Hildebrand's pithy answer is, "Yes, but not always" (652). But it's clear that Ellison's interest in Burke focuses on the most pragmatic strains in his thought—as Hildebrand identifies them: his "assault on the neutrality feigned by scientific and philosophical traditions" (633), his view of the universe as an "active theater where countless dramas continually unfold" (636), his characterization of "humans in terms that stress practical, social and creative aspects" (637), and of course his view of language as a form of action.

23. "The Rhetoric of Hitler's 'Battle'" is in Burke, *Philosophy of Literary Form,* 191–220. Ellison's note of thanks is quoted from Timothy L. Parish, "Ralph Ellison, Kenneth Burke, and the Form of Democracy," *Arizona Quarterly* 52, no. 3 (autumn 1995), 119. Parish's essay is an important, indeed catalyzing, contribution to this growing discussion about Burke and Ellison. While I am in basic agreement with his description of Burke's influence, I would want to make what I consider a key distinction between his critique and my own. Parish makes three somewhat casual references to Emerson's relation to Ellison that are essentially analogies rather than discussions of Ellison's actual reading of Emerson. Likewise, there is a similar analogy of Emerson, James, and Burke. While the specificity of Parish's inquiry is a perfectly good explanation for these cursory connections, there are, I think, two problematic consequences to his method. First, the lack of a specific recognition of how Ellison was affected by Emerson's most pragmatist/democratic thinking leads to the utterly peculiar assertion toward the end of the essay that the final lines of *Invisible Man* do not represent "a gesture of with-drawal, of uppity Emersonianism." Emerson's methodology is so integral to the rhetorical strategies at work in Ellison's final lines that, as I suspect Parish knows, vague and inaccurate characterizations such as "uppity Emersonianism" only serve to cloud the issue; such characterizations rely on an ahistorical view of Emerson with which Ellison would have wholly disagreed. What Parish describes as the "Burkean process in which 'doing' can become its own 'undoing' in the name of a revised 'doing,'" Ellison would have recognized as an Emersonian process. Secondly, once our eye is drawn away from Ellison's actual signifying on Emerson, it is that much more difficult to describe Ellison's connection of American philosophy and jazz, since, at least in the context of *Invisible Man,* that connection is worked out through Emerson more so than Burke. See Parish, "Ralph Ellison, Kenneth Burke, and the Form of Democracy," 118, 121–23, 125, 141. For more discussion of Ellison and Burke, see Robert G. O'Meally, "On Burke and the Vernacular: Ralph Ellison's Boomerang of History," in *History and Memory in African American Culture,* eds. Genevieve Fabre and Robert G. O'Meally (New

York: Oxford University Press, 1994), 244–60. See also Berndt Ostendorf, "Ralph Waldo Ellison: Anthropology, Modernism and Jazz," in *New Essays on Invisible Man,* ed. Robert G. O'Meally (New York: Cambridge University Press, 1988), 105. Ostendorf asserts that Ellison "is a radical American pragmatist. . . . In his social philosophy he stands in an American moral tradition that includes Emerson, Whitman, James, Dewey and Mead," but his essay is not designed to elaborate on this assertion. More recently, James M. Albrecht's article "Saying Yes, Saying No: Individualist Ethics in Ellison, Burke, and Emerson," appeared in *PMLA* (January 1999), 46–63. While I am in agreement with Albrecht regarding the intensity of connections between Emerson, Burke, and Ellison, we differ significantly on the nature of those connections. I would cite two central differences: 1) Albrecht emphasizes Burke's "comic frame of acceptance" rather than his "rhetorical theory of form"; as a result the issue of langauge as symbolic action, so crucial to Ellison's sense of both Emerson and Burke, remains obscured; and 2) though Albrecht admits that for Emerson the self "exists through its social and historical engagements," he fails to address Emerson's most relevant "engagement"—his abolitionism, about which Ellison was keenly aware. These two differences are crucial because without the connections I have emphasized, it is impossible to understand Ellison's view of pragmatism and jazz as related forms of democratic symbolic action.

24. Frank Lentricchia, *Criticism and Social Change* (Chicago: University of Chicago Press, 1983), 19.

25. Indeed, Ellison had his own description of this phenomenon, in the form of "The Little Man at Chehaw Station," who frustrates all attempts to make a priori assumptions about value and to construct hierarchies based on those assumptions. "In this country there'll always be a little man hiding behind the stove," he recalls a teacher telling him, "and he'll know the music, and the tradition, and the standards of musicianship required for whatever you set out to perform." Of this suggestion, Ellison writes, "the little stove warmer has come to symbolize nothing less than the enigma of aesthetic communication in American democracy. I especially associate him with the metaphoric character of the general American audience, and with the unrecognized and unassimilated elements of its taste." See Ralph Ellison, *Going to the Territory* (New York: Vintage, 1986), 4, 6. Hereafter cited as GT. Parish's essay "The Form of Democracy," contains an excellent reading of "The Little Man at Chehaw Station." Parish discusses "antagonistic cooperation" (128), a phrase that appears in Ellison's story (7).

26. West's quote is from *American Evasion of Philosophy,* 5. Not included in West's genealogy is Ellison, and I believe that this omission is partly the consequence of West's mistaken view of Emerson as a "typical nineteenth-century North American 'mild racist'" (27), a view that it seems keeps West from recognizing Ellison's dialogue with Emerson as a key genealogical link rather than a tacit repudiation.

27. Burke's passage is in *Philosophy of Literary Form,* 89–90. Dewey's quotation is in *Art as Experience,* which precedes Burke's statement by seven years. See John Dewey *The Later Works, 1925–1953,* ed. Jo Ann Boydston, 17 vols. (Carbondale: Southern Illi-

nois University Press, 1984), 10:114. Hereafter cited as LW with volume and page number. For more discussion of Burke's ties to pragmatism, see Giles Gunn, *Thinking across the American Grain: Ideology, Intellect, and the New Pragmatism* (Chicago: University of Chicago Press, 1992), 1–2, 14–16. Parish, in his discussion of Burke and Ellison observes that "Following Emerson's observation in 'The Poet' that 'We are symbols and inhabit symbols' and William James' insistence that we see our ideas and interpretations as actions, Burke maintains that our words are activating agents which also encode the agents subsequent actions." See "The Form of Democracy," 123. For a more developed analysis of Burke's relationship to Dewey in particular, see "Kenneth Burke: Modernism and the Motives of Rhetoric" in Paul Jay, *Contingency Blues: The Search for Foundation in American Criticism* (Madison: University of Wisconsin Press, 1997), 109–41. Jay describes Burke's "commitment to a pragmatic or rhetorical theory of form," and though he wants to distinguish Burke from Dewey by the difference in the reception they give the avant-garde movements of their day (Burke being significantly more receptive), he neglects the fact that Burke's theoretical acceptance of, say, New York dada, is largely predicated on his reading of Dewey. As Burke himself writes, "It is not gratuitous that Professor Dewey has written so brilliantly of art" (388).

28. Livingston has written brilliantly on this concept of form in relation to Frederic Jameson: "The morality of form, I would then say, is this anticipatory arena where actuality and possibility, past and present, are allowed to collaborate on a history of the future. Hence to suggest that form or genre should be treated as the 'immanent ideology' or the 'political unconscious' of fictional discourse, as Frederic Jameson does in *The Political Unconscious: Narrative as Socially Symbolic Act* (Ithaca, N.Y.: Cornell University Press, 1981), is not to remint the coinage of base and superstructure, it is instead to suggest that *form* is to fictional discourse what *paradigm* is to non-fictional discourse—that is, a historically specific protocol that naturalizes an observable reality and constitutes a social relation between practitioners (writers) and their potential publics." See Livingston, *Pragmatism and the Political Economy,* 343. As Livingston well knows, Jameson's idea of the political unconscious (note his subtitle) owes a deep debt to Burke. Ellison, it should be said, has a nearly identical concept of form: "The novel is rhetorical. For whatever else it tries to do, it must do so by persuading us to accept the novelist's projection of an experience which, on some level or mixtures of levels, we have shared with him, and through which we become empathetically involved in the illusory and plotted depiction of life which we identify as fictional art" (GT 243). To this sense of the novel Ellison adds that "the American audience [is] far more than a receptive instrument. . . . While that audience is eager to be transported, astounded, thrilled, it counters the artist's manipulation of forms with an attitude of antagonistic cooperation; acting, for better or worse, as both collaborator and judge" (7).

29. Dewey writes that the artist is "a born experimenter . . . because he has to express an intensely individualized experience through means and materials that belong to the common and public world. . . . Only because the artist operates experi-

mentally does he open new fields of experience and disclose new aspects and qualities in familiar scenes and objects" (LW 10:148–49).

30. *Trading Twelves: The Selected Letters of Ralph Ellison and Albert Murray,* eds. Albert Murray and John F. Callahan (New York: Modern Library, 2000), 117.

31. Geertz, *Interpretation of Cultures,* 449.

32. Ellison, "Schweitzer Program," 3–4.

33. Ralph Ellison, *Shadow and Act* (New York: Vintage, 1964), 102. Hereafter cited as SA.

34. Nathaniel Mackey, *Discrepant Engagement: Dissonance, Cross-Culturality, and Experimental Writing* (New York: Cambridge University Press, 1993), 303. Hereafter cited as DE. Mackey's examples of eclectic individuals are principally jazz musicians: Thelonious Monk, Ornette Coleman, Cecil Taylor, and others. Mackey has suggested to me in conversation that Ellison's antiphonal model of jazz, whereby the individual plays both "within and against the group," was the precedent for his own description of the individual–group dynamic quoted above.

35. Ellison, "Schweitzer Program," 2.

36. "Praise then the interruption of our composure" is Duncan's full phrase. Robert Duncan, *Bending the Bow* (New York: New Directions, 1968), ix.

37. Little's discussion is from an interview in *Metronome* with Robert Levin, quoted in the liner notes to *Eric Dolphy at the Five Spot,* a live recording from July 16, 1961, reissued by Prestige, 1991. Little goes on to say of his idea of "integration": "I'm interested in putting sounds against sounds and I'm interested in freedom also. But I have respect for form," a statement that is obviously cousin to Ellison's central artistic concerns.

38. This is Burke's characterization of "the pragmatist" in *Philosophy of Literary Form,* 382.

39. Ellison, "Schweitzer Program," 4.

40. Kenneth Burke, *Permanence and Change: An Anatomy of Purpose,* 3rd ed. (Berkeley: University of California Press, 1984), 119, 121. Hildebrand has a valuable discussion of "planned incongruity" vis-à-vis pragmatism. See "Was Kenneth Burke a Pragmatist?" 642–43.

41. Comparisons between Ellison's rhetoric and that of other pragmatists highlight this important change. Take the following description of the mind by James, "Every experience undergone by the brain leaves in it a modification which is one factor in determining what manner of experiences the following ones shall be. . . . As our brains and minds are actually made, it is impossible to get certain m's and n's in immediate sequence and keep them pure. . . . The second object is not n pure, but n-as-different-from-m" (WJ 8:471). While I would say that one of the motives behind James's description of the mind as hybrid and integrative is clearly his desire for a "democratic" psychology, it is interesting to note what Ellison does with the same basic premise about the mind. "I'm not a separatist," Ellison says. "The imagination is inte-

grative. That's how you make the new—by putting something else with what you've got. And I'm unashamedly an American integrationist" (CE 235). Notice how Ellison erases distinctions between his psychological point and his social one, assuring that the practice of psychology can't be isolated from its cultural implications, particularly in regard to race relations.

42. I take this phrase from Stanley Crouch: "The jazz band put democracy into aesthetic action." Of course Crouch would readily admit that he arrived at this phrase via Ellison's lexicon. See Stanley Crouch, *The All-American Skins Game, or, the Decoy of Race: The Long and Short of It, 1990–1994* (New York: Vintage, 1995), 15. I feel compelled to add that in the past decade, Crouch's writings on race and jazz have become increasingly essentialist and thus anathema to the tradition of Ellisonian pragmatism he often claims as his own.

43. Quoted in Paul Mariani, *William Carlos Williams: A New World Naked* (New York: McGraw-Hill, 1981), 518.

44. *The Selected Letters of William Carlos Williams,* ed. John C. Thirwall (New York: McDowell, Obolensky, 1957), 224. Hereafter cited as SL.

45. William Carlos Williams, *Imaginations* (New York: New Directions, 1970), 175, 195. Hereafter cited as I.

46. *The Autobiography of William Carlos Williams* (New York: New Directions, 1967), 391. Hereafter cited as A.

47. Though Williams disliked the term "free verse," I take it here to be suggestive of a line of writers with whom Williams would have happily included himself. In his essay "Notes Apropos 'Free Verse,'" Williams's great admirer Robert Creeley cites "Yvor Wintors' tracking of 'impulse' as informing principle in Emerson's discussions of poetry, as equally in Whitman, and then in Crane's," and the example he ends his essay with is Williams. See *The Collected Essays of Robert Creeley* (Berkeley: University of California Press, 1989), 492, 485. Not surprisingly, Creeley has also called Burke "an exceptional critical intelligence" (522).

48. *The Dial* 68, no. 6 (June 1920), 688. Mike Weaver discusses the essay and Williams's interest in it in *William Carlos Williams: The American Background* (New York: Cambridge University Press, 1971), 32–34. For Williams's very funny "The Spirit of '76" and a brief commentary on it see *The Collected Poems of William Carlos Williams,* ed. A. Walton Litz and Christopher MacGowan, 2 vols. (New York: New Directions, 1986), 1:128, 491–92. For Williams's commentary on the title for *Al Que Quiere!* see pages 480–81.

49. William Carlos Williams, *The Embodiment of Knowledge,* ed. Ron Loewinsohn (New York: New Directions, 1974), 123. Hereafter cited as EK. For comparison's sake one might go to Dewey's essay "From Absolutism to Experimentalism" in *The Philosophy of John Dewey,* ed. John J. McDermott (Chicago: University of Chicago Press, 1973), 1–12, though sentiments such as those expressed by Williams above can be found almost anywhere in Dewey's work.

50. William Carlos Williams, *In the American Grain* (New York: New Directions, 1956), 230. Hereafter cited as AG. Williams is speaking here of Poe, but it applies, of course, equally to himself.

51. Henry James, *Portrait of a Lady, Complete Text with Introduction and Historical Contexts,* ed. Jan Cohn (Boston: Houghton Mifflin, 2001), 23. Of course some might argue that James's portrait is almost as purposeful and funny a dig at English speech as Williams's is.

52. Brian A. Bremen, "Attitudes Toward History," in *Critical Essays on William Carlos Williams,* eds. Steven Gould Axelrod and Helen Deese (New York: G. K. Hall, 1995), 184. Those interested should also see Bremen's excellent book *William Carlos Williams and the Diagnostics of Culture* (New York: Oxford University Press, 1993).

53. In a 1961 interview with Walter Sutton (which I will reference again later for its relevance to Williams's view of jazz) Williams elaborates: "I've been insisting that since the day of Pound a cultured American language, which was different from English, which was not recognized by Pound, has grown up. . . . It had not been recognized as a poetic language at all, and all our generation was rejected, because we didn't speak English, the English of the schools. But we were—I was talking a language I was familiar with, that I got from—Polish people, we'll say, any man that would talk to me at all. Pound would want to take it to Harvard or some such place." See Linda Wagner, ed., *Interviews with William Carlos Williams:"Speaking Straight Ahead"* (New York: New Directions, 1976), 44. This same passage is quoted in Sergio Rizzo's fine essay "The Other Girls of *Paterson*—Old and New," in *William Carlos Williams Review* 20 no. 1 (spring 1994), 48.

54. I'm thinking here in particular of something Williams wrote in *The Embodiment of Knowledge:* "The Language is the storehouse of the people. Language is not stable. Leaks occur and—though they are aware of it or not—the lives of people are modified" (117).

55. Aldon Nielsen, *Reading Race: White American Poets and the Racial Discourse in the Twentieth Century* (Athens: University of Georgia Press, 1988), 80. Hereafter cited as RR.

56. Aldon Nielsen, "Whose Blues?" in *William Carlos Williams Review* 15 no. 2 (fall 1989), 6.

57. For "Ol' Bunk's Band" see Williams, *Collected Poems of William Carlos Williams,* 2:149. *Man Orchid* is collected in full in Williams, *The Massachusetts Review* 14 (1973), 77–117.

58. For Mariani's discussion of these incidents see Mariani, *A New World Naked,* 512–16 and his essay "Williams' Black Novel" in *The Massachusetts Review* 14 (1973), 67–75. I have already mentioned Rizzo's "The Other Girls of *Paterson*." An abbreviated version, "Can 'Beautiful Thing' Speak? Race and Gender in *Paterson,*" appears in Axelrod and Deese, *Critical Essays on William Carlos Williams,* 199–212. Mackey's discussion appears in DE 240–53.

59. See Williams, *Man Orchid,* 111. Mackey is making reference to Mailer's essay

196 NOTES TO PAGES 41-50

"The White Negro," which can be found in Norman Mailer, *Advertisements for Myself* (Cambridge: Harvard University Press, 1992), 337-58.

60. Nielsen puts it this way: "For Williams from the outset, as in so many of his writings on blacks, *Man Orchid* was a repository for libidinal longings, a refuge from the worn restrictions of puritanism, and an opportunity to oppose what he saw as the pure American impulse of jazz, as represented in Bunk Johnson's music, to the agonized and Anglicized wasteland of Eliot" (RR 81).

61. See the liner notes to The Cecil Taylor Quartet, *Looking Ahead!* Contemporary Records S7562, 1959.

62. Ellison notes how "Armstrong and any other jazz musician of that period would take a theme and start improvising. Then he would pay his respects to [Verdi's] *Aida*, to any number of operas, to light opera, or to religious music. All this came out in the course of improvisation" (CE 90). In addition, I'm thinking of a wonderful moment in Ornette Coleman's composition "Congeniality" in which, during a solo, Coleman quotes Tchaikovsky's 1st Piano Concerto and runs it into the typical melody of the American folk expression "shave and a haircut, two bits."

63. "Brathwaite provides an interesting counterpoint, picturing Eliot and black music as allies when he notes the influence of Eliot's recorded readings in the Caribbean: 'In that dry deadpan delivery, the riddims of St. Louis . . . were stark and clear for those of us who at the same time were listening to the dislocations of Bird, Dizzy, and Klook. And it is interesting that on the whole, the Establishment couldn't stand Eliot's voice—far less jazz!'" (DE 249).

64. Nielsen notes a reference Williams makes to black entertainer Bert Williams in *American Grain* (209), reminding us that Williams "often was required to black up with burnt cork so that his face would be dark enough to meet the expectations of his white audiences" (RR 75).

65. Mariani, "Williams' Black Novel," 73; and *A New Word Naked*, 516.

66. Rizzo, "Can 'Beautiful Thing' Speak?" 202-05.

67. William Carlos Williams, *Paterson* (New York: New Directions, 1992), 125. Hereafter, references cited as P.

68. Wagner, *Interviews with William Carlos Williams*, 55. For Williams's letter to Baraka see Mariani, *A New World Naked*, 848.

CHAPTER 2

1. See also Gougeon, *Virtue's Hero*, 220.

2. Jonathan Levin, *The Poetics of Transition: Emerson, Pragmatism, and American Literary Modernism* (Durham: Duke University Press, 1999). Levin distinguishes his view from West's in noting that "West's narrative . . . ignores the unsettled, unsettling quality of the Emersonian moment of transition" (xii). What I am arguing is that Emerson saw that very unsettling as the predicate of a democratic politics. I will discuss Emerson's

use of the concept of "transition" (as well as another word focused on by Levin, "abandonment") in his anti-slavery writings later in this chapter. See also West, *American Evasion of Philosophy,* 5.

3. Stanley Cavell, "What's the Use of Calling Emerson a Pragmatist?" in *The Revival of Pragmatism: New Essays on Social Thought, Law, and Culture,* ed. Morris Dickstein (Durham: Duke University Press, 1998), 75. I do not disagree with the distinction that Cavell draws. At the same time I don't believe that distinction is the central one when considering the question of whether Emerson can be called a pragmatist. It seems clear to me that Emerson is both a pragmatic artist, as Dewey defined that term in *Art as Experience* (1934), and a pragmatic "philosopher of democracy," as defined in Dewey's "Philosophy and Democracy" (1918). For *Art as Experience* see LW 10. That Emerson extends Dewey's emphasis on unpredictability to the very fabric of his language (as Dewey, by and large, does not) hardly makes him less of a pragmatist. Indeed I would say (and I believe Dewey himself agrees on this point) it makes him the pragmatist par excellence.

4. Ralph Ellison, *Invisible Man* (New York: Vintage, 1952), 6. Hereafter cited as IM. Of course Ellison himself borrows the phrase in part from Emerson's "Circles": "Our life is an apprenticeship to the truth that around every circle another can be drawn; that there is no end in nature, but every end is a beginning" (CW 2:301).

5. Harold Bloom, *Agon: Towards a Theory of Revisionism* (New York: Oxford University Press, 1982), 145–78; Barbara Packer, *Emerson's Fall: A New Interpretation of the Major Essays* (New York: Continuum, 1982); Evan Carton, *The Rhetoric of American Romance* (Baltimore: Johns Hopkins University Press, 1985); and Levin, *Poetics of Transition.* Stanley Cavell and Richard Poirier have of course written numerous books and articles on this subject. A brief list of those most important to me would include Cavell, *This New Yet Unapproachable America: Lectures after Emerson after Wittgenstein* (Albuquerque: Living Batch Press, 1989) and "Aversive Thinking: Emersonian Representations in Heidegger and Nietzsche," in *New Literary Theory: A Journal of Theory and Interpretation* 22, no. 1 (1991); and Poirier, *The Renewal of Literature* (New York: Random House, 1987), *Poetry and Pragmatism* (Cambridge: Harvard University Press, 1992,) and *Trying it Out in America* (New York: Farrar, Straus and Giroux, 1999), 204–18.

6. It is clear in consulting the *Oxford English Dictionary* that both meanings would have been operative in Emerson's day. "To pass" as in either "to pass by, to move along" or "to die" were common; "to pass for" as in "to be accepted as" has some interesting precedents, not least of which is this, from Shakespeare's *Merchant of Venice,* i.ii: "God made him, and therefor let him pass for a man." Equally interesting is Addison's use of the phrase in regard to racial identity in 1711: "I sometimes pass for a Jew in the Assembly of Stock-Jobbers at Jonathans." Needless to say, Emerson's complex phrase destabilizes all such attempts to distinguish between true and fabricated identities.

7. Bloom, *Agon,* 174.

8. Juliana Spahr, *Everybody's Autonomy: Connective Reading and Collective Identity* (Tus-

caloosa: University of Alabama Press, 2001), 12–13. Spahr's chief examples are Gertrude Stein, Bruce Andrews, Lyn Hejinian, Harryette Mullen, and Theresa Hak Kyung Cha.

9. Emerson goes on to identify these American rhetoric and rituals as specifically democratic, employing the fancifully colloquial metaphor of the "liberty-cap": "If we never put on the liberty-cap until we were freemen by love and self-denial, the liberty cap would mean something. I wish to see America not like the old powers of the earth, grasping, exclusive and narrow." That a model of self-reliance must necessarily include a measure of self-denial became a key component of his later thinking on the subject.

10. Geertz, *Interpretation of Cultures,* 449, 91.

11. Gougeon, *Virtue's Hero,* 4. See also "Emerson's Emancipation Address" and "The Fugitive Slave Act" in Robert D. Richardson, Jr., *Emerson: The Mind on Fire: A Biography* (Berkeley: University of California Press, 1995), 395–99, 495–99. Richardson, in brief, and Gougeon, in great detail, describe the damaging misconceptions about what was actually Emerson's extremely committed career as an abolitionist. Richardson explains the genesis of such misconceptions: "First, his principal notebook on the subject ("WO Liberty") was lost from 1903 until 1966. Second, many of his antislavery talks are still in manuscript, and when those that were published were gathered together, they were put in a volume harmlessly called *Miscellanies,* when it might have been *The Fugitive Slave Law and Other Papers.* Finally, both [Oliver Wendell] Holmes and [James Eliot] Cabot, the authors of the most influential Emerson biographies before [Ralph] Rusk's, made careful and conscious efforts to underplay Emerson's antislavery work" (497–98). Thus supportive facts such as that Emerson actively campaigned for Free Soil candidate John G. Palfrey in 1851; that, from 1854 until the Great Emancipation, Emerson's home was a designated stop on the Underground Railroad; that he "entertained John Brown at his home, raised money for him, and spoke on his behalf"; that he was intimate friends with all of the "Secret Six" who helped Brown plan the Harpers Ferry raid and harbored one of them, Franklin Sanborn, as a fugitive in his home— have gone largely unnoticed by critics of both Emerson and pragmatism. As an example of how pervasive and problematic this lack of notice has been, see West, *American Evasion of Philosophy,* 22–35. West, who is generally quite nuanced in his reading of pragmatism and race, describes Emerson as a "typical nineteenth century North Atlantic 'mild racist' " and mistakenly concludes that "unlike Thoreau" there was "relatively little risk" to his abolitionism. For critical precedent West relies almost exclusively on Philip Nicoloff, *Emerson on Race and History: An Examination of English Traits* (New York: Columbia University Press, 1961), written before the rediscovery of the "WO Liberty" notebook. Gougeon has further addressed this critical misconception by republishing many of the essays in *Miscellanies* as well as other, previously unpublished antislavery essays in Len Gougeon and Joel Myerson, ed., *Emerson's Antislavery Writings* (New Haven, Conn.: Yale University Press, 1995). Hereafter cited as ASW.

12. In addition to Gougeon's *Virtue's Hero,* Albert von Frank's more recent *The Trials of Anthony Burns: Freedom and Slavery in Emerson's Boston* (Cambridge: Harvard University

Press) provides invaluable information on and analysis of Emerson's role in the abolitionist movement. Von Frank fleshes out the importance of Emerson's "aggressively noninstrumental thought" (282), arguing that "Emerson was a force in antislavery because of his idealism, not in spite of it" (327). I myself am more inclined to mark a shift in Emerson's thought brought on by his abolitionism, whereby he began to think of "noninstrumental thought" specifically as a form of socially symbolic action.

13. See Gay Wilson Allen, *Waldo Emerson: A Biography* (New York: Viking Press, 1981), 619. John Carlos Rowe notes the event and quotes from Allen in John Carlos Rowe, *At Emerson's Tomb: The Politics of Classic American Literature* (New York: Columbia University Press, 1997), 17.

14. Anita Haya Patterson, *From Emerson to King: Democracy, Race, and the Politics of Protest* (New York: Oxford University Press, 1997), 12.

15. Rowe, *Emerson's Tomb*, 22.

16. Albert von Frank, "Mrs. Brackett's Verdict: Transcendental Antislavery Work," in *Transient and Permanent,* eds. Charles Capper and Conrad Edick Wright (Boston: Massachusetts Historical Society, 1999), 395. See also von Frank, *Trials of Anthony Burns,* 327.

17. Rowe, *Emerson's Tomb*, 19.

18. The quote is from James's critique of Kant in *The Principles of Psychology* (1890), which comprises volumes 8, 9, and 10 of the collected *Works,* corresponding to volumes 1 and 2 of the original publication as well as a third "index" volume. James called Kant's transcendental ego "as ineffectual and windy an abortion as Philosophy can show" (8:345).

19. It is symptomatic of Rowe's case that while he goes to great effort to connect Emerson to "the literary modernism that would find its primary critical function in the aesthetic irony practiced by the high moderns and theorized by Anglo-American New Criticism," (1) he never once cites or discusses the American thinkers who by their own admission and, indeed, self-evidently are Emerson's most assiduous readers: James, Dewey, and Burke.

20. While Poirier rightly notes that in a short passage in the sixth section of "Experience," "Emerson adumbrates no less than three ideas that were to become central to James" and to pragmatism, I am even more struck by James's indebtedness to "Montaigne." The following seems to me a veritable miniature of the opening passages of James's *Pragmatism:* "The abstractionist and the materialist thus mutually exasperating each other . . . there arises a third party to occupy the middle ground between these two" (CW 4:154–55). See Poirier, *Poetry and Pragmatism,* 41.

21. Frederick Douglass, *Narrative of the Life of Frederick Douglass, An American Slave, Written By Himself* (1845; reprint, New York: W. W. Norton, 1997), 26.

22. For an interesting discussion of Emerson's sense of language as "vehicular" see Carton, *Rhetoric of American Romance,* 82. "Neither by nor in language are vehicle and object, symbol and fact, fully united or finally solved; rather, they are held in the kind

of volatile solution that is the agent of experimentation and the stuff of possibility"
(82). I would only add that Emerson increasingly brought this observation to bear on
his concurrent view that language is socially symbolic action.

23. More often than not, contemporary criticism of Emerson's rhetorical strategies has taken its cue from the historicist work of Bercovitch and Jehlen. Jehlen emphasizes the way in which Emerson's rhetoric affirms "an ultimate transcendent rec-
onciliation of all apparent oppositions," a view that is dependent on the line Bercovitch
draws between Emerson and the doctrinaire Puritans who "enlisted the covenant of
grace as a vehicle of social control," as well as on a more general sense of how "ideology
in America requires a constant conflict between self and society," conflict that is nonetheless innocuous, what Jehlen calls "non-antagonistic rhetorical dualism." See Myra
Jehlen, *American Incarnation: The Individual, The Nation, and The Continent* (Cambridge:
Harvard University Press, 1986), 108, 110; and Sacvan Bercovitch, *The American Jere-
miad* (Madison: University of Wisconsin Press, 1978), 47, and *The Office of The Scarlet
Letter* (Baltimore: Johns Hopkins University Press, 1991), 145. Patterson reproduces
this logic in arguing that "both Emerson and the founders designed a rhetoric that
would create a consensus over the meaning of self-ownership, and both resolve conflict
by arriving at a self-contradictory formula for representation that precludes the possibility of denial" (19). Bloom, Poirier, Cavell, and others do a strong job in arguing
against this interpretation from a structural point of view, and I am indebted to them
as such. However, it seems equally if not more important that Emerson's abolitionist
activity and the writing identified with it calls into question the historicist position
from a *historicist* point of view. Gougeon's book receives a single, tellingly brief footnote in *From Emerson to King:* "a useful history of Emerson's involvement in the abolitionist movement." That history does not seem to have been of much use to Patterson.
See also Christopher Newfield, *The Emerson Effect: Individualism and Submission in America*
(Chicago: University of Chicago Press, 1996). Newfield gives Gougeon similar treatment, a single footnote that comprises one sentence (258 n. 62), though he draws
extensively on Philip Nicoloff's "more critical" (and forty-year-old) study, *Emerson on
Race and History,* a study that, as I have said, was conducted without the benefit of
Emerson's most extensive consideration of slavery and race—his "WO Liberty" notebook, which was lost between 1903 and 1966. Newfield, following suit, makes no reference to the "WO Liberty notebook" in his discussion of Emerson's "liberal racism"
(174–208). He does give Emerson his due in noting his vehement abolitionism; but as
I discuss in a later footnote he persists in a view of Emerson's thorough-going racism
which is simply contrary to the facts. Moreover, neither Patterson nor Newfield cite
Richardson's crucial recent biography, *Mind on Fire.*

24. Newfield, *Emerson Effect,* 196; Patterson, *From Emerson to King,* 93.

25. Patterson, *From Emerson to King,* 152–53.

26. Patterson notes that DuBois quoted Emerson's second motto from "History"
("I am the owner of the sphere / Of the seven stars and the solar year; / Of Caesar's

hand, and Plato's brain, / Of Lord Christ's Heart and Shakespeare's strain") to the National Colored League of Boston in 1891 as evidence that "the living bequest of a million souls is the property of you" (163). Again, Patterson, believing Emerson to be a racist, sees this as ironic, but it is not ironic in the least. In fact, one wonders whether DuBois, in quoting from "History," also has in mind the quatrain from "Boston Hymn" regarding the slave's self-ownership that I quoted earlier—whether, that is, DuBois had read through Emerson's antislavery writings, as Ralph Ellison would later.

27. This, along with countless other examples, puts the lie to Newfield's argument that Emerson "attached racial hierarchy to the permanent order of things" (196). Newfield distinguishes this from any claim that Emerson believed African Americans were destined "to bear their biologically fated racial death" (196); but in implying Emerson's guilt by association to Agassiz's biology-based "racism and hatred for social equality" (Agassiz, Newfield surmises, "must have been . . . hard . . . for Emerson to ignore" 198), and in implying that Emerson trafficked in a sort of proto–Social Darwinism whereby African Americans would "go the way of natural law" (196), Newfield renders moot the question of whether "fate" is for Emerson biological or social. In concluding that there is "no indication that Emerson ever conceived of the possibility of black-white social equality" (197), Newfield ignores all evidence to the contrary: such evidence would include Emerson's observation that "the negro has saved himself and the white man very patronizingly says, I have saved you" (JMN 9:126), a sentiment that veritably explodes Newfield's whole argument. In the same vein, I would ask, once Emerson has quoted Montesquieu (repeatedly) saying "it would not do to suppose that negroes were men, lest it should turn out that whites were not" (CW 11:140), are not any arguments for the inferiority of blacks marched out in the course of Emerson's *overall* argument suffused with irony? Finally, I would say that Newfield's ultimate conclusion that, biology aside, Emerson's "racism hinged on naturalizing black passivity and on the natural hierarchies of meritocracy" (201) is undone by, among many other things, Emerson's positing of the black soldier and reader as the "true American Genius" in 1864, something I will discuss later in the chapter.

28. Patterson, *From Emerson to King*, 6.

29. Charles Woodbury, *Talks with Emerson* (New York: Baker and Taylor, 1890), 28. Hereafter cited as TE.

30. Richard Poirier, "The Question of Genius," *Raritan: A Quarterly Review* 5, no. 4 (1986), 79.

31. Just prior to this quote Emerson provides an early formulation of the relationship between reading and self-reliance: "Books are the best of things, well used; abused, among the worst. . . . The [abused] book, the college, the school of art, the institution of any kind, stop with some past utterance of genius. This is good, say they, let us hold by this. They pin me down" (CW 1:89—90).

32. Jacques Derrida, "Structure, Sign, and Play in the Discourse of the Human Sciences," in *The Critical Tradition: Classic Texts and Contemporary Trends*, ed. David H. Rich-

202 NOTES TO PAGES 62–66

ter (New York: St. Martin's Press, 1989), 961. For comments on this connection between Emerson and post-structuralism see Rorty, *Essays on Heidegger*, 2–3; and Poirier, *Poetry and Pragmatism*, 135, 149, 156. Poirier goes so far as to suggest that much of what we consider post-Nietzschean language theory is a consequence of Nietzsche "assiduously reading Emerson," a suggestion given some weight by the following observations from Frederick Ives Carpenter, *Emerson Handbook* (New York: Hendricks House, 1953), 247: "These facts are established: that Nietzsche always carried a volume of Emerson with him when he traveled, beginning about 1862 and continuing for more than twenty years until 1882; that Nietzsche owned about four volumes of Emerson which he annotated heavily, and is known to have borrowed others; that he actually composed the first drafts of fragments of his works in the margins of Emerson's books; and that many sentences of his have been identified as free adaptations of Emerson's. . . . During the most creative years of his life Nietzsche read Emerson more frequently, continuously and deeply than any modern writer after Goethe; and he praised him more enthusiastically." Henry LeRoy Finch quotes this same passage from Carpenter in his introduction to *Talks with Emerson*, xvi–xvii. See also Gunn, *Thinking across the American Grain*, 1–2. Gunn makes a similar argument for the connection between pragmatism in general and post-structuralism. For a specific reading of Emerson in relation to post-Nietzschean philosophy see Cavell, "Aversive Thinking." More recently an entire volume of *ESQ: A Journal of the American Renaissance* has been devoted to this issue. See *ESQ* 43:1–4 (1997).

33. Packer, *Emerson's Fall*, 142.

34. Cavell, *Unapproachable America*, 81. See also "Aversive Thinking."

35. Joseph Slater, ed., *The Correspondence of Emerson and Carlyle* (New York: Columbia University Press, 1964), 185. Hereafter cited as CEC.

36. Emerson elaborates, "Behind every individual, closes organization. . . . Liberation of the will from the sheaths and clogs of organization which he has outgrown, is the end and aim of this world" (CW 6:35–36). See also Poirier, *Poetry and Pragmatism*, 40.

37. Poirier, *Poetry and Pragmatism*, 152–53. Poirier has shown how this is one of Emerson's major contributions to pragmatism, leading as it does to William James's discussions of grammar. Of James, Poirier notes, "His ideal grammar leads to his politics, and not the other way round. The grammar he proposes is already anti-imperialist, anti-patriarchal, while never becoming directly focused on political or social structures. . . . The rejection of logocentrisms, and the rejuvenations that go with them, are articulated within confines having essentially to do with language use." I would agree that Emerson can be read similarly, with the exception that, as I will discuss later, Emerson was increasingly interested in blurring the line between a focus on political structures and a focus on language, and highly aware of the fact that, in a nation whose politics were ostensibly based on written documents, all political questions are questions of language, or, more specifically, of reading.

38. That Woodbury's book itself clearly involved this burden and pleasure of nar-

NOTES TO PAGES 68–69   203

rating an "Emerson" is not lost on me. I read these sentences of Emerson's aware that they may not be exact transcriptions but convinced that Emerson authorized the entire process, and that the de-authorizing rhetoric here is in keeping with the rhetoric of his published essays.

39. The first quote is from Coverdale's Bible of 1535; the second from King James and Webster; the third from King James. All three employ styles with which Emerson, the former minister, would have been readily familiar.

40. Walt Whitman, *Prose Works, 1892*, ed. Floyd Stovall, 2 vols. (New York: New York University Press, 1963–64), 2:517–18. The full quote is as follows: "The best part of Emersonianism is, it breeds the giant that destroys itself. Who wants to be any man's mere follower? lurks behind every page. No teacher ever taught, that has so provided for his pupils setting up independently—no truer evolutionist." See also 1:281–82, where Whitman provides a telling description of the results of a "talk" with Emerson. Emerson was giving Whitman advice on whether or not to include the controversial "Children of Adam" in *Leaves of Grass*. Whitman writes, "During those two hours he was the talker and I the listener. It was an argument-statement, reconnoitering, review, attack, and pressing home. . . . More precious than gold to me that dissertation—it afforded me, ever after, this strange and paradoxical lesson: each point of E.'s statement was unanswerable, no judges charge ever more complete or convincing, I could never hear the points better put—and then I felt down in my soul the clear and unmistakable conviction to disobey all and pursue my own way. 'What have you to say then to such things?' said E., pausing in conclusion. 'Only that while I can't answer them at all, I feel more settled than ever to adhere to my own theory and exemplify it,' was my candid response. Whereupon we went and had a good dinner at the American House." I've tried to show how Emerson's prose itself provokes such responses.

41. The quotes from Dewey in this paragraph are from *The Quest for Certainty* (1929), in LW 4:19–20. I am in agreement with Frank Lentricchia regarding this aspect of Dewey's thinking, which he says is "at once a political critique of classical, spectator epistemology and an alternative to it," and I am obviously locating the beginnings of this critique and alternative, and as such the beginnings of pragmatism itself, in Emerson's work. "Pragmatism," Lentricchia continues, "is a rejection of hierarchical structure itself, of the stabilizing (kingly) forces of structure, which would always stand safely outside structure—outside the game, but ruling the game. Pragmatism is a commitment to the openness of time and a chance for change; pragmatism, then, is the expression of the radical democrat and the experimental method, or scientific spirit of democracy." See Lentricchia, *Criticism and Social Change*, 3. But in arguing that the chief sociopolitical manifestation of Emerson's proto-pragmatism is his abolitionism, I hope to complicate the second half of Lentricchia's dialectic by which he criticizes pragmatism for what he considers its most prominent public expression, namely, "the self-centered capitalist spirit of rugged-individualism" (3). Lentricchia's critique, like that of a host of pragmatist sympathizers critiquing pragmatism, is dependent on a

genealogy of pragmatism that plays itself out in Rorty's work: "the problem, here, as before, with the fathers of American pragmatism, is that there is only a rarefied, liberal idea of society or history at work in Rorty's position" (16). But Emerson's pragmatism is in dialogue with the abolitionist's reckoning of society and history from its adolescence, and this fact suggests an alternative genealogy, one that leads, both directly and via Burke, to Ralph Ellison and subsequently to Albert Murray, Cornel West, and others, a rather different, hybrid tree. This branch of pragmatism is characterized by a view of the cultural conversation that is neither Manichean (as the vulgar Marxist's) or cacophonous (as Rorty's) but, rather, antiphonal.

42. "Our young people have written much on labor and reform, and for all that they have written, neither the world nor themselves have gotten on a step. Intellectual tasting of life will not supersede muscular activity. If a man should consider the nicety of the passage of a piece of bread down his throat he would starve. At Education-Farm, the noblest theory of life sat on the noblest figures of young men and maidens, quite powerless and melancholy. It would not rake or pitch a ton of hay; it would not rub down a horse; and the men and maidens it left pale and hungry" (CW 3:58).

43. Gougeon, Virtue's Hero, 182. Gougeon notes that both Theodore Parker and James Freeman Clarke persisted in their belief in the inferiority of the African race.

44. Poirier, Trying it Out in America, 213. Patterson reads this passage as "the dismantling of possibilities for effective, meaningful forms of public action—including public expressions of protest against slavery" (92). I read in between the two by suggesting that the passage is a prelude to his entrance into abolitionist politics. See also George Kateb, Emerson and Self-Reliance (Thousand Oaks, Calif.: Sage, 1995). I would agree with Poirier that Kateb's defense of this passage against charges of selfishness is hampered by "the defensiveness of Kateb's rhetoric, and his evident feeling that he needs to protect Emerson from the charge of callousness and insensitivity by a laying on of rhetorical pieties" (212). Kateb's defensiveness seems the product of an inability to decide the precise connection between Emerson's philosophy and his political activity. Hence Emerson's politics are accepted grudgingly ("he quietly broke the law, I suppose"), and Kateb's insistence that "the advocacy of violence is inconsistent with the theory of self-reliant activity" seems offered as a curious apology for Emerson's radical politics (185). I, on the other hand, do not see any contradiction between Emerson's theory of self-reliance and his later theory of self-government attained, if necessary, by violent means. Indeed, the latter seems to me both an expansion of the logic of "Self-Reliance" and a correction of past hesitancy.

45. "For non-conformity the world whips you with its displeasure" (CW 2:55–56). "I cannot sell my liberty and my power, to save their [his friends] sensibility" (2:73–74). "I cannot consent to pay for a privilege where I have intrinsic right" (2:53). By the end of "Self-Reliance," Emerson seems squarely to make an argument against the compatibility of self-reliance and slavery: "the reliance on Property, including the reliance on governments which protect it, is the want of self-reliance. . . . [A] cultivated man be-

comes ashamed of his property, out of new respect for his nature. Especially he hates what he has, if he sees that it is accidental,—came to him by inheritance, or gift, or crime; then he feels that it is not having; it does not belong to him, has no root in him, and merely lies there, because no revolution or no robber takes it away" (2:87–88).

46. Also interesting in this regard is his comment two years earlier regarding Harriet Beecher Stowe's *Uncle Tom's Cabin:* "It is the distinction of 'Uncle Tom's Cabin,' that, it is read equally in the parlor & the kitchen & the nursery of every house" (JMN 13:121). Compare this to Hawthorne's contemporaneous statement regarding "scribbling women," and one begins to understand how flawed are the arguments that have homogenized the "classic" writers of the "American Renaissance." Emerson's statement also bears comparison to this statement of Carlyle's, from 1853: *"Uncle Tom's Cabin* is the mania of *this* season; what will that of the *next* be? . . .* [T]o me for one, it seemed a pretty perfect sample of Yankee-Governess Romance, & I fairly could not and would not read beyond the first hundred pages of it" (CEC 489–90). Incidentally, Emerson's comment would seem to complicate substantially Newfield's argument regarding Emerson's "feminizing [of] unappealable authority" (137–43) whereby women are allowed a nonpolitical divine agency, a brand of self-reliance that is "done in self-forgetting" (142).

47. Kenneth Cmiel, *Democratic Eloquence: The Fight over Popular Speech in Nineteenth-Century America* (New York: William Morrow, 1990), 55. Emerson anticipates Cmiel's observation that "When eighteenth-century linguists located linguistic authority in the speech of gentlemen . . . it certainly wrote off the language of at least nine tenths of the human race as 'vulgar and not to be taken seriously.'" In contrast, "the stylistic *bricolage*" of popular newspapers "made it maddeningly hard to divide the world into the few and the many, impossibly difficult to see which men were 'truly' gentlemen, which women 'really' ladies. Terms like refined and vulgar, which formerly had distinct sociological resonance, in the nineteenth century became vaguer allusions to cultural styles" (15). As I will later explain in detail, Emerson's aesthetic disagreements with infamous newspaper hater Carlyle during the 1850s and 1860s were precisely disagreements over what constituted "democratic eloquence." Interestingly, Cmiel quotes Holmes as having said that "The use of slang . . . is at once a sign and cause of mental atrophy" (55). Had Emerson heard Holmes say it, he would no doubt have linked the sentiment to Holmes's proslavery sentiments, which he understood as explicitly antidemocratic.

48. Compare this similar, vitriolic passage from the "WO Liberty" notebook: "[Slaveholders] do not eat men, but only steal them & steal their earnings. . . . Pleasant, is it not? Manly, is it not? Right, is it not?" (JMN 14:388).

49. Here I have an obvious difference of opinion with von Frank, who suggests that "Emerson's position seems to a modern reader even more abstract and disengaged than perhaps it really is because of the notable absence of any direct sympathy or fellow-feeling for the slave." See von Frank, *Trials of Anthony Burns,* 332. While von Frank's

intention is to rescue Emerson's thought from its critics, I believe that in this instance he is too willing to concede the point. The fact is that there are many instances in writing and action that reveal Emerson's fellow feeling for the slave and, more importantly in this context, that fellow feeling had a substantial influence on Emerson's thought. To my mind, this fact only bolsters von Frank's central premise. As von Frank himself puts it, whether Anthony Burns's name appears in Emerson's writing or not, "his identity, his meaning for America, is borne out in every word" (333).

50. Gougeon, *Virtue's Hero*, 306.

51. Cary Wolfe, *The Limits of American Literary Ideology in Pound and Emerson* (New York: Cambridge University Press, 1993), 151–52. Wolfe seizes on a journal entry Emerson wrote when he was twenty-one—"Aristocracy is a good sign"—but this hardly represents Emerson's mature view. Likewise Wolfe's claim that Emerson is "wholly unsympathetic to the Jacksonian masses" is more than hyperbolic; it ignores, for instance Emerson's letter to Carlyle, quoted earlier, extolling (in very un-Nietzschean, un-Carlylean terms) the "sublime lessons I have once & again read on the Bulletin-boards in the streets," as well as this 1847 journal entry: "A course of mobs was recommended to me by [abolition journalist] N. P. Rogers to correct my quaintness and transcendentalism. . . . [He] spoke more truly than he knew, perchance, when he recommended an Abolition campaign to me. I doubt not, a course of mobs would do me a world of good" (JMN 10:28).

52. von Frank, "Mrs. Brackett's Verdict," 385–86.

53. Wright suggested that Carlyle's words "would have delighted John C. Calhoun," a sentiment repeated by Emerson in his journal in 1858: "'masterly inactivity' 'wise passiveness' see how much has been made of that feather stolen from the plume of Carlyle by Calhoun & others" (JMN 14:192). Wright was at the center of the controversy set off by Carlyle's 1850 pamphlet, "The Present Time," where he scoffs at abolitionism and democracy and calls Americans "Eighteen Millions of the greatest *bores* ever seen in this world." Wright replied with a pamphlet entitled "Perforations in the 'Latter Day Pamphlets' by One of the 'Eighteen Millions of Bores,'" attacking Carlyle. Emerson's friend Samuel Ward refused to visit Carlyle following this incident, and Emerson himself called this "fine vengeance." For his part, Carlyle wrote Emerson a letter calling Elizur Wright a "little dog," saying of his response, "I have not read a word of it, nor shall ever read," and attempting to justify his position by distinguishing between the "eighteen million bores" and the "eighteen thousand noble-men" (CEC 463–64)—a line of argumentation that, by 1850, would have been thoroughly unpersuasive to Emerson.

54. Woodbury elaborates in saying that Emerson "was deeply sensitive to the many-sidedness of truth, and the impossibility of uttering in regard to it the complete word. How this contrasts with Carlyle! With what tempests of humour that, as Emerson said, 'floated everything,' the great Scotchman would sweep opposition away; or,

quite as likely, with what electrical violence he would destroy it!" (144). I am also reminded, in this same vein, of the poet Arthur Hugh Clough's words to Emerson during Emerson's visit to England in 1848. Upon Emerson's departure, Clough said, "You leave all us young Englishman without a leader. Carlyle has led us into the desert, and he has left us there." Emerson noted worriedly, "This is what all the young men in England have said to me." See L 3:424.

55. That the theorist of "self-reliance" should recommend that one "postpone one-self" seems counterintuitive, but that stipulation was latent in Emerson's conception of self-reliance from the beginning. As I've suggested, its origin lies in his deep distrust for stable representations of selfhood and his equally deep desire to spur others toward self-reliance. Anyone who wishes to posit a connection between "self-reliance" and "rugged individualism" needs to explain how he or she works around the theoretical and practical implications of this concept of "postponement." Such an explanation would necessarily include an engagement with Emerson's criticism of "an easy self-reliance that makes [one] self-willed and unscrupulous . . . pampered by finer draughts, by political power and by the power in the railroad board, in the mills, or the banks" and his connection of "liberty" with "self-denial" in "The Fortune of the Republic" (11:522). Perhaps his clearest statement on the subject is the one I have used for an epigraph to this chapter.

56. Gougeon, *Virtue's Hero,* 304. See also ASW 140. Compare this statement to Emerson's contemporaneous journal entry: "Channing thinks Carlyle does not recog-nize the people in 'Life of Friedrich'" (15:355). Describing Southern society as a kind of grotesque imitation of English aristocracy became a common practice for Emerson in the journals and notebooks of the 1850s. Statements similar to the one on "English nationality" appear in JMN 11:399 and 15:174. In 1862 Emerson wrote, "All nationality soon becomes babyish, even in Carlyle." In 1864, in a somewhat triumphant, but also regretful, letter to Carlyle, he wrote, "Ten days residence in this country would have made you the organ of the sanity of England & of Europe to us & to them, & have shown you the necessities and aspirations which struggle up in our Free States, which, as yet, have no organ to others, & are ill & unsteadily articulated here. In our today's division of Republican & Democrat, it is certain that the American nationality lies in the Republican Party (mixed & multiform though that party be;) & I hold it not less certain, that, viewing all nationalities in the world, the battle for Humanity is, at this hour, in America" (CEC 541). See also JMN 15:438, where a similar statement ends with the conclusion, "hence the weakness of English & European opposition." Inter-estingly, Whitman voices a remarkably similar opinion of Carlyle vis-à-vis American democracy in "Carlyle from American Points of View." See Walt Whitman, *Prose Works,* 1:254–62.

57. As Emerson's critique of Carlyle is in this instance largely a critique of his "3rd Volume of Friedrich," we should also be reminded of Emerson's claim that "Webster

thinks this union is a vast Prince Rupert's drop," which recalls Prince Rupert himself, the German son of Frederick V, nephew of Charles I, a royalist and general in the English Civil War. Webster, Emerson suggests, has marked himself as a royalist, however he might hope to convince the people otherwise, and Carlyle's own defenses were no more convincing. Emerson's critique of Carlyle does not appear in any of the published versions of "The Fortune of the Republic," all of which were assembled by Cabot from various versions of his lecture. By the time the piece was first published in 1879, Emerson was cognitively unable to edit his own work.

58. Perhaps the statement most representative of his feelings regarding Carlyle during this period is this one: "If Genius were cheap, we should do without Carlyle; but in the existing population, he cannot be spared" (JMN 15:82), though this generosity was always tempered by his general critique of Carlyle's opinions and his growing sense that the category of "genius" was expanding.

59. The OED lists this 1840 usage: "As he no longer did the duty of coxswain . . . he was not entitled to the rating," as well as this resonant usage from 1623: "It was referred to the king to rate how much he should pay." In his more jovial moments, Emerson enjoyed drawing himself and Carlyle as Revolutionary War combatants in caricature, noting, for instance, that Carlyle had "reprimanded with severity the rebellious instincts of the native of a vast continent which made light of the British islands" (JMN 10:334).

60. Robert Duncan, Fictive Certainties: Essays (New York: New Directions, 1985), 227.

61. My argument here, as will become clear, runs directly against Newfield's argument that Emerson's employment of the rhetoric of inevitability in his abolitionist writings amounts to a "wholesale denial of anti-slavery agency" (203).

62. Livingston, Pragmatism and the Political Economy, 164.

63. Victor Turner, Dramas, Fields, and Metaphors: Symbolic Action in Human Society (Ithaca: Cornell University Press, 1974), 232, 248. Emerson was keen, too, to the process by which even liminal "forms generated in some experiences of communitas get repeated in symbolic mimesis and become routinized forms of structure" (249), and that recognition helps explain his insistence on a perpetually renewable union.

64. Gougeon, Virtue's Hero, 315.

65. Gougeon, Virtue's Hero, 330.

66. To the second quote Emerson adds ominously, "take away his motive & growth & he dwarfs & dies," a further indication that his new thinking took into account social force and restraint.

67. See also a similar passage on "Toussaint and the Haitian heroes" in "Emancipation in the British West Indies" (CW 11:144). In discussing Emerson provoking a logical gap and then making a transition, I'm thinking of Poirier's description of Emersonian pragmatists: "for them the evidence of a gap or an abyss is an invitation simply to get moving and keep moving, to make a transition." Poirier, Poetry and Pragmatism, 149. Where I try to extend Poirier's idea is in suggesting that Emerson doesn't simply

recognize cultural, linguistic, logical, gaps—he *provokes* them as a way to open up possibilities for transition, and his motives for doing so are often political in nature.

68. See Gougeon, *Virtue's Hero*, 300, 305, 332. Emerson raised money for the Massachusetts 54th Regiment, read them his "Boston Hymn," and later memorialized those soldiers who died at Fort Wagner in his poem "Voluntaries," which appeared in the *Atlantic Monthly* in October 1863. Note how this quatrain of Emerson's "flips" racial terms in the manner I've been describing: "I am not black in my mind / But born to make black fair / On the battle field my master find,—/ His white corpse taints the air" (JMN 15:213). The soldier who is a "man of transition" is using a transitional vocabulary whereby black is becoming fair, and white, the symbol of death and putrescence.

As regards Douglass, it's worth at least thinking about how close the subversive model of reading he describes in *Narrative of the Life of Frederick Douglass* is to Emerson's ideal model. Remember that Douglass reverses the logic by which he is forbidden to read (that reading "would spoil the best nigger in the world," that "if you teach that nigger . . . how to read, there would be no keeping him. It would forever unfit him to be a slave"), turning it into instruction rather than censure. What he later seizes on is "one of Sheridan's mighty speeches on and in behalf of Catholic Emancipation," which he freely applies to his own situation, mining the speech for the vocabulary it can provide him in his own fight against slavery. See Douglass, *Narrative of the Life of Frederick Douglass,* 20–35. Later still, he makes arguments similar to Emerson's regarding the liminal state of the union ("I am glad, fellow citizens, that your nation is so young"); perhaps only Douglass attacks the incongruency between the nation's cultural and social structures with more verve than Emerson: "Must I argue the wrongfulness of slavery? Is that a question for republicans?" he asks bitterly in "What to the Slave is the Fourth of July." And like Emerson, he attacks the "nonsense we had been wont to hear and to repeat on . . . the 4th of July," noting, "To say *now* that America was right and England was wrong is exceedingly easy. . . . Men seldom eulogize the wisdom of their fathers, but to excuse some folly or wickedness of their own . . . [but] they who did so were accounted in their day, plotters of mischief, agitators and rebels, dangerous men." This last statement is nearly identical in its point to Emerson's various attacks of Webster. And both men emphasized a vision of the Declaration of Independence as tool *for* liberty rather than as a representation *of* liberty. As Douglass put it, "the principles contained within this instrument are saving principles." See Frederick Douglass, "What to the Slave is the Fourth of July" in The *Norton Anthology of African American Literature,* eds. Henry Louis Gates, Jr., and Nellie McKay, eds., (New York: Norton, 1997), 380, 381, 382, 385, 387.

69. I feel justified in bringing this Kaluli myth to bear on Emerson's philosophy and aesthetic mostly because Mackey has argued its relevance to a host of literary figures related to or influenced by Emerson and pragmatism, among them, Douglass, William Carlos Williams, Ellison, and Robert Duncan. Though Mackey's knowledge

of and interest in world cultures is far greater than my own, his method in this case is similar to mine; that is, he is working more or less by analogy rather than attempting to argue for a specific material or historical connection between these writers and Kaluli myth. And I believe, as he does, that the analogy is a functional and helpful one.

70. Poirier, *Poetry and Pragmatism,* 139, 146. Poirier notes the success of words with the prefix "some," in particular, in re-instating the vague: someone, something, somewhere. See his discussion of Frost (145).

71. Cavell, "Aversive Thinking," 142.

CHAPTER 3

1. As an example, Mackey quotes West as saying "Ellison's existentialist blues novelistic practices, with their deep sources in Afro-American music, folklore, Western literary humanism, and American pluralist ideology, are concealed by subsuming him under a 'post-Wright school of black writing.'" See Cornel West, "Minority Discourse and the Pitfalls of Canon Formation," *The Yale Journal of Criticism* 1, no. 1 (fall 1987), 198—99.

2. I've already begun to discuss how Ellison would have linked Emerson to the pragmatist tradition. It is also clear that in connecting him with Lincoln and the tradition of the Constitution, the Declaration of Independence, and the Bill of Rights in his course on the American vernacular, Ellison must have been aware of Emerson's antislavery writings. Even the most cursory search of these terms in Emerson's writings would have turned up all the antislavery lectures in *Miscellanies.* With the publication of Ellison's second novel, *Juneteenth: A Novel* (New York: Random House, 1999), we have new evidence of his careful reading of and interest in Emerson's antislavery writings. At one point in the novel, one of its two central characters, the Reverend A. Z. Hickman, tells his congregation that God "means for us to be a new kind of human. Maybe we won't be that people," he says, "but we'll be a part of that people, we'll be an element in them, amen" (128). Hickman, who reads Emerson to his adopted son Bliss and calls Emerson "a preacher . . . just like you" (45), is undoubtedly referring to Emerson's prophetic statement in "Emancipation in the British West Indies" that "The First of August marks the entrance of a new element into modern politics, namely, the civilization of the negro. . . . The black man carries in his bosom an indispensible element of a new and coming civilization" (CW 11: 140, 144). "Juneteenth" is the celebration of June 19, 1865, the day two and a half years after the Emancipation Proclamation was decreed in which Galveston, Texas, slaves found out that they were free. The relevance of signifying on Emerson's "Emancipation" address is obvious. For further discussion of Ellison's *Juneteenth* as it relates to my concept of democratic symbolic action, see Michael Magee, "Constituting Ellison: *Juneteenth* as a Function of American Democracy," *Review* 22 (2000), 37—55.

3. The first position is Leonard Deutsch's; the second, Alan Nadel's; the third,

Kun Jong Lee's. See Deutsch, "Ralph Waldo Emerson and Ralph Waldo Ellison: A Shared Moral Vision," *CLA Journal* 16 (1972), 160. Deutsch's reading suffers from a failure to recognize Invisible Man's "hole" as a liminal space where his identity is in a state of unsettled transition. He has no total awareness of selfhood but rather "a certain necessary faith in human possibility before the next unknown" (GT 317). See also Alan Nadel, *Invisible Criticism: Ralph Ellison and the American Canon* (Iowa City: University of Iowa Press, 1988), 118. Still the best piece on Emerson and Ellison, Nadel finally links Ellison to "that strain of Emersonianism honed on the distortions propagated by the ersatz followers of Emerson" (123), a position that, while certainly true, doesn't allow for a description of Ellison's meticulous involvement with Emerson's actual writings. Kun Jong Lee's piece is "Ellison's *Invisible Man:* Emersonianism Revised," *PMLA,* 107 (March, 1992), 331–32. Lee's assumptions are, I can only guess, the result of limited reading in Emerson's works.

4. Gates discusses Ellison as a signifier in Henry Louis Gates, Jr., *The Signifying Monkey* (New York: Oxford University Press, 1988). "Ellison," Gates writes, "is a complex Signifier, naming things by indirection and troping throughout his works" (105). I am, of course indebted to the model of signifying that Gates outlines in his seminal book. And Gates is obviously indebted to Ellison's model of vernacular discourse ("the Signifying Monkey, stands as the rhetorical principle in Afro-American discourse," 44). I am particularly interested in Gates's discussion of how African American signifying traditions stand in contradistinction to the literate, written uses of the standard English (46) and in how the *Signifying Monkey* stories can be read as a kind of democratic symbolic action, since they play on presumed hierarchies between Monkey, Lion, and Elephant, and since they end with the symbolic "dethroning" of the "King of the Jungle." See pages 51–64.

5. Green, *Deep Democracy,* viii–ix, 83. Green is thinking specifically of Emerson and Dewey.

6. Quoted in Livingston, *Pragmatism and the Political Economy,* 197. The second italics are mine. As an aside, it's worth noting that Jameson's assertion in *The Political Unconscious* that "the effectively ideological is also, at the same time, necessarily utopian," his description of how "a *functional* method for describing cultural texts is articulated with an *anticipatory* one," is deeply indebted to the pragmatist concept of "narrative as socially symbolic act," which he takes from Burke. Though Jameson has in mind a Marxist utopia of collective unity (of a "properly socialist legality"), his sense of how the utopian gesture functions is pragmatic. As such it is useful reading for anyone trying to make sense of the function of democratic utopian gestures in the work of pragmatists. See Jameson, *Political Unconscious,* 286, 296, 298.

7. "The end is in the beginning and lies far ahead" (IM 6), and "I would take up residence underground. The end was in the beginning" (571).

8. Consider this connection between Emerson and Douglass around the idea of naming in relation to the following quote from Gates: "Douglass's major contribution

to the slave's narrative was to make chiasmus the central trope of slave narration, in which a slave object writes himself or herself into a human-subject through the act of writing." See Gates, *Signifying Monkey,* 172.

9. Whitman, *Prose Works,* 2:517—18.

10. While this argument that Ellison's play on "initial" represents an act of conscious signifying may seem extreme to some, I firmly believe that such remarkably subtle allusions, puns, winks, are part of Ellison's methodology. I've mentioned Gates's discussion of that methodology. Certainly Nadel's *Invisible Criticism* is based on this very premise. Though it is off the subject, and though pursuing it would constitute another essay entirely, the best evidence I know for Ellison's complex use of extratextual reference occurs in the scene with Sybil in chapter 24: encouraged by Sybil to play the role of the simultaneously menacing and eroticized black rapist, Invisible Man instead "write(s) furiously across her belly in drunken inspiration: SYBIL, YOU WERE RAPED / BY / SANTA CLAUS / SURPRISE" (522). This is Ellison's joke, whereby Invisible Man recognizes that his identity is being organized around a time-honored and insidious caricature and tropes his way out of that organization. He does so by alluding to Joe Christmas, the protagonist from Faulkner's *Light in August* who is asked by his white lover Joanna Burden to play this identical role, and who ends up killing her out of frustration. Invisible Man's signifying represents a refusal to play the role asked of him as well as a refusal to react violently (which would simply perpetuate the stereotype from a slightly different angle and which would lead, as it did for Christmas, to his own demise). Moreover, Ellison is troping on Christmas's complex racial identity that, again, he can see only as an endless frustration. This, too, is refused by Invisible Man. Instead he adopts the pragmatist's model of social change whereby, as Poirier has suggested, "instead of trying to revoke or revere or repeat the past," one can "renew it by troping the language." See William Faulkner, *Light in August* (New York: Vintage, 1990), chapters 11—12. See also Poirier, *Poetry and Pragmatism,* 39.

11. Nadel, *Invisible Criticism,* 113.

12. His characterization of Bledsoe's authority as whiplike is only one of many instances in which Ellison implies that so-called progressive educators such as Bledsoe and Norton are dependent on the still powerful metaphors of slavery. Norton frames the Founder as Master, as plantation owner with thousands of dependents whose justification is "the fruits produced by the land that your great Founder has transformed" (45). Bledsoe ominously tells Invisible Man "You've got to be disciplined, boy" (141) and, in one of the most stunning passages in the novel, tells him "I'll have every Negro in the country hanging on tree limbs by morning if it means staying where I am" (143).

13. Richardson, *Mind on Fire,* 500—501.

14. As I've argued in chapter 1, Emerson's insistence on fusing ideas and action during this period mark his transition into a fully pragmatist mode of thought. In a line that would have tickled Ellison, Emerson says of Brown, "It is easy to see what a favorite he will be with history, which plays pranks with temporary reputations" (269).

15. Indeed, Norton's name itself may well be Ellison's craftiest signifying gesture against Norton's claims to an allegiance with Emerson. It may be, that is, an allusion to Andrews Norton. A prominent Unitarian minister and one of Emerson's most vocal critics, Norton had written a blistering attack of Emerson's "Divinity School Address," calling it "a great offense" to the "highly respectable officers" of Harvard University. Following the controversy over his address, Emerson considered Norton little more than a bore and a bother. Norton's name is then, perhaps, the signifying gesture that trumps all. See Richardson, *Mind on Fire,* 298. See also CEC 196, 214, where Emerson and Carlyle joke about Norton's criticisms. In a journal entry from 1855, Emerson remembered, "It seemed enough to damn any book, I remember, to his students, when old Andrews Norton said, 'I have never read it.' And yet, I suppose, this was nothing but that omniscience which every boy attributes to his first tutor" (JMN 13:413).

16. I have decided that the "Trueblood episode," which propels Ellison's narrative toward the Golden Day chapter, doesn't merit an extended discussion within the text proper. Nonetheless it is compatible with the general tendency I am describing. When Trueblood says that during his blues improvisation "I makes up my mind" (IM 66), Ellison intends for his reader to consider the possibility that this vernacular expression should be taken *literally*—that Trueblood makes up his mind (decides) to make up his mind (invent a mind, a self, that is *made up,* false in the traditional sense but true insofar as he treats his improvised self as an evolving reality). When Trueblood asserts that "I ain't nobody but myself" (66), he is asserting not an established and invariable persona but an Emersonian model of selfhood that marries the invocation "insist on yourself" (CW 2:83) to a belief that the self *becomes,* that it "resides in the moment of transition" (2:69). As Huston Baker has noted, Trueblood's "self . . . is in many ways the obverse of the stable, predictable, puritanical, productive, law-abiding ideal self of the American industrial-capitalist society." The blues singer is a symbolic activist, an organic intellectual, who reminds the community of the material limitations of circumstance while at the same time emphasizing the contingency of those limitations and offering a transitional vocabulary that might ultimately take their place. How can Trueblood be an Emersonian? This is the social paradox that fascinates Ellison. See Houston A. Baker, Jr., *Blues, Ideology, and Afro-American Literature: A Vernacular Theory* (Chicago: University of Chicago Press, 1984), 190. Baker himself might not agree with my comparison of Trueblood and Emerson, but I'm confident in arguing that Ellison would have.

17. Orrin Keepnews, *The View from Within: Jazz Writings, 1948–1987* (New York: Oxford University Press, 1988), 62, 64. "Storyville," Keepnews explains, "was the legally fixed area within which prostitution flourished in New Orleans between 1896 . . . and November 14, 1917. . . . [It] also housed a multitude of assorted saloons, gambling joints, dives and cabarets, and in all these there was music" (63–64).

18. Recall, too, Invisible Man's description of the Brotherhood marching military style: "falling into columns of four, and I was alone in the rear, like the pivot on a drill team. . . . [S]uddenly I was blinded" (338).

19. How long, how long,
   has that evening train been gone?
   How long, baby, how long, how long?

   . . . .

   I could holler like a mountain jack,
   go up on the mountain and call my baby back.
   How long, how long, how long?

20. Jean Francois Lyotard, *The Postmodern Condition* (Minneapolis: University of Minnesota Press, 1984), 17.

21. The passage is worth quoting at length: "The student is to read history actively and not passively; to esteem his own life the text and books the commentary. . . . I have no expectation that any man will read history aright, who thinks that what was done in a remote age by men whose names have resounded far, has any deeper sense than what he is doing to-day. . . . He must sit solidly at home, and not suffer himself to be bullied by kings or empires, but know that he is greater than all the geography and all the government of the world; he must transfer the point of view from which history is commonly read, from Rome and Athens and London to himself, and not deny his conviction that he is the court, and if England or Egypt have anything to say to him, he will try the case; if not, let them forever be silent."

22. Ostendorf, "Modernism, Anthropology and Jazz," 105.

23. "Ko-Ko" can be found on *The Genius of Charlie Parker,* Savoy/Denon: 0104, 1945–48. Martin Williams has written, "I know of no other Parker solo which shows how basic and brilliant were Parker's rhythmic innovations," and he speculates interestingly that the first take of "Ko-Ko"—which includes portions of the "Cherokee" melody—is cut short "because if it had gone on someone would have had to pay Ray Noble some royalties." See Martin Williams, *The Jazz Tradition,* rev. ed. (New York: Oxford University Press, 1983), 149–50, and *Jazz Changes* (New York: Oxford University Press, 1992), 232. Keepnews notes a 1949 interview in which Parker actually suggests that "bop was born" during a spontaneous improvisation on "Cherokee" in "the back room of a Harlem chili house" in 1939. See Keepnews, *View from Within,* 91. Ellison sites this same interview with Parker (SA 229). Perhaps most relevant is Eric Lott's stipulation that "Ko-Ko" "suggested that jazz was a struggle which pitted mind against the perversity of circumstance, and that in this struggle blinding virtuosity was the best weapon." See Lott, "Double V, Double-Time: Bebop's Politics of Style," in *Jazz among the Discourses,* ed. Krin Gabbard (Durham: Duke University Press, 1995), 243. Lott's characterization of Parker links him very readily, I would say, to Ellison, and I'll have more comment on this possibility later in the chapter.

24. The doctor-vet calls Norton "only a man" (86), "a trustee of consciousness" (89), and tells him, "To some, you are a great white father, to others the lyncher of souls" (93). Of Invisible Man, he says "He's invisible" and tells Norton, "He'll do your

bidding, and for that his blindness is his chief asset" (94–95). Invisible Man, not yet hip to the vet's good advice, thinks that he is "acting toward the white man with a freedom which could only bring trouble" (93), and Bledsoe says of him, "A Negro like that should be under lock and key" (140).

25. See the 1969 interview where Ellison describes the process whereby one "master[s] a technique or discipline which will get them to a point where they can actually see that it's not what they want or that something else is demanded" (CE 181).

26. Something similar to this insistent refusal to distinguish the "real" self from the self's manipulation of appearances seems to be behind Emerson's statement "We live amid surfaces, and the true art of life is to skate well on them," living well defined as "skill of handling and treatment" of these surfaces (CW 3:59–60).

27. Ostendorf has framed Ellison's perspective on Armstrong succinctly in writing, "if one accepts masking not only as a temporary necessity but as a constant existential fact, then even the role playing of Louis Armstrong may hold deeper secrets." See Ostendorf, "Anthropology, Modernism and Jazz," 104. For a sense of how names can function as masks in Ellison's symbolic economy, note the following:

> "A small brown bowlegged Negro with the name 'Franklin D. Roosevelt Jones' might sound like a clown to someone who looks at him from the outside," said my friend Albert Murray, "but on the other hand he just might turn out to be a hell of a fireside operator. He might just lie back in all that comic juxtaposition of names and manipulate you deaf, dumb and blind—and you not even suspecting it, because you're thrown out of stance by his name! There you are, so dazzled by the F. D. R. image—which you know you can't see—and so delighted with your own superior position that you don't realize that it's Jones who must be confronted." (SA 150)

F. D. R. Jones's mask, like R. W. Ellison's, is his name—but it functions much like those masks Armstrong used to "take liberty . . . with Presidents."

28. I've summarized much, and though I don't believe a discussion of Emerson, Sr., and Emerson, Jr., is warranted in the text proper, they are worth briefly discussing here. I believe that Ellison employs these names in dissonant juxtaposition to his allusions to Emerson's writings. One might say that the senior Emerson represents a name grown famous and, as such, indicative of what Packer has called "the natural tendency toward ossification" that "will transform the purest truth into the deadliest falsehood." Neither the senior nor the junior Emerson attempts anything resembling the gesture toward linguistic dissonance represented by Ellison's changing "Waldo" to "W." In the course of chapter 9, it becomes clear that Emerson, Sr., does not represent Emerson's philosophy any more than John D. Rockefeller does. He stands instead as the inaccessible, unengageable patriarch, as remote and socially tame as the Emerson of whom Norton speaks: the Emerson who transforms self-reliance into "a most worthy virtue"

(108) and thus a means not to "practical power" (CW 3:86) but to containment via the same societal norms that include "race manners" (SA 55). Emerson, Jr., struggles under this remote and rigid patriarchal authority. While Lee accuses Emerson, Jr., of "quasiliberalism" and suggests that Ellison "satirizes [him] as a decadent hypocrite," it seems more accurate to say that the young Emerson is pathetically under his father's thumb. He wants to "throw off the mask of custom and manners that insulate man from man" and makes a vaguely homosexual invitation to Invisible Man to join him at "the Club Calamus" (185–86), an allusion to Whitman's erotic poems ("in this secluded spot I can respond as / I would not dare elsewhere. . . . To tell the secrets of my nights and days, / To celebrate the needs of comrades," Whitman writes in "In Paths Untrodden"). He makes a gesture of connection toward the narrator, saying, "A number of my friends are jazz musicians, and I've been around," and he confesses, "I'm afraid my father considers me one of the unspeakables" (188). One might say that he serves as a kind of innocuous, corporate version of the early beat generation; he has a claim to marginality and a connection with the speaker that certainly Norton does not, but he is ultimately not courageous or imaginative enough to plunge outside the system that contains him. Emerson, Sr., is his father "though he would have preferred it otherwise" (190), and the younger Emerson is seemingly too "afraid" to run out from under the patriarch's shadow. Still, Ellison does allow him to participate in the sound advice already given to Invisible Man by the vet: "Don't blind yourself" (192). Ultimately, the exchange seems to me an allegory for the differences between genetic and literary kinship.

29. Turner, *Dramas, Fields and Metaphors,* 232, 248. Turner's notion is even more applicable to Ellison's thinking than it is to Emerson's, since in Ellison's case there is a historically situated connection, given the fact that both Turner and Ellison develop their concept of symbolic action out of their reading of Burke. For more commentary on the connection between Turner and Ellison, see Ostendorf, "Anthropology, Modernism and Jazz," 97–100.

30. The factory hospital seems to me something like the evil twin of Harlem's Lafargue Psychiatric Clinic, which Ellison became interested in at the time he was writing *Invisible Man.* For Ellison, the clinic "represents an underground extension of democracy" that "rejects all stereotypes" while assisting Harlem residents in their "search for answers to the questions: Who am I, What am I, Why am I, and Where" in "a world so fluid and shifting that often within the mind the real and the unreal merge, the marvelous beckons from behind the same sordid reality that denies its existence." See Ellison, "Harlem is Nowhere" (SA 295–97).

31. Nicknaming is one of Ellison's deep and lasting preoccupations, as he says, "a concern with names and naming was very much a part of that special area of American culture from which I come" (149). In a 1961 interview he says of a childhood friend, "I don't remember his family name even though his father was pastor of the leading Episcopal church in Oklahoma City at that time, but his nickname was Hoolie and for

kids of eight or nine that was enough" (4). Ellison of course loves the idea that the name given Hoolie by his pastor-father is supplanted in the course of these children's group improvisation. And he goes on to describe how this practice is extended, how he and his nicknamed playmates would further apply nicknames to the jazz-shaped world around them, "laughing at the impious wit of applying church titles to a form of music which all the preachers told us was the devil's potent tool." Such wit was most evident among their jazz heroes, who they applauded in such pronouncements as "Now that's the Right Reverend Jimmy Rushing preaching now, man" (243), a style of nicknaming that Ellison himself will apply to "Rev. B. P. Rinehart, *Spiritual Technologist*" in his novel. I would argue that the nicknaming described by Ellison is a kind of democratic symbolic activity of fundamental similarity to Emerson's process of gazetting old words in favor of "find[ing] new ones" (JMN 9:117). What they have in common is a recognition that the maintenance of old terminologies is in effect a strategy for constraining logical possibility, not only in regard to the individuality of the self but to the eccentricity of groups, both of which act to sustain egalitarian activity generally.

32. I'm reminded, too, of the fact that in a 1973 interview, Ellison defined "circling" as "the back and forth play" (CE 253).

33. Mackey suggests that Tarp's link is "a gesture recalling the protective root Sandy gives Frederick Douglass in the latter's *Narrative*" (DE 245).

34. Leonard Harris, ed., *The Philosophy of Alain Locke: Harlem Renaissance and Beyond* (Philadelphia: Temple University Press, 1989), 71. For further discussion of Locke's quote, see Green, "Alain Locke's Multicultural Philosophy of Value," 89.

35. The distinction drawn here between blues and jazz is in some sense a false one, though I believe it is useful enough to pursue. Ellison would likely see it as a difference in degree or intensity rather than in form, where the jazzman heightens the emphasis on the revisability of cultural material and the speed with which such revision might be performed through improvisation. The first quote is from Lott's discussion of Parker in "Bebop's Politics of Style," 243. For James's discussion of time see James, *Principles of Psychology* (WJ 8:591—94): "what is past, to be known as past, must be known *with* what is present, and *during* the 'present' spot of time" (593). Ellison describes Armstrong as having "a slightly different sense of time, you're never quite on the beat. Sometimes you're ahead and sometimes behind. Instead of the swift and imperceptible flowing of time, you are aware of its nodes, those points where time stands still or from where it leaps ahead. And you slip into the breaks and look around" (IM 8). Again, describing time as having nodes from which it can stand and leap, where one might slip in and look around, necessarily spatializes time.

36. Albert Murray, *The Omni-Americans: New Perspectives on Black Experience and American Culture* (New York: Outerbridge and Dienstfrey, 1970), 13.

37. Gates, *Signifying Monkey*, 105. Gates cites the Morton quote as appearing in Library of Congress conversations with Alan Lomax, recorded on *Discourse on Jazz*, Riverside RLP9003, side 1.

38. For another fascinating example of Ellison's use of the riff, follow the changes in the meaning of the term "law-abiding" in Invisible Man's speech during the Harlem eviction (276–84).

39. OED provides us with two resonant definitions for "rounder": 1b: "A Methodist local preacher." A preacher, that is, who *makes the rounds* rather than maintaining a parish. This example is provided from 1820: "Many . . . prefer . . . even the rounder, whether male or female . . . to the accredited and licensed minister." 1d: "One who makes the round of prisons, workhouses, drinking saloons, etc.; a habitual criminal, loafer, or drunkard." This definition first arrives in print, interestingly, in 1854, and we should keep in mind that Ellison is working out of a tradition that gives positive value to statements such as Whitman's "I loaf and invite my soul, / I lean and loaf at my ease" and Emerson's "there is no crime to the intellect" (CW 3:80). OED quotes as an example the following dialogue from Zora Neale Hurston, *Mules and Men* (1970), i. iv. 93: " 'What make de rooster crow every morning at sun-up?' 'Dat's to let the pimps and rounders know de workin' man is on his way.' " Rinehart literally brings all these definitions together: he is numbers runner, pimp and minister, "Rev. B. P. Rinehart, *Spiritual Technologist*" (495). Another character identified as a "rounder" by Ellison is Peetie Wheatstraw: "I'm a piano player and a rounder, a whiskey drinker and a pavement pounder" (176). "My name is Peter Wheatstraw, I'm the Devil's only son-in-law, so roll 'em!" Wheatstraw says, signifying on a notorious passage from "Self-Reliance," where Emerson asserts: "If I am the Devil's child, I will live then from the Devil. No law can be sacred to me but that of my own nature. Good and bad are but names very readily transferable to that or this; the only right is what is after my constitution, the only wrong what is against it. A man is to carry himself in the presence of all opposition, as if everything were titular and ephemeral but he. I am ashamed to think how easily we capitulate to badges and names, to large societies and dead institutions" (CW 2:50–51). Emerson, then, is the devil's son; Wheatstraw, the son-in-law. As such, Ellison highlights Wheatstraw's un-asked-for predicament, the necessity of his having to marry into—through the legal system—Emersonian self-reliance. But Ellison also provides Wheatstraw with an important kind of agency, the ability to trope all over Emerson's prose. If Emerson says, "Good and bad are but names very readily transferable to that or this," Wheatstraw takes the transvaluation of good and bad a step further in promising Invisible Man, "I'll teach you some good bad habits. You'll need 'em." One of these "habits," I'd suggest, is the vernacular reversal of making "bad" mean "good," a joke on the fact that what might be good for the boss (or indeed, theoretically, for Emerson) might be bad for Wheatstraw or Invisible Man. Invisible Man can't resist Wheatstraw's self-affirming improvisation: "he had me grinning despite myself," he says, "I liked his words" (176). Nor could Ellison have resisted the pun on "constitution" in Emerson's statement and its contrast with "dead institutions." Ellison clearly based his character at least in part on the real Peetie Wheatstraw. Born William Bunch in 1902, Wheatstraw, also known as the Devil's Son-in-Law, was an influential and

popular blues artist of the 1920s and 1930s who died in 1941. Ellison was familiar with his music. For more information on Wheastraw, see Paul Garon, *The Devil's Son-in-Law: The Story of Peetie Wheatstraw and His Songs* (London: Studio Vista, 1971).

40. Ellison, "Schweitzer Program," 2.

41. Turner, *Dramas, Fields and Metaphors,* 248.

42. For example, see O'Meally's comment that Ellison is "deaf to virtually all jazz beyond Basie and Ellington" in Robert G. O'Meally, *Craft of Ellison,* (Cambridge: Harvard University Press, 1980), 169.

43. See Crouch, *Skins Game,* 182; and Crouch's liner notes to *Fats Navarro Featured with the Tadd Dameron Band,* Milestone, MCD 47041, 1977.

44. I am reminded here of Daniel Nevers's characterization of King Oliver as a "man of transition . . . his transition, one of those moments of privilege, such as the sudden discovery of eternity in a face." See liner notes to the reissue of *King Oliver and His Orchestra* (1929–1930), RCA/Jazz Tribune, 66538–2, 1979. Like Oliver's groups, in which he, Armstrong, Sidney Bechet, Kid Ory, Johnny Dodds, and others defined jazz by inventing it, the bop originators discovered a new definition of jazz in the course of improvisation. "What we know," Ellison says, "is that which was then becoming" (SA 203).

45. Mackey takes as his cue Jacques Attali's discussion of noise in *Noise: The Political Economy of Music* (Minneapolis: University of Minnesota Press, 1985): "A noise is a resonance that interferes with the audition of a message in the process of emission . . . a signal that interferes with the reception of a message by a receiver" (26).

46. LeRoi Jones (Amiri Baraka), *Blues People* (New York: Morrow, 1963), 231.

47. See Coleman's preface to the liner notes to *Beauty Is a Rare Thing,* Rhino/Atlantic, R2 71410, 1993.

CHAPTER 4

1. Ellison, "Schweitzer Program," 4.

2. *The Collected Poems of Frank O'Hara,* ed. Donald Allen (Berkeley: University of California Press, 1971), 498. Hereafter cited as CP.

3. Richard Poirier, "The Scenes of the Self," *New Republic,* August 2, 1993, 33–39. This book review of Brad Gooch's biography of O'Hara, *City Poet,* was pointed out to me by Andrew Epstein. Epstein delivered a paper entitled "'My Force Is in Mobility': Frank O'Hara and the Pragmatist Strain" at the Midwest Modern Language Association Conference on November 6, 1998, as part of the William James session. I am indebted to him for the many conversations we've had regarding both O'Hara and pragmatism.

4. A less intense, though perhaps pertinent, interest of O'Hara's would be Louis Zukofsky. Zukofsky, as a student of Dewey's at Columbia and a devotee of the pragmatist Charles S. Peirce, was, among other things, an important messenger to younger poets regarding pragmatism's aesthetic philosophy. Zukofsky's essay "A Statement for

Poetry" included in Donald Allen's anthology, *The Poetics of the New American Poetry* (along with essays by Stein, Williams, and O'Hara, among many others), contains the following statement: "No verse is 'free,' however, if its rhythms inevitably carry the words in contexts that do not falsify the function of words as speech." Zukofsky seems to be adapting Peirce's pragmatic notion that "the test of truth is both social and contextual," that "we do not understand ideas in isolation; we understand something in terms of how we relate it to other things," to words and speech. See Donald Allen and Warren Tallman, eds., *The Poetics of the New American Poetry* (New York: Grove Press, 1973), 146. For the connection to Peirce, see Sandra Kumamoto Stanley, *Louis Zukofsky and the Transformation of a Modern American Poetics* (Berkeley: University of California Press, 1994), 95. Of course Peirce's notion is also James's notion, Dewey's notion, and both of these latter philosophers had already argued for the relevance of a pragmatic view of truth to one's view of speech. For O'Hara's appreciation of Zukofsky, see Frank O'Hara, *Standing Still and Walking in New York* (San Francisco: Grey Fox Press, 1983), 21. Hereafter cited as SS.

5. Brad Gooch, *City Poet: The Life and Times of Frank O'Hara* (New York: Knopf, 1993), 318. Hereafter cited as CPT. The term "New American Poets" stems from Donald Allen's anthologies, *Poetics of the New American Poetry* and Donald Allen, ed., *The New American Poetry* (New York: Grove Press, 1960). Allen separated the poets in this latter anthology into five groups: the Black Mountain group (which included Olson, Creeley, Duncan, and Levertov and centered around Black Mountain College and the *Black Mountain Review*); the San Francisco Renaissance (where Duncan also figured prominently); the Beat Generation (which included Ginsberg); the New York School (which included O'Hara and Ashbery); and a nongeographical catch-all group for younger poets (which included LeRoi Jones [Amiri Baraka]). I will discuss later O'Hara's relation to the Black Mountain group as well as to Jones.

6. These quotes from O'Hara on Stein come from three unpublished letters. The first, from O'Hara to his family is dated 12/11/46. The second and third—to Kenneth Koch, 6/30/55, and to Vincent Warren, 1/18/61—are contained in "Frank O'Hara Letters Vols. 1 and 2," Don Allen boxes 2 and 3, Archives and Special Collections Department, Thomas J. Dodd Research Center, University of Connecticut Libraries. All subsequent mention of letters written by O'Hara refer to these volumes unless otherwise specified. As I have suggested, there are much more obvious reasons for O'Hara to have felt an affinity with Stein—most notably her connection to modern painters such as Picasso and Matisse, which O'Hara saw as mirroring his own relationship to the first- and second-generation abstract expressionists in New York. Likewise her role as a pioneering gay writer—though even into this sphere O'Hara seems to strangely want to insert West: "Mae really did invent the small-town faggot psychology I'm convinced, and in that she is a real pioneer like Stein."

7. Paul Goodman, *Speaking and Language: Defense of Poetry* (London: Wildwood House, 1973), 33.

8. These words are Ellison's from "Schweitzer Program," 3–4. Ellison once said that Stein's work involved "reshaping [American literature's] values and its styles in the 'revolution of the word'" (CE 114). It is worth noting that, as Mackey and Charles Bernstein have both pointed out, Stein's "Melanctha" reveals many of the same strengths and weaknesses as Williams's work in regard to its use of black cultural expression in relation to experimental writing. "Melanctha," Mackey argues, "recalls minstrelsy in that Stein uses one form of marginality, blackness, to mask another, to mask two others in fact—the avant-garde linguistic experimentation . . . and, albeit much less evident, lesbianism" (DE 282–83). Conceding that Stein's story does employ racist stereotypes, Bernstein focuses on the "counter-racist currents that flow through [Stein's] linguistic explorations." "In her own or possibly her parents' broken English and, more important, the spoken language of African-Americans, Stein found a linguistic utopia—a domain not colonized by England, not Island England's sovereign subject." See Charles Bernstein, *A Poetics* (Cambridge: Harvard University Press, 1992), 148–49.

9. Gertrude Stein, *The Autobiography of Alice B. Toklas* (New York: Vintage, 1933), 78–80. This passage contains an interesting account of James's visit to Stein's salon, where he reacted to paintings by Cezanne, Picasso, and Matisse by gasping and exclaiming, "I always told you that you should keep your mind open." Also mentioned is the fact that James heavily annotated his copy of Stein's *Three Lives*. See also Poirier, *Poetry and Pragmatism,* 129–70, where Poirier discusses Stein in reference to Jamesian pragmatism and "the vague"; and Jay's *Contingency Blues,* where Jay argues for the similarity of Stein's philosophy and aesthetic to that of James, Dewey, and Burke.

10. As a student in James's graduate psychology seminar, Stein would have undoubtedly given the psychology a meticulous reading. Two quotes from the first volume suggest the impact it had on her style:

To sum up, certain kinds of verbal associate, certain grammatical expectations fulfilled, stand for a good part of our impression that a sentence has meaning and is dominated by the Unity of one Thought. Nonsense in grammatical form sounds half-rational; sense with grammatical sequence upset sounds nonsensical; e.g., "Elba the Napolean English faith had banished broken to he Saint because Helena at." (8:255)

The relations [between words] are numberless, and no existing language is capable of doing justice to all their shades.
    We ought to say a feeling of *and,* a feeling of *if,* a feeling of *but,* a feeling of *by,* quite as readily as we say a feeling of *blue* or a feeling of *cold.* Yet we do not: so inveterate has our habit become of recognizing the existence of the substantive parts alone, that language almost refuses to lend itself to any other use. (8:238)

11. Jay, *Contingency Blues,* 117. This is Jay's definition of the "pragmatic or rhetorical theory of form" (120).

12. Williams's statement is from his introduction to "The Wedge" in Williams, *Collected Poems of William Carlos Williams,* 2:54. Rorty's statement is from *Essays on Heidegger,* 13. For further evidence that O'Hara read "Introduction to the Wedge," see his comments on Williams's "diatribes against the sonnet" (SS 26) in reference to Williams's assertion that "all sonnets say the same thing of no importance." The belief shared by Williams and O'Hara that "face to face" activities should determine the course and meaning of the linguistic code is often expressed as an emphasis on *the local* that, as I argue in chapter 1, has its precedent in Dewey's work. O'Hara undoubtedly read the acknowledgment to Dewey that appears in *Paterson,* vii.

13. O'Hara typically thought of his own work as in the line of Williams, and John Ashbery's work as in the line of Wallace Stevens, and he explained the distinction by noting, "mine is full of objects" (268). O'Hara was of course aware of Williams's central role (along with Zukofsky, George Oppen, and Charles Reznikoff) in the "objectivism" movement. Oppen interestingly describes the basic premise of the movement in the following, very Jamesian, way: "Whatever may be doubted, the actuality of consciousness cannot be doubted. 'Therefor consciousness in itself, of itself, carries the principle of actualness' This is indeed the law and the prophets. It can happen in the poem. Perhaps this should have been the meaning of 'objectivism.'" See *The Selected Letters of George Oppen,* ed. Rachel Blau DuPlessis (Durham: Duke University Press, 1990), 290.

14. Goodman, *Speaking and Language,* 19, 28. Williams's admiration of James is suggested by the line of praise he receives in "Choral: The Pink Church": "O Dewey! (John) / O James! (William) / O Whitehead! / teach well!" See Williams, *Collected Poems of William Carlos Williams,* 2:179. As another reference point for Williams's poetic model, see Charles Olson's description of "open field" poetics in "Projective Verse," specifically the description of "the kinetics of the thing," in Charles Olson, *Selected Writings,* ed. Robert Creeley (New York: New Directions, 1966), 16.

15. Goodman, *Speaking and Language,* 5, 7, 124. As a reference point, compare Burke's description of a "pragmatic" approach to the poem, quoted in chapter 1. For a full view of Goodman's position vis-à-vis Burke, see the entire chapter "Speaking as Action, Speech as Thing" (19–55). Goodman was a careful reader of not only James but Dewey and Burke as well. Also worth mentioning is the fact that Goodman's description of Jamesian pragmatism as "in the American grain" is a conscious connection of James to Williams through Williams's book *In the American Grain.*

16. These references to Goodman appear in two letters to Freilicher dated 6/6/51 and 8/1/51 respectively. Goodman's essay "Advance-Guard Writing, 1900–1950" is found in *The Kenyon Review* 13, no. 3 (summer 1951), 357–80. Hereafter cited as AW.

17. Burke, *Philosophy of Literary Form,* 89.

18. Another explanation for Goodman's similarity to Ellison on this point might

be Goodman's interest in black vernacular expression. See Goodman, *Speaking and Language,* 67: "Black argot began to become slang through the jazz musicians, but now it has come in strongly through the civil rights and black liberation movements, and the association of blacks with the youth of the white majority. . . . Slang creates new language just like poetry, and it can be regarded as a kind of folk poetry. . . . Whitman says, 'Slang is the lawless germinal element below all words and sentences and behind all poetry'."

19. The statement on consistency that O'Hara paraphrased is "a foolish consistency is the hobgoblin of little minds, adored by little statesmen and philosophers and divines. With consistency a great soul has simply nothing to do. He may as well concern himself with his shadow on the wall. Speak what you think now in hard words, and to-morrow speak what to-morrow thinks in hard words again, though it contradict everything you said to-day."

20. "The Artist," Goodman suggested, "is to invent ways needfully to throw himself on the mercy of the audience. . . . The advance-guard artist . . . more than any other needs accomplices, not only *post factum* but as collaborators *in delictu,* in constructing the social art-object" (AW 372, 380).

21. O'Hara originally intended to call the essay "Personalism," a title that connected the essay to his poem "Personal Poem," and which would have made the link to Goodman's call for "personal writing" more visible. See Joe LeSueur, "Four Apartments," in *Homage to Frank O'Hara,* eds. Bill Berkson and Joe LeSueur (Berkeley: Creative Arts Book Company, 1980), 54. The young O'Hara glossed this advice by writing, "you could fit the people I write for into your john, all at the same time without raising an eyebrow." See letter to Freilicher dated 6/6/51.

22. See *The Journal of the Charles Olson Archives* 2 (fall 1974), 37. Though his teaching tenure at Black Mountain College was brief, Goodman was in regular correspondence with Olson, Creeley, and Duncan—and his standing in that community was such that Creeley asked him to be a contributing editor to the *Black Mountain Review.* See Creeley, *Collected Essays of Robert Creeley,* 511. In comparing the Black Mountain premise that "the American language and culture are departures from the Western norm" to Ellison's own premises, I am thinking, again, of such statements as "the language which we speak is not English" (GT 317), which Ellison explains by describing how Americans "were improvising themselves into a nation, scraping together a conscious culture out of various dialects, idioms, lingos, and methodologies of America's diverse people's and regions" (CE 336).

23. In a 1964 interview that I'll discuss in more depth toward the end of this chapter, Creeley confirms Duncan's connection of Emerson, Dewey, and Olson. See *Kulchur* 16 (winter 1964/65), 12–13, 15.

24. Creeley, *Collected Essays of Robert Creeley,* 369–70. The previous quotes from Duncan can be found in Duncan, *Fictive Certainties,* 68, 204–5, 227–28, emphasis added. In connecting Emerson and Dewey to Olson, Duncan continues, "In this aes-

thetic, conception cannot be abstracted from doing." In positing Emerson as the fore-runner of "open form" aesthetics, Duncan is suggesting his relevance to Olson's semi-nal essay, "Projective Verse." Projective verse—which Olson also calls "open verse"—is based largely on the use of the breath of the poet to indicate the form of the poem; in this way it is "opposed to inherited line, stanza, over-all form." See Olson, *Selected Writings*, 15–16. Duncan would locate the origins of "Projective Verse" in such state-ments as Emerson's that "it is not metres but a metre-making argument that makes a poem" (CW 3:9–10) or in the following from Dewey's *Art as Experience:* "Experiencing, like breathing, is a rhythm of intakings and out-givings. . . . Space is room. . . . The very word 'breathing space' suggests the choking, the oppression that results when things are constricted. . . . Lack of room is denial of life, and openness of space is affirmation of its potentiality" (LW 10:62). It is also worth noting how remarkably similar the opening of "Projective Verse" is to Burke's description of a "pragmatic view of the poem" quoted in chapter 1. Olson writes, "I want to . . . suggest a few ideas about what stance toward reality brings such verse into being, what that stance does, both to the poet and to his reader" (16). While O'Hara's "Personism: A Manifesto" has often been taken as a parody of "Projective Verse," I believe this has been exaggerated. If anything, O'Hara objected to Olson's masculine bravado, but he was in clear agree-ment with the principles behind "open form" and "projective verse." As evidence, I'd cite the following, from a 1965 interview: "It seemed to me that the metrical, that the measure let us say, if you want to talk about it in Olson's poems . . . comes from the breath of the person. . . . So therefor the point is really more to establish one's own measure and breath in poetry . . . rather than fitting your ideas into an established order, syllabically and phonetically and so on" (*SS* 17). Earlier, in a letter to Kenneth Koch dated 4/56, O'Hara had written, "I've also been reading some of Charles Olson's things, which are more attractive than most." I lay out these various quotes because I believe they are the subtext for the conversation Duncan and Creeley were having about O'Hara's "Personism: A Manifesto" as quoted above. Duncan is clearly describ-ing personism as akin to Emerson and Dewey's "aesthetic [in which] conception cannot be abstracted from doing." Lastly, I would note that I take O'Hara's and Duncan's an-tagonistic personal relationship (CPT 319–21) as immaterial to their shared aesthetic convictions. Duncan clearly admired O'Hara's work, and I take at face value Ginsberg's characterization of their falling out: O'Hara, Ginsberg notes, believed that poetry "was totally democratic. So that there were no kings and queens of poetry." When Duncan wrote O'Hara an admiring letter in 1958 regarding his poem "In Memory of My Feel-ings," O'Hara saw Duncan "as the Queen of Poetry, giving him the scepter, and he said, 'Well, I don't want a scepter from that old queen!'" See Berkson and LeSueur, *Homage to Frank O'Hara*, 63. In any case, Duncan's claim that "O'Hara was absolutely intolerant of my existence" seems exaggerated in the extreme.

25. James Livingston puts it this way: "When the belief that knowledge is active and operative takes hold of men, the ideal realm is no longer aloof and separate; it is

rather that collection of imagined possibilities that stimulates men to new efforts and realizations." See Livingson, *Pragmatism and the Political Economy,* 197.

26. Another moment in this text that Duncan clearly has in mind (and that he previously had cited in reference to Olson) is Dewey's stipulation that "Art is a quality of doing and of what is done" (LW 10:218). See also his discussion of how "everything depends upon the way in which the material is used when it operates as a medium" (LW 10:69).

27. Goodman, *Speaking and Language,* 206.

28. Paul Goodman, *Collected Poems,* ed. Taylor Stoehr (New York: Vintage, 1977), 307–8.

29. If there is a difference between O'Hara's rhetorical strategies and Goodman's, it lies in O'Hara's even more strenuous attempt to erase the writer/reader hierarchy. O'Hara, for instance, would in all likelihood avoid the largesse of Goodman's "to whom is given to declare / among Americans." "Chatter," rather than declaration, is more in line with O'Hara's motives.

30. Spahr, *Everybody's Autonomy,* 113.

31. This quote appears in a letter from O'Hara to Kenneth Koch dated 7/25/57 where O'Hara outlines an idea for a play called "Susan B. Anthony in Sodom." The drama would surround Anthony's attempt to "win for fairies equal rights with suffragettes." In an e-mail to me dated 1/9/99, O'Hara's good friend, poet Bill Berkson, notes of O'Hara's idea, "there wouldn't have been a written play, just Frank's way of following an impulse in chat with a friend," but it remains an interesting insight into O'Hara's concerns.

32. Berkson and LeSueur, *Homage to Frank O'Hara,* 217. In an e-mail to me dated 1/12/99, Berkson identified the "Jim" in this text as Jim Brodey. Brodey, Berkson explained, "had taken some (I think) mescaline and saw a 'flashing bolt.'" Another interesting reference to the telephone comes in a letter from O'Hara to Vincent Warren dated 4/2/60 where O'Hara describes how Ava Gardner "built herself a beautiful isolated house outside the city but she couldn't get a telephone installed there, so she sold it and moved to Rome. Isn't that grand?"

33. Dewey quoted in Livingston, *Pragmatism and the Political Economy,* 197.

34. Livingston, *Pragmatism and the Political Economy,* 155.

35. See CPT 175. See also Larry Rivers, *What Did I Do? The Unauthorized Autobiography* (New York: HarperCollins, 1992), 44–46: "I swear to God, my name was given to me by a night club emcee," Rivers says, though, interestingly, he also compares the change to the way black poets and musicians such as Baraka and Sahib Shihab adopted African and Muslim names.

36. I've linked the two passages according to the implicit logic of O'Hara's discussion of "risked identity," which appears in both. Recall also Goodman's insistence that "all original composition . . . risks . . . something unknown" (AW 357).

37. Berkson's comment is from an email to me dated 1/12/99. He continues, "By

the way, the only time I ever met Ellison was at Robert Motherwell & Helen Frankenthaler's house in the mid 60s; I don't recall if Frank was present, but it may not have
been the only, or first, time Ellison attended one of their parties." O'Hara was a regular
attendee at Motherwell and Frankenthaler's, and the idea that he and Ellison may have
conversed probably merits more investigation.

38. O'Hara's characterization of the "free, glamorous Village" is in a letter to Kenneth and Janice Koch dated 1/29/57. Interestingly, Goodman's discussion of "personal
writing," which had so engaged him in 1951, returns at this time in a letter to John
Ashbery dated 3/27/57. LeSueur's characterization of O'Hara appears in the letter to
me dated 12/12/98.

39. For O'Hara's introduction to *Yugen,* see the letter dated 11/11/58. This would
have been *Yugen* 2, which featured poems by Baraka as well as Gregory Corso, whose
influence on O'Hara I will discuss later. In the spring of 1959, O'Hara's poems appeared in *Yugen* 4 alongside work by Olson, Creeley, Baraka, Corso, Ginsberg and Jack
Kerouac. The reference to Jones as "a saint" appears in a letter to John Ashbery dated
10/29/59. His praise for Spellman and Baraka's *The System of Dante's Hell* appears in a
letter to Vincent Warren, 7/17/61. He undercuts the formal, hyberbolic quality of his
praise for *The System of Dante's Hell* with the self-effacing comment, "I'm getting like
J. Donald Adams." For O'Hara's reading of *The Toilet* see his letter to Larry Rivers dated
4/7/63. Baraka's play appeared shortly thereafter in *Kulchur* 9 (spring 1963), 25—39.
For O'Hara's solicitations for the civil rights issue of *Kulchur* see his letter to Rivers
dated 7/21/63. The issue itself was *Kulchur* 12 (winter 1963) and the quote from
Baraka's "Expressive Language" appears on page 79.

40. Creeley, *Collected Essays of Robert Creeley,* 531—532.

41. I am struck by how different the phrase "I consider myself to be black" is from
"I am black." There seems a suggestion in its syntax that "I" and "myself" are separate
entities and that "to" should be read as "in order to." Read this way, the phrase seems
to be a gesture toward DuBois's idea of double-consciousness. Baraka, in a letter to
me dated 1/3/99, relates DuBois's concept to the Greenwich Village culture of this
period as well as to jazz generally: "The music, Jazz, like anything hooked up with black
people, is non conformist at base, because it is the music of Americans who have never
been allowed to be that. So it comes, like WEB's double consciousness, as the amalga-
mated expression of a 'twoness' (his word). So with an idealism ubiquitous in GV, at
that time, I could find a parallel between the bohemian 'outness,' proclaimed and the
actual outness of the music." For DuBois's explanation of double-consciousness see
W. E. B. DuBois, *The Souls of Black Folk: Authoritative Text, Contexts, Criticism,* ed. Henry
Louis Gates, Jr., and Terri Hume Oliver (New York: W. W. Norton, 1999), 10—11.

42. Burke, *Philosophy of Literary Form,* 90.

43. Leigh Witchel has written two articles relevant to a more specific discussion
of ballet: "Racism and Dance" (5/2/96), written for the USENET group alt.arts.ballet

and available at http://members.aol.com/lwitchel/dance.htm; and "Four Decades of Agon," *Ballet Review* 25, no. 3 (1997), 53–78. In the former, Witchel suggests the difficulties involved in any attempt to make democracy and ballet conform: "The style that I know as classical has an entire aesthetic and power structure that has to be accepted and embraced in order to make it resonate. It's not a veneer. You can't just look classical—you have to buy into its values; hook, line and sinker. In a telling comment made in the sixties (OTTOMH) [off the top of my head] Arthur Mitchell was asked how he thought about the elegance necessary to do Divertimento No. 15. 'Think White' he responded. Are blacks not elegant? A ridiculous thought. But are they elegant in that way? That is a question of cultural values."

44. See Baraka's letter to me dated 1/3/99.

45. Monk and Coltrane played the Five Spot during a six-month stretch from July to December 1957. Monk returned again for the summer and fall of 1958, with Coltrane sitting in during September. In an 8/26/57 letter to Mike Goldberg, O'Hara lamented, "How I long for the Five Spot," and a 9/19/57 letter to Larry Rivers indicates that he was in the Five Spot the night of September 18th.

46. J. J. Johnson, quoted in Eric Nisenson, *Ascension: John Coltrane and His Quest* (New York: St. Martin's Press, 1993), 46.

47. John Coltrane, quoted in Nisenson, *Ascension,* 45–46.

48. Thinking specifically of Monk and Coltrane's run at the Five Spot, Nisenson sounds a note that is remarkably similar to the passages from O'Hara and Ellison that I compare at the outset of this essay: "Picture a jazz musician walking on the stand, knowing exactly what he is after musically, but having no idea what he will play until the notes come out of his instrument, and you can perceive the paradox that is at the heart of jazz. In addition, he will be interacting with the other members of his group, who will also be improvising, and they will force him to alter his musical conception in order to create an apposite group sound. Is jazz the music of the individual or that of the group consciousness? Once again it is both simultaneously." See Nisenson, *Ascension,* 53–54.

49. The quote from "A True Account of Talking to the Sun at Fire Island"—spoken by the sun—is followed interestingly by the sun speculating, "Maybe we'll speak again in Africa, of which I too am specially fond." The poem was written 7/10/58, the day after "Ode: Salute to the French Negro Poets" (CP 305), where he writes, "if there is fortuity it's in the love we bear each other's differences / in race." "Bathroom" was written 6/20/63 as O'Hara was helping prepare the special civil rights issue of *Kulchur.*

50. Letter from O'Hara to Corso dated 3/20/58. O'Hara's feeling that jazz didn't "go with" his poems is expressed in a letter to Grace Hartigan dated 12/20/57.

51. Lott, "Bebop's Politics of Style," 248. Lott reads bebop as a reaction to this co-optation.

52. Creeley, *Collected Essays of Robert Creeley,* 591.

53. Monk, among other jazz innovators, was sometimes referred to as "neurotic." See Keepnews, *View from Within*, 111. Here O'Hara turns the term into a positive via its counterintuitive ability to "cohere."

54. The related definitions of the pragmatic self are all Livingston's from *Pragmatism and the Political Economy*, 138, 209, 236. His discussion of the concept of "reciprocal exteriority" of the fully contingent and yet social self occurs in the course of a broader discussion of Henri Bergson's relation to pragmatism. My reading of "Ode: Salute to the French Negro Poets" runs counter to that of Aldon Nielsen in his generally excellent *Reading Race*. Nielsen reads the lines "the love we bear each others differences / in race which is the poetic ground on which we rear our smiles" in shortened form: "race which is the poetic ground on which we rear our smiles" and concludes that O'Hara is "seeking some white equivalent of Cesaire's poetics of 'negritude'" (157). I would argue that confronting the complexity of a phrase such as "each others differences" as well as the specifics of O'Hara's social ground are essential to reading the poem. O'Hara was, as I argue, aware of the ongoing debates about race relations within jazz culture; he was also aware of and interested in African liberation movements, a fact surely relevant to our reading of his representation of Cesaire. In "For the Chinese New Year and For Bill Berkson" (CP 389–93), published in *The Floating Bear* in 1961, he wonders about the fate of Patrice Lumumba, the first (and only) democratically elected prime minister of the independent Republic of the Congo, who had been assassinated the month before O'Hara wrote his poem.

55. Miles Davis with Quincy Troupe, *Miles: The Autobiography* (New York: Touchstone, 1989), 141.

56. LeRoi Jones (Amiri Baraka), *Blues People: Negro Music in White America* (New York: William Morrow, 1963), 213. Hereafter cited as BP. See also Baraka's description of the "deadly cool of '50's 'West Coast' jazz," in Baraka, *The Autobiography of LeRoi Jones* (Chicago: Lawrence Hill, 1997), 260.

57. Letter from O'Hara to Rivers dated 10/4/62. See also Rivers, *What Did I Do*, 455–56, where Rivers recalls O'Hara bringing up the jazz/poetry night issue again in 1966, as part of a very complicated exchange involving a racially volatile sculpture of Rivers's called "Lampman Loves It," which depicted "a black man fucking a white woman" (the face of jazz musician Bob Wails and the body of *Playboy* playmate Jo Collins). Rivers's difficulties included Sidney Janis's refusal to show the piece and Collins's threat to sue him. The way Rivers remembers it, O'Hara suggested he be practical and have a black actress O'Hara knew model for him in place of Collins—though it doesn't seem to me that O'Hara's motive was as simple as practicality. O'Hara reminded Rivers of an incident at one of the Five Spot jazz/poetry events in which some of the musicians, including Mal Waldron, expressed uncomfortability with playing "funny music" behind Kenneth Koch's funny poetry. Rivers, O'Hara reminded him, had argued that the performance would not reflect on their identity as jazz musicians. While Rivers recalls O'Hara validating his point in 1966, that recollection seems dubious to

me given the hesitancies expressed in the 10/4/62 letter—though it is certainly possible that O'Hara imported the Five Spot anecdote to new purposes in 1966 because it was expedient to do so at the time. In any event, the motives for his nervousness circa 1962 seem clear and will become more so in the pages that follow and in the next note.

58. O'Hara's comment about Holliday ("Well, I guess she's *better* than Picasso") was made after seeing her at the Loew's Sheridan in the summer of 1957 (CPT 327). Holliday's comment to Koch is mentioned by Bill Berkson in his e-mail to me dated 1/4/99. This may have been the same night referred to by Koch in his contributors note to *The New American Poetry:* "Last year Larry Rivers and I tried to kill poetry-and-jazz by parodying it" (440). In an odd reversal, David Shapiro recalls "Kenneth Koch walking out of Frank's place one night when LeRoi Jones had all these people together about to play blues. Kenneth said something like 'I'm not going to take this cliché.'" It's safe to say that, in terms of what would be classified as cliché when it came to racial expression, O'Hara would have supported Baraka. Despite being "intimate friends" with Koch, O'Hara was not afraid to say "I hate his social ideas," and he bristled at what he once called Koch's "sophomoric intellectual snobbishness involving ideas of 'people who matter' and 'what is really interesting.'" See O'Hara's letter to Freilicher dated 4/54. These complaints would seem to complement Baraka's recent comparison of O'Hara and Koch: "Frank at least had a political sense. Kenneth Koch and Kenward Elmslie and all those people were always highly anti-political, which is why I couldn't get along with them longer than two minutes" (CPT 425).

59. LeRoi Jones (Amiri Baraka), *Home: Social Essays* (New York: William Morrow, 1966), 113. Mackey discusses this juxtaposition in DE 2.

60. These two views are represented in Mutlu Konuk Blasing, *Politics and Form in Postmodern Poetry* (New York: Cambridge University Press, 1995), 50; and Andrew Ross, "The Death of Lady Day," in *Frank O'Hara: To Be True to a City,* ed. Jim Elledge (Ann Arbor: University of Michigan Press, 1990), 385–88. Blasing's reading of the poem seems particularly ahistorical; her view that O'Hara's "concept of the artist and art is as 'bourgeois' as you can get"—besides being needlessly hyperbolic and fundamentally inaccurate—seems to prevent her from addressing the most obvious contexts for the poem, namely, his friendship with Baraka and the Five Spot itself. Ross, despite his claims to having "comb[ed] through O'Hara's entire oeuvre," ignores an awful lot in order to come to the conclusion that "jazz almost never figures into the taste milieu within which [O'Hara] represented himself." He quotes Amiri Baraka's poem "Jitterbugs" as if it were a corrective to O'Hara's view of jazz without mentioning that at the time he wrote "The Day Lady Died," O'Hara and Baraka were close friends. He questions the relevance of O'Hara's work to the civil rights movement without mentioning that Baraka and O'Hara put together a special civil rights issue of *Kulchur* in the early sixties. In short, Ross's mapping of "a highly romantic form of Racism" onto "The Day Lady Died" overlooks much evidence to the contrary. He finally wants to see O'Hara's

"white intellectual" as ironized (invoking O'Hara's "camp ethic" as his saving grace), but, as will become clear, I'm arguing that his identity as mediated by events in the Five Spot is, in fact, much more radical.

61. James explains that experience is marked by *attention* rather than receptivity and that one's attention within the stream of experience is emblematic of the "fact that subjective experience may, by laying its weighty index-finger on particular items of experience, so accent them as to give to the least frequent associations far more power to shape our thought than the most frequent ones possess" (WJ 8:381). But our subjective attention, our reactive spontaneity, does not leave us unchanged, since "every experience undergone by the brain leaves in it a modification which is one factor in determining what manner of experiences the following ones shall be" (472).

62. Creeley, *Collected Essays of Robert Creeley,* 576. See also "Notes Apropos Free Verse," 492–95, for further discussion of Creeley's connection of poetic verse and jazz changes.

63. See Crouch's liner notes to *Thelonious Monk, At the Five Spot,* Milestone M-47043, in Tom Piazza, *Setting the Tempo: Fifty Years of Great Liner Notes* (New York: Anchor Books, 1996), 261.

64. Keepnews, *View from Within,* 116; and Rivers, *What Did I Do?* 342.

65. Berkson's mention of Taylor appears in his e-mail to me dated 1/4/99. The characterizations of Taylor's music are from Nat Hentoff's liner notes to Taylor's *Looking Ahead!* Contemporary S7562, 1959.

66. Monk, quoted in Keepnews, *View From Within,* 112.

67. This expression of purpose appears in a statement entitled "Statement to the Ford Foundation" found in "The Frank O'Hara Letters" and dated "late 1959." O'Hara was proposing to write a libretto. Among his suggestions for collaborators was Morton Feldman, whose music, Berkson has said, "felt close to Monk (did he agree? I never had the temerity to ask)." See Berkson's e-mail to me dated 1/4/99. Berkson's apprehensiveness belies the cultural distance mediating against his multiracial hearing. O'Hara of course was notorious for his attempts to bridge cultural distance. In any event, my point is not to argue for an analogy between Feldman's and Monk's work so much as to point out that if O'Hara was developing "ideas about suitable prosody for musical setting of American diction" with Feldman in mind then the music he was hearing at the Five Spot during this period may well have figured into his considerations.

68. See A. B. Spellman, "Genesis of the New Music—III: Ornette Coleman," *Evergreen Review* 47 (June 1967), 80. Spellman began reviewing music in *Kulchur* in 1962, at the same time that Baraka made O'Hara the art editor.

69. Coleman himself designed the song titles on his LP *To Whom Keeps a Record* in the form of a joke only a pragmatist could make; when read in succession, the titles make the sentence, "Music Always Brings Goodness To Us All. P.S.: Unless One Has Some Other Motive For Its Use." See *To Whom Keeps a Record,* Warner Pioneer P-10085A, 1975.

70. See Berkson's e-mail to me dated 1/4/99. Berkson's reading of Monk and Coleman might be usefully compared to Ellison's description of dissonance and flexibility, as discussed in chapter 1.

71. There is a fascinating moment in *Yugen* 7, for instance, where—in the middle of a book review of Robert Lowell's *Life Studies* of all things!—Baraka glosses his experience of watching Coltrane perform with the last stanza of Creeley's "I Know a Man." See page 5.

72. LeSueur has written to me restating what Gooch makes clear in his biography, namely, that "Frank was himself very attracted to black men," and suggesting that O'Hara's conversations with Powell were most likely about her relationship with Coleman rather than about Coleman's music. See LeSueur's letter dated 12/12/98; see also CPT 195–96. I would argue that Baraka is the more authoritative voice regarding O'Hara's interest in Coleman and, in any event, that we should be cautious about categorizing O'Hara's sexual relationships and desires as *merely* sexual, particularly as they took place in late 1950s Greenwich Village; as Berkson explains, "that downtown scene permitted what seemed at the time very specific, uncategorizable relations: race relations, gender relations, sexual-orientation relations, & alllikethat. It was after all in that context as well as in the permissive Arcadia of my own self-image that Frank & I acted as we did with each other." See Berkson's e-mail to me dated 2/3/99. The ambiguity of O'Hara's relationship with Berkson was not unlike the ambiguity of his relationship with Baraka. See CPT 337.

73. These quotes are contained in Baraka's letter to me dated 1/3/99.

74. Coleman's Atlantic LPs during this period were *The Shape of Jazz to Come*, Atlantic 1317, released 12/59; *Change of the Century*, Atlantic 1327, released 6/60; *This is Our Music*, Atlantic 1353, released 2/61; *Free Jazz*, Atlantic 1364, released 9/61; *Ornette!* Atlantic 1378, released 2/62; and *Ornette on Tenor*, Atlantic 1394, released 12/62. All of the music is contained in a single set, *Beauty Is a Rare Thing: The Complete Atlantic Recordings*, Rhino R2 71410, 1993. Mingus's comment appears in the liner notes to *Beauty Is a Rare Thing*, 28. Spellman's appears in "Genesis of the New Music," 79. Schuller's is from the liner notes to *Free Jazz* (deluxe edition). The title track, "Free Jazz," is a thirty-seven-minute piece directed ad hoc by Coleman and performed simultaneously by two separate quartets using similar instrumentation with a polyphonic freeness and nontonal idiom, the result of Coleman's request that each musician go as "far out" as possible. The idea, Coleman says, "was for us to play together, all at the same time, without getting in each other's way."

75. Martin Williams, *Jazz Masters in Transition, 1957–69* (New York: MacMillan, 1970), 56.

76. See also Baraka's description of O'Hara as "one of the most incisive and knowledgeable critics of painting in New York at the time," in Baraka, *Autobiography of LeRoi Jones*, 233.

77. Speaking of Williams, Baraka himself sounds a lot like Ellison: "Williams was a

common denominator because he wanted American speech, a mixed foot, a variable measure. He knew American life had out-distanced the English rhythms and their formal meters. The language of this multinational land, of mixed ancestry, where war dance and salsa combine with country and western, all framed by African rhythm-and-blues confessional." See Baraka, *Autobiography of LeRoi Jones,* 233.

78. Baraka, *Autobiography of LeRoi Jones,* 205.

79. The first quotation, on "abstraction" is from the poem "An Explanation of the Work" in LeRoi Jones, *Black Magic: Sabotage, Target Studies, Black Art: Collected Poetry, 1961–1967* (Indianapolis: Bobbs-Merril, 1969).

80. See Baraka's letter to me dated 1/3/99. See also CPT 338.

81. *Transbluesency: The Selected Poems of Amiri Baraka/LeRoi Jones (1961–1995)* (New York: Marsilio, 1995), 118. It has been suggested to me that the "Dewey" in Baraka's poem could be Thomas rather than John. I find it hard to believe that Baraka would include Republican Thomas Dewey (running against Truman from his Right and largely responsible four years later for getting Eisenhower nominated) alongside progressives such as Henry A. Wallace (founder of the Progressive Party and sometime admirer of Soviet communism) and Wendell Wilkie as inheritors of Lincoln's legacy. (In 1940, Chester Franklin, owner and publisher of the *Kansas City Call* [largest black newspaper west of Chicago] and chairman of the Colored Citizen's Committee for the Election of Wendell Wilkie as President, said, "Just as Abraham Lincoln said that the United States could not exist half-slave and half-free, so this great country cannot have prosperity with one-half of its people employed and one-half of its people unemployed. I support Mr. Wilkie for President because I believe that ONLY under his leadership can America secure employment for that now jobless portion of American citizens of which the Colored race, of which I am a member, forms a large part.") *John* Dewey simply makes more sense in this context.

82. See *Kulchur* 16 (winter 1964/65), 12–13, 15. Again, for "this concept of 'energy,'" see also Goodman, *Speaking and Language,* 19.

83. *West, American Evasion of Philosophy,* 5.

84. See the liner notes to Coleman, *Beauty Is a Rare Thing.*

EPILOGUE

1. *Webster's New Universal Unabridged Dictionary,* 140, 345, 418, 487, 488, 644, 650, 1332, 1403, 1604.

2. Douglass, *Narrative of the Life of Frederick Douglass,* 26.

3. DuBois, *Souls of Black Folk,* 157.

4. Nan Aron, "The Problem with 'Strict Constructionist' Judges," *The Hill,* April 17, 2002. Aron is president of the Alliance for Justice (http://www.afj.org/).

5. Spahr, *Everybody's Autonomy,* 24, 13.

6. *Tripwire* 5 (Fall 2001). This issue, subtitled "Expanding the Repertoire: Conti-

nuity and Change in African-American Writing," developed out of a three-day conference hosted by Small Press Traffic and held at New College in San Francisco in April 2000.

7. Lorenzo Thomas notes that "while the movement rejected mainstream America's ideology, deeming it inimical to black people, Black Arts poets maintained and developed the prosody that they had acquired from Black Mountain and the Beats." See Lorenzo Thomas, *Extraordinary Measures: Afrocentric Modernism and Twentieth-Century American Poetry* (Tuscaloosa: University of Alabama Press, 2000), 201.

8. See *Kulchur* 16 (winter 1964/65), 12–13, 15.

9. This is in an interview in Olson's *Muthologos* 2:71. Mackey also quotes it in *Discrepant Engagement*.

10. Creeley, *Collected Essays of Robert Creeley*, 494.

11. Gunn, *Thinking across the American Grain*, 12.

12. Harryette Mullen, *Muse & Drudge* (Philadelphia: Singing Horse, 1995).

13. Susan Howe, *My Emily Dickinson* (Berkeley: North Atlantic Books, 1985), 11. Howe is also referring here to Dickinson.

14. *Combo* 1, 48.

15. Susan Howe, *The Birth-mark: Unsettling the Wilderness in American Literary History* (Hanover, N.H.: Wesleyan University Press, 1993), 181. Hereafter cited as BM.

16. Susan Schultz, "Exaggerated History," *Postmodern Culture* 4, no. 2 (January 1994), 2.

17. Howe is herself clearly a student of classical pragmatism. Brian Lennon remarks on "the affinity [Howe's] projects display for the goals of philosophical pragmatism as formulated by Peirce, James, and John Dewey. Beginning with Peirce's notion of truth as a function of practical 'effect,' pragmatists devised a theory of art-as-experiment. . . . The pragmatist poet begins with the practice indicated or suggested by theory-constructing a provocation of theory, an invitation to more theory (and hence more practice) rather than theory as bête noire." See Brian Lennon, "Pierce-Arrow, Susan Howe," *Boston Review* (October/November 1999). In the fall of 2002, Howe taught a graduate seminar on "Poetry and Pragmatism" at the University at Buffalo, in which I had the opportunity to guest lecture, discussing some of the materials that appear in chapter 1 of this book. In her recent book *Pierce-Arrow* (New York: New Directions, 1999), Howe unsettles pragmatism itself by focusing her attention on the unpublished manuscripts of Charles Sanders Peirce, who, though he coined the term "pragmatism," is the least recognized and recognizable of the classical pragmatists. We might think of Peirce's manuscripts, as Howe seems to, as the "unclassified residuum" in classical pragmatism and note what James says about the unclassified residuum as such: "If there is anything which human history demonstrates, it is the extreme slowness with which the ordinary academic and critical mind acknowledges facts to exist which present themselves as wild facts, with no stall or pigeon-hole, or as facts which threaten to break up the accepted system. . . . Anyone will renovate his science who

will steadily look after the irregular phenomena. And when the science is renewed, its new formulas often have more of the voice of the exceptions in them than of what were supposed to be the rules" (WJ 223–24).

18. Susan Howe, *The Nonconformist's Memorial* (New York: New Directions, 1993), 11.

19. *Tripwire* 6 (Fall 2002), 43–44.

Index

"Cherokee" (composition by Noble), 109, 214n. 23

"Choral: The Pink Church" (Williams), 222n. 14

"Circles" (Emerson), 63, 93, 99–100, 108

civil rights movement, 164; civil rights issue of *Kulchur,* 172; its connection with advance-guard art, 149–50

Clarke, James Freeman, 204n. 43

Clarke, Kenny, 125

Clough, Arthur Hugh, 207n. 54

Cmiel, Kenneth, 74, 205n. 47

Coleman, Ornette, 128, 170, 174–75; *Change of the Century* (recording), 167; "Congeniality" (composition), 196n. 62; "Free Jazz" (composition), 231n. 74; *Free Jazz* (recording), 166–67; his arrival as "the greatest furor," 165–69; his pragmatist joke, 230n. 69

Coleman, Wanda, 180

Color and Culture (Posnock), 180

Coltrane, John, 46, 152, 227n. 45

Constitution, 2, 19, 22, 53, 54

"cool jazz," 155–56

Corso, Gregory, 154

Crane, Hart: O'Hara's admiration for, 130

Creeley, Robert, 137–38, 173; on "Black Mountain" philosophy, 180–81; connection between poetry and jazz, 181–82; debt to black expressivity and women's writing, 181; "the Negro consciousness" as *the* dominant reality, 149; stuttering in the work of, 183; on Williams, 194n. 47

Cremer, Jan, 172

Crouch, Stanley, 125, 159, 194n. 42

cutting session, 27, 106, 113, 115–17

Dameron, Tadd, 124–25

Davis, Miles: on "cool jazz," 155

"The Day Lady Died" (O'Hara), 157–58, 160–66

Declaration of Independence, 2, 22, 54,

209n. 68; postponement of its promise, 107

de Kooning, Willem, 153

Denby, Edwin, 150–51

Derrida, Jacques, 62

Deutsch, Leonard, 211n. 3

Dewey, John, 11–12, 28, 29, 84; "Americanism and Localism," 29–30; *Art as Experience,* 40, 138–39, 143, 197n. 3; "Art is a quality of doing," 225n. 26; artist as experimenter, 62; belief in Emerson's commitment to abolitionism, 2; continuity between events and works of art, 157; idealism as a functional strategy, 100; influence of his ideas on philosophy and democracy on Ellison, 17–18; "Philosophy and Democracy," 29, 197n. 3; philosophy as a form of desire, 18; race and ethnicity not explicitly relevant to democracy, 21–22; re-instatement of the vague, 95; sociopolitical description of action, 20–22; spectator theory of knowledge, 69; on transformation of philosophy into a democratic philosophy, 23

Dickinson, Emily, 32, 233n. 13

dirge. *See* "Voluntaries" (Emerson)

Douglass, Frederick, 92, 211n. 8; his name, 102; meeting with Lincoln, 176; *Narrative,* 56, 217n. 33; reading in *Narrative,* 209n. 68; "What to the Slave is the Fourth of July?" 181, 209n. 68

DuBois, W. E. B., 11, 57, 200n. 26; debt to description of "double consciousness" in Emerson's "Fate," 58; his idea of double consciousness, 226n. 41

Duchamp, Marcel: *Nude Descending a Staircase,* 35

Duncan, Robert, 25, 84, 137–39, 145; on O'Hara and Dewey's *Art as Experience,* 138

Egyptian mythology, 156
"Elegy on Causality in the Five Spot Café"
    (O'Hara), 154–56
Eliot, Charles W., 1
Eliot, T. S., 41; Ellison's approach to, 42
Ellington, Duke, 148
Ellison, Ralph: African American culture
    and democratic symbolic action, 169;
    allegiance with and difference from
    Emerson, 101; "The American Vernacu-
    lar as Symbolic Action" (course), 14;
    belief in Emerson's commitment to
    abolitionism, 2; blackness as a con-
    struct, 42; broad scope of his thought,
    26; buried puns, 103, 212n. 10; "The
    Charlie Christian Story," 116–17,
    146–47; critical views of his "kin-
    ship" with Emerson, 97–98; educated
    by Emerson and Louis Armstrong,
    120; Emerson and, 10–12; first to
    link pragmatism to cultural identity,
    22; on frustration of attempts to con-
    struct hierarchies, 191n. 25; "Hidden
    Name and Complex Fate," 102–3; his
    changes to pragmatism's vocabulary,
    23–25; his concept of form similar
    to Jameson's, 192n. 28; his jazz meta-
    phors, and dissonance vis-à-vis pragma-
    tist tradition, 25–27; on improvisations
    at Minton's, 127; influenced by Burke's
    concept of language as symbolic ac-
    tion, 14–16; influenced by Dewey's
    ideas on philosophy and democracy,
    17–18; inheritor of "the language of
    Emerson," 10–11; interest in Emer-
    son's antislavery writings, 210 n. 2;
    ironic position of African Americans,
    60; jazz and democracy, 167; June-
    teenth: A Novel, 210 n. 2; language,
    culture, and ethnic diversity, 12–13;
    linking of psychology to culture and
    race, 194n. 41; "The Little Man at
    Chehaw Station," 191n. 25; name

change, 102–3, 112, 183, 215n. 28;
    named after Emerson, 10, 102; on
    names, 216n. 31; on names as masks,
    215n. 27; New York as local context of
    his symbolic activities, 127–28; "The
    Novel as a Function of American De-
    mocracy," 23–24; "On Bird, Bird-
    Watching, and Jazz," 115; on racial
    inequality and democratic symbolic
    action, 100–101; review of Baraka's
    Blues People, 169–70; vernacular im-
    provisation and democracy, 19–20.
    See also Invisible Man
"Emancipation in the British West Indies"
    (Emerson), 53, 73, 85–88, 208n. 67,
    210 n. 2
The Embodiment of Knowledge (Williams), 30
Emerson, Ralph Waldo, 150; agency of
    the fugitive slave, 6, 75–76; aim of
    disrupting spectator theory of knowl-
    edge, 69–70; allusion by Ellison to
    "Self-Reliance," 218n. 39; America
    as idea of emancipation, 8–10; be-
    lief that language is material, 56;
    and "black-white social equality,"
    201n. 27; blurred emphasis of his
    call to all people, 94–95; "Boston
    Hymn," 55, 200n. 26, 209n. 68; Car-
    lyle, democracy, and the illusion of
    stable signification, 76–85; "Circles,"
    63, 93, 108; comment on Uncle Tom's
    Cabin, 205n. 46; commitment to aboli-
    tionism minimized, 198n. 11; compari-
    son of the self-reliant man to the Afri-
    can American slave, 73–75; connection
    between social change and linguistic
    change, 99–100; critical views of, 1;
    critical views of his "kinship" with El-
    lison, 97–98; critical views of his poli-
    tics and abolitionism, 54–56; critique
    of consistency in language use, 188n. 9;
    cultural texts as contingent, 2–4; de-
    fense of abolitionists, 188n. 10; depen-

dence of democratic structures on
a collaborating reader, 49–51; on
Douglass, 60; "Emancipation in the
British West Indies," 53, 73, 85–88,
208n. 67, 210 n. 2; Emerson-as-sign
and the unnamable self in *Invisible Man,*
98–99; "Experience," 72, 199n. 20;
experiments with language, 85–87;
"Fate," 57–60; foregrounding of the
contingent nature of language, 65–69;
"The Fortune of the Republic," 9–10,
53, 76, 80–81, 92, 208n. 57; "Fugitive
Slave Law (1851)," 71, 74–75; "Fugitive Slave Law (1854)," 73–74; his fellow feeling for the slave, 206n. 49; his
"flipping" of racial terms, 209n. 68;
his influence on pragmatism, 8, 10; his
"nimble" terms, and critics' misconceptions, 56–60; his "noninstrumental
thought," 199n. 12; "History," 61, 63,
200n. 26; history called into question, 63–64, 92–93; incompatibility
of self-reliance and slavery, 204n. 45;
incomplete selfhood and abolitionism,
87–88; insistence on a perpetually
renewable union, 208n. 63; involvement with Underground Railroad, 75;
and James's discussions of grammar,
202n. 37; on John Brown, 212n. 14;
language as "vehicular," 199n. 22; and
later experimental writers, 179–80;
"Lecture on Slavery," 59; Manifest Destiny, disapproval of, 57; *Miscellanies,* 2;
"Montaigne," 53, 199n. 20; *Nature,* 55;
a new way of speaking as a new reality,
90–91; onus of connection is on the
reader, 51–53; "orator for freedom,"
satire on, 5–7; the orphan, and abandonment as the general state of things,
93–94; "The Poet," 90; "postponement" and self-reliance, 207n. 55; and
post-structuralism, 202n. 32; pragmatic artist and pragmatic philosopher,

197n. 3; reading and self-reliance,
201n. 31; relationship with Charles
Woodbury, 65–68; remedy for Church
and government, 187n. 5; research on
slavery, 72; research on West Indian
emancipation, 75; revisability of the
body politic, 95–96; *Second Series* essays, 53; "Self-Reliance," 61, 63, 71–73,
84, 99, 104, 136, 204n. 44, 204n. 45;
self-reliance and self-denial, 198n. 9;
self-reliance and self-government,
204n. 44; slavery, law, and a revised
definition of "local," 70–73; on Southern culture, 104; speech for Massachusetts 54th Regiment, 93–94; strategy
of altering balance of authority in a
text, 61–65; style of, and democracy,
18–19; on subjective nature of history, 1; "sublime lessons" in the
streets, 206n. 51; symbolic activities
of African Americans, and history's
fables exposed, 91–93; symbolic activity and the agency of fugitive slaves,
88–90; tautology, 52, 64; texts as sites
of social contestation, 53–54; theory
of social change similar to Geertz's, 7;
from transcendentalist to pragmatist,
55–56, 94; the uncategorizable fugitive reader, 89–90; "Voluntaries," 176–
78, 209n. 68; "WO Liberty" notebook,
2, 205n. 48

From Emerson to King (Patterson), 54–55
Espinasse, Francis, 76–79
Everett, Edward: criticized by Emerson,
5–6, 9
Everybody's Autonomy (Spahr), 179–80
"Experience" (Emerson), 72, 199n. 20
"Expressive Language" (Baraka), 149

"Fate" (Emerson), 57–60
Feldman, Morton, 230n. 67
feminism: "Portrait of a Lady" as feminist
poem, 33